Edinburgh University

Books may be recalle
if so you will be con

_____
Due Date

ITALIAN WOMEN WRITERS

KATHARINE MITCHELL

Italian Women Writers

Gender and Everyday Life in Fiction and Journalism, 1870–1910

UNIVERSITY OF TORONTO PRESS
Toronto Buffalo London

ISBN 978-1-4426-4641-4

Toronto Italian Studies

Library and Archives Canada Cataloguing in Publication

Mitchell, Katharine, 1976–, author
Italian women writers : gender and everyday life in fiction and journalism,
1870–1910 / Katharine Mitchell.

(Toronto Italian studies)
Includes bibliographical references and index
ISBN 978-1-4426-4641-4 (bound)

1. Italian fiction – Women authors – History and criticism. 2. Women and
literature – Italy – History – 19th century. 3. Italian fiction – 19th century –
History and criticism. I. Title. II Series: Toronto Italian studies

PQ4173.M58 2014   853'.8099287   C2014-900694-2

This book has been published with assistance from grants from Lucy
Cavendish College, Cambridge; the Carnegie Trust for the Universities of
Scotland; and the School of Humanities, University of Strathclyde, Glasgow.

University of Toronto Press acknowledges the financial assistance to its
publishing program of the Canada Council for the Arts and the Ontario Arts
Council.

Canada Council   Conseil des Arts
for the Arts   du Canada

ONTARIO ARTS COUNCIL
CONSEIL DES ARTS DE L'ONTARIO
50 YEARS OF ONTARIO GOVERNMENT SUPPORT OF THE ARTS
50 ANS DE SOUTIEN DU GOUVERNEMENT DE L'ONTARIO AUX ARTS

University of Toronto Press acknowledges the financial support of the
Government of Canada through the Canada Book Fund for its publishing
activities.

For Dad, Liz, Jess, and Mum

Contents

Preface

Feminist theory needs to know how to find its way back to the ordinary and the every-day, where our political battles are actually fought.

Toril Moi, *Sexual/Textual Politics* (2002)

Popular fiction written by women for middle-class women readers began to emerge in the eighteenth century. Arguably the chick lit of its time, by the nineteenth and twentieth centuries some women writers were denouncing the "woman's novel." George Eliot (1819–1880) famously criticized the "Silly Novels by Lady Novelists," and her sentiment was echoed a century later by the Italian feminist writer Sibilla Aleramo (1876–1960), who dismissed Italian women's fiction as "stupid."[1] Writing on mass-produced fantasies for women in the twenty-first century, Tania Modleski detects in chick lit an "underlying sense of disillusionment that makes [it] of interest to feminism."[2] I argue in this book that the same can be said of Italian women writers' popular domestic fiction and journalism for women from the late nineteenth century. While Elizabeth Merrick has suggested that chick lit's formula "numbs our senses," Modleski, as well as Janice Radway, have highlighted the pleasure women readers take in reading about, and identifying with, the complexities of modern-day middle-class heterosexual relationships.[3]

Domestic fiction in the newly unified Italy draws on the nineteenth-century French literary school of realism and refers to novels and short stories by women writers who typically depicted middle-class adolescent girls and young women whose lives revolved around the domestic sphere, home, and family. In this book, through an examination of journalism addressed to a female readership, essays, and conduct books by La Marchesa Colombi, Neera, and Matilde Serao read alongside their domestic fiction, I show how these offered late-nineteenth-century women writers and readers an implicit feminist intervention and a legitimate means of addressing and engaging with the burning social and political issues of the day regarding the "woman question" – women's access to education and the professions; their legal rights; female suffrage, and so on.

Though Italian domestic fiction is undoubtedly a precursor of today's chick lit (in the same way as nineteenth-century women's journals are precursors of contemporary women's magazines), it needs to be read through its socio-historical and geo-political context. At the time of Italian Unification, adolescent girls were generally ignorant about the life cycles of womanhood, relationships, and personal struggles in a way in which they are not today due to the pervasiveness of mass popular culture. It played an important didactic role, educating women in good manners, social etiquette and relationships with the opposite sex. Yet Italian domestic fiction and chick lit are both ambivalent about making claims for feminism. While the not-very-flattering portraits of domesticity which emerge from Italian domestic fiction are testimony to a critique of women's social condition, at the same time, the fiction's preservation of the status quo is an indicator of middle-class women's acceptance of their prescribed roles as wives and mothers. Similarly, chick lit may endorse a conservative, post-feminist approach to romance and domesticity while teaching the female reader to "read" men. That this ambivalent cultural strategy on the part of female authors and creators of popular culture still persists in the twenty-first century is something that feminists should begin to reflect upon.

Acknowledgments

Many friends and colleagues have given me encouragement and constructive feedback during the years I have been working on this book. I would especially like to thank the president, Professor Janet Todd OBE, and fellows of Lucy Cavendish College, Cambridge, where I worked as a research fellow from 2008 to 2011, the Carnegie Trust for the Universities of Scotland, and the School of Humanities, University of Strathclyde, Glasgow, for their generous financial assistance. I thank my editor, Richard Ratzlaff, and my former editor, the late Ron Schoeffel, for their patience and guidance, as well as staff in Italian studies at the Universities of Warwick, Cambridge, and Strathclyde, Glasgow, for supporting my frequent visits to the Biblioteca Nazionale in Florence and the Biblioteca Nazionale Braidense in Milan. I thank in particular my dear friend and colleague Danielle Hipkins, whose moral support, good advice, and kindness know no bounds. I am infinitely grateful to her, as well as to Penny Morris, Ursula Fanning, Janet Todd, Helena Sanson, and Elspeth Jajdelska for their careful readings of earlier versions of parts of this book, as well as to my PhD supervisor Professor Ann Caesar.

I also thank my students, and friends and colleagues working in the humanities whose scholarship has inspired me: Pierpaolo Antonello, Ferzina Banaji, Roberto Bigazzi, Jenny Burns, Kenneth Clarke, Phil Cooke, Joanna Drugan, Simon Gilson, Ruth Glynn, Robert Gordon, Stephen Gundle, Faye Hammill, Michael Higgins, Anne Holloway, Jonathan Hope, Laura Lepschy, Mirca Madianou, Isabelle McNeill, Catherine O'Rawe, Loredana Polezzi, Charlotte Ross, Catherine Ramsey-Portolano, Lucia Re, Susan Rutherford, Katsura Sako, Mark Seymour, Stuart Taberner, Hayden White, Nicola Wilson Mathias, and my undergraduate professors Dick Andrews and Brian Richardson. My loving thanks go to my family, and to Julie, Lauren, and Sofia Gilson, Beth Buxton, Laura Pritchard Mellor, Ruth Thomas, Nick Wake, Tanya Barker, and Louise Mor for their friendship, and Rosaria Angeletti and the rest of my Italian "family" in Rome, as well as Patrizia and Lanfranco in Milan for providing relief from the pursuit of scholarship with their understanding, good humour, and laughter. During the writing of this book I lost my paternal grandmother, Fanny Mitchell (née Liversage, 1913–2005); her wonderful plain speaking and particular way of retelling anecdotes from her past assured frequent visits to her home in London to work in the British Library were relaxing and happy. I remember also with great fondness my maternal grandfather Victor Lown (1920–2012), a kindred spirit who is sorely missed. Finally, I would like to thank my parents, Paul and Susan, and my sisters Jessica and Elizabeth, for their love. This book is dedicated especially to Lizzie, for her strength and courage.

ITALIAN WOMEN WRITERS

Introduction

The Italian feminist movement in the 1970s triggered a renewed interest, from both writers and critics, in the lives and works of Italian women writers from the late nineteenth century. Studies published over the last forty years have reintroduced forgotten female authors into the Italian literary canon, and have tended to regard women writers as belonging to a homogeneous group, engendering what Elaine Showalter has described as "a literature of their own" in a given period.[1] They have pointed to particular qualities of women's writings which are perceived as different from men's in portrayals of characters, narrative style, and subject matter. They have also attempted to draw parallels between women's experience as represented in the novels by female authors of this period and contemporary social and historical reality.

Many women writers from late-nineteenth-century Italy, including La Marchesa Colombi, Neera, and Matilde Serao, whose domestic works I examine in this book, had been forgotten since the onset of fascism, during which time legislation granting women rights as workers and better access to the professions during the period 1860 to 1927 was vetoed. An important landmark in the revival of these authors can be seen in Natalia Ginzburg's autobiographical novel *Lessico famigliare* (Family sayings, 1963). In one section of the book, the author's mother, who was acquainted with Anna Kuliscioff (1857–1925), the socialist and activist in the movement for women's emancipation, praises highly La Marchesa Colombi's writings, which she remembers reading as a young girl, and encourages her daughter to recommend her work to the publisher Einaudi.[2] In 1973, Einaudi published La Marchesa Colombi's *Un matrimonio in provincia* (A small-town marriage, 1885) in its collection "Centopagine," which was edited by Italo Calvino with a preface by Ginzburg. This rediscovery was not simply of historical interest: early-twentieth-century women writers were also reappraised as significant talents. Some years later, for example, writing in an article in *La Stampa*, which appeared on 6 January 1977, Ginzburg identified what she thought were Serao's strengths:

> Serao is wonderful when she moves in the light of day, when she watches and observes. She needs concreteness, she needs to wander between solid and tangible objects and places, and among people linked to problems that are simple, clear and real; her gaze is so alive that it can give life to feelings and temperaments of any one of her characters and render them memorable, and yet at times we conserve of some of her stories and novels the deep and intense memory not only of a human trait but of a state of mind or a colour.[3]

Neera also receives high praise from another critic writing in the 1970s, Luigi Baldacci. In his introduction to Neera's *Teresa* (1886), which he reprinted in 1976, Baldacci describes the work as "one of the best Italian novels of the last twenty years from the last century."[4]

It is these three nineteenth-century women writers, rediscovered in the 1970s, that I discuss in this book, looking at their domestic fiction and non-fiction writings (journalism, which addressed a female readership, essays, and conduct books). These women were well known in their day and wrote about a common set of subjects. They shared similar socio-cultural backgrounds, and corresponded with one another: all three were married at certain stages during their careers, and Serao and Neera were also mothers. Their works cut across regional divides, thus addressing a national readership in formation – Neera was Milanese, La Marchesa Colombi was from Piedmont, whilst Serao was Neapolitan. While each differed in her use and style of language – La Marchesa Colombi's and Serao's use of language is playful, direct, and ironic, while Neera's tends to be earnest, more intent on describing the female psyche, and is characterized by a moralizing tone – the writers eschewed dialect and regionalism, writing instead in an accessible Italian.[5] (The Italian language, which is based on Tuscan from the 1300s, was codified as a written language in the sixteenth century. When it was adopted as the newly established written and spoken national language at the time of Unification, it had to be acquired through study.) In an interview she gave with the writer Ugo Ojetti (1871–1946), which was published in 1895, Serao reveals how she consciously adopted an accessible Italian:

> If my language is incorrect, if I don't know how to write, if I admire those who write well, I confess that if by chance I were to learn how to do it, I wouldn't. I believe that with the liveliness of that uncertain language and with that broken style I infuse in my works *warmth*, and warmth not only gives life but preserves people from the corruption of time.[6]

Through a reading of the writers' domestic fiction alongside their journalistic works for women, their essays, and their conduct manuals, this book argues that these genres offered women writers a means of addressing and engaging with the social and political issues of the day vis-à-vis the "woman question" during the period 1870 to 1910 – a time when unprecedented political, economic, cultural, and social change was taking hold in the new Italy. It is my contention that Italian domestic fiction and journalism that addressed a female readership contributed to more liberal thinking concerning women's "proper" roles as wife and mother in the collective consciousness, and in particular among women readers. The writers whose works I consider in this book employ a *verist* poetics, focusing on the realistic and objective description of specific settings and individual situations, often with a regionalist touch.[7] This highly visual form of literature enabled women writers to depict an almost exclusively all-female world that taught women readers to deal with their limitations and predicaments as wives and mothers. Realist fiction purports to describe the "extratextual" world in an apparently faithful way, and in this respect we might think of it in similar terms to reportage. Regardless of whether non-fiction succeeds in representing reality, its professed referent is the extratextual world, which sharply distinguishes it from those pieces of writing that declare themselves fiction. The writers' predominantly conservative stances concerning the "woman question" are clear from their non-fictional works which address a predominantly male readership. Despite this, an examination of the recurring themes of the domestic fiction – the typical experience of adolescent middle-class girls, such as a young woman's attendance at an opera or theatre performance; her over-emotional investment in a relationship with a man who courts her yet whom, for financial reasons, she cannot marry; her limited access to education and her confinement to the domestic sphere compared with boys' education and access to knowledge – reveals the writers' engagement (conscious or otherwise) with the issues with which the moderate emancipationists were concerned, such as better access to education and the professions. The authors' declarations that they did not support the movement for female emancipation (in particular Neera's and Serao's), which feature in a selection of their journalism and essays, are called into question by an examination of their contributions to journals for women, as well as their correspondence with a few exceptional women in the public eye: these reveal the same sympathy with and concern for women that is to be found in the domestic fiction, and bear witness to the writers' sense of solidarity with contemporary women writers, female performers, and their forebears. Read together, the writers' domestic fiction and journalism presents a subtle and sustained engagement with the construction of womanhood in the new Italy.[8]

My theoretical and methodological approach is guided by an analysis of discursive practices in late-nineteenth-century Italy – education and employment for women, the gendering of public and private spheres, the medicalization of women, and the shame surrounding the figure of the spinster. Writing about the fiction and non-fiction by these writers in particular stems from an awareness that, unlike Caterina Percoto (1812–1887), who wrote about peasant life in Friuli, Grazia Deledda (1871–1936), who wrote on the popular traditions of her home town, Nuoro, in Sardinia, and Carolina Invernizio (1851–1916), who wrote gothic stories, they were writing in the same genre. While this study would undoubtedly have been reinforced by an analysis of the aforementioned writers' fiction and non-fiction, there is simply not room for their inclusion. Nor is there space to go into much depth on the creative output of male artists and authors whose works conveyed a clear social message of sympathy for the underdog. (One thinks of the *macchiaioli*, the Florentine impressionist painters, who painted women engaged in their daily work; the *scapigliati*, the bohemian or "dishevelled" group of young artists, which included poets, writers, musicians, and painters from Milan who were disillusioned with what they perceived as the bourgeois lifestyle in the new Italy; the writers of *verismo*, members of the late-nineteenth-century literary movement that stressed the representation of squalid themes such as poverty, despair, violence; and the writers of naturalism who pitied women and the lower classes, such as Giovanni Verga, Luigi Capuana, and Federico De Roberto.)[9]

Regarding the issue of genre, one important point to note at this juncture is the difference with which women were portrayed by men writers and artists of *verismo* and the social. As Ann Hallamore Caesar and Michael Caesar note:

> [In the late nineteenth century] women become increasingly aberrant in Italian literature – possessed as in the case of Malombra, sexually preda-tory and hysterical as in Tarchetti's *Fosca*, sick as in Capuana's *Giacinta*, rapacious as in the protagonist of Oriani's *Gelosia* (*Jealousy*). Women's sus-ceptibility to music, to literature and to the theatre was initially seen as a cause of disorder and waywardness and ended as evidence of it, while medical and moral discourses permitted the representation of women as erotic and sadistic. Men by contrast become increasingly helpless or hopeless and the relationship between the sexes becomes one of predator (female) and prey (male).[10]

In the context of nineteenth-century Italy, the Other woman, or *femme fatale*, was the woman who transgressed bourgeois norms of "proper" behaviour and social mores by being "dangerously" attractive, and consciously and deliberately leading men to do things they would not normally do. With the exception of Neera's *Lydia* (1887), male authors were more inclined than female authors to make the Other woman the protagonist of their novels. Women writers of domestic fiction were preoccupied with depicting the everyday lives of ordinary women rather than centring their narratives on women who were male con-structs, or who existed only in an elevated fantasy form whose pur-pose was to control women's sexuality. Thus, their female protagonists are not marked as transgressive, and are entirely conventional; what characterizes them most of all is their tendency to form ill-fated emo-tional attachments with the opposite sex, to fantasize about an "unat-tainable" marriage partner, and to experience the inevitable depressive states of mind when faced with the necessity to adhere to the social prescriptions, monotony, and limitations of everyday life in early post–Unification Italy.

Culture, Gender, and the Everyday in the New Italy

Following Gayle Rubin, my premise for this book is that every society has a "sex/gender system," a "mode of reproduction" or "patriarchy," that is, "a set of arrangements by which the biological raw material of human sex and procreation is shaped by human, social intervention and satisfied in a conventional manner, no matter how bizarre some of the conventions may be."[11] Gender is a socially imposed division of the sexes and a product of the social relations of sexuality. I concur with Judith Butler's conceptualization of gender as "the effects of a subtle and politically enforced performativity," "an 'act' ... that is open to splittings, self-parody, self-criticism, and those hyperbolic exhibitions of 'the natural' that, in their very exaggeration, reveal its fundamentally phantasmatic status;"[12] the categories of woman and of man are being continuously contested and (re)defined.

These theories of gender can help us to reach a better understanding of constructions of masculinity and femininity in everyday life in late-nineteenth-century Italy. The "everyday" as an object of theory emerged in the post–Second World War era following Henri Lefebvre's 1947 publication *Critique de la via quotidienne* (Critique of everyday life). While earlier thinkers such as Lukács and Heidegger had presented the everyday as a mundane, ordinary, repetitive existence, Lefebvre argued that the everyday was also a primal arena for meaningful social change, "an inevitable starting point for the realization of the possible."[13] In its very triviality lay its seriousness; in its humdrum routine lay the potential for creative energy. For Lefebvre, the everyday weighed more heavily on women and the working classes.[14] Lefebvre's notion of the everyday as a modern Western bourgeois phenomenon emerged with the rise of the middle classes in European cities at the beginning of the nineteenth century. Sometime during the 1830s in French art and literature (which, according to Lefebvre, have better grappled with understanding the everyday), there was a recognizable and conscious movement known as realism, which became a definite trend in the latter part of the century. Indeed, as previously mentioned, one tends to think of literary realism as documenting the everyday in an apparently "faithful" way. If, as Lefebvre argues, the everyday is the place where ordinary people creatively use and transform the world they encounter from one day to another, and it is also – as Michel De Certeau has asserted – the creativity and productivity of ordinary consumers as they move across the dominated landscape of cultural production,[15] we might consider professional women writers and women readers in late-nineteenth-century Italy as discursive producers and consumers of culture and as benefitting socially, politically, and economically from their active engagement in everyday life.[16] As it shall become clear in the ensuing chapters, through a close reading of the domestic fiction by women writers from late-nineteenth-century Italy and their journalism that addressed a female readership, women in the new Italy participated in the everyday – its humiliations and tediums as well as its pleasures – very differently from men. And it was this very difference in experience of documenting in journalism and in realist fictional form, from a female perspective *for the first time* in the new Italy, which contributed in no small measure to improvements in women's civil status, in both the workplace and the domestic sphere of the home.

Economic change contributed to this through a rise in female literacy. Though still predominantly rural compared with its European neighbours, Italy experienced an unprecedented period of political, economic, and social change following the Risorgimento – the political and social process of Unification that began in the early nineteenth century and was completed between 1861 and 1870. The period saw the rise of the middle classes, an expansion in the production and consumption of print culture, and increased access to education and professions for women, particularly in urban areas.[17] According to the general census of 1861, female illiteracy was on average around 86 per cent in rural areas and 77 per cent in towns and cities.[18] In 1901, 62 per cent of Italian women were illiterate, and still ten years later 40 per cent of Italians could neither read nor write.[19] Although these figures testify to a gradual rise in literacy levels towards the end of the century, it is important to bear in mind that they may be misleading, since if a person could merely write their name legibly and read a short passage they were regarded as literate. The gradual rise in literacy rates took place in part thanks to the opening up of schools to girls and the government's efforts to widen access to education.

As in other countries, literacy was associated with political change. Although suffrage was extremely restricted at the time of Unification – only 2 per cent of the population, or 600,000 males, had the right to vote – 7 per cent (slightly more than 2 million adult males) were enfranchised in 1882, and in 1912, a new law gave the vote to all males over thirty who had served in the forces. In addition, the railway networks were rapidly expanding while periodicals and newspapers became more widely available to a growing readership. People from the south – the majority of whom were landless peasants tending large estates belonging to noble landlords in a system not unlike that of feudalism – migrated to the cities and the increasingly prosperous north, as well as abroad. Italy experienced an unprecedented industrial take-off between 1896 and 1913, during which time new sectors such as the engineering, chemical, metal-working, and hydro-electric industries and the banking sector expanded, leading to the development of the "industrial triangle" of Turin, Genoa, and Milan. Milan was one of the first European cities to use electricity for streetcars, street lighting, and industrial power, and in 1895, the first Italian automobile was made in Turin.[20]

Yet the period was one of ambiguity and paradox for many women: legally, economically, and socially, women were subordinate to men and had limited autonomy, while the climate favoured the emergence of professional, financially independent women, such as La Marchesa Colombi, Neera, and Serao. The two latter writers in particular positioned themselves as ideologically opposed to the ideals put forward by the emancipationists, which at the time signified "cultivating one's own genius, providing for one's own future without depending on marriage, marrying without selling oneself, remaining a spinster without feeling anxious, being a widow capable of being independent,"[21] yet theirs and La Marchesa Colombi's fiction and non-fiction writings are shot through with contradictory evidence of their views of women's "proper" roles as wife and mother in the new Italy.[22] According to feminist historian Franca Pieroni Bortolotti, the movement for women's emancipation in Italy did not gain momentum until the 1880s and 1890s, and was associated with the idea of revolutionary social renewal carried out by women and workers.[23] Radical emancipationists were mainly followers of democrat and republican Giuseppe Mazzini (1805–1872). They upheld the model of the independent, emancipated woman, educated but also politicized, demanding political rights and committed to social and economic change or revolution. For Mazzini, they were "patriot mothers," that is, politicized women who were devoted not only to their families but also to the cause of a democratic republic, and among them were foreigners such as Jessie White Mario (1832–1906) and Giorgina Craufurd Saffi (1827–1911). They were outsiders in a Catholic country and were met with opposition by moderate feminists, such as the poet Erminia Fuà Fusinato (1834–1876), who stressed that women should be educated in order to further social progress. According to the moderates, education would enhance women's status and prepare them to better fulfil their family duties, which included the need to earn a living, preferably as a teacher. Women should be self-sufficient, but should shun political involvement. The moderates were social or practical emancipationists who not only aimed at equal rights but also posited essential biological differences between the sexes and sought to transform society through the influence of qualities particular and seemingly natural to women, such as motherhood.

The "woman question" in Italy was debated among emancipation-ists, politicians, writers, and intellectuals to varying degrees during the period with which this book is concerned. Giuseppe Pisanelli's Civil Code, passed on 25 June 1865 under law number 2358, delegated all authority to male heads of the household, legally sanctioning women's subordination to men. The Code generally resembled the Napoleonic Code that was imposed during the period of French rule and, in some regions (e.g., Lombardy, Tuscany, and the Austrian territory), women lost previously held privileges: prior to the Code's introduction, women in these regions had full rights to dispose of their property without needing to obtain their husband's permission, and in both Lombardy and Tuscany they enjoyed limited electoral rights. The Code introduced the *maritalis auctoritas*, which meant that although married women across the nation could own, inherit, and bequeath property, they were not permitted to have a bank account without their husbands' permission, and they were required to seek their husbands' authorization in all economic transactions and legal matters, including inheritance (the *maritalis auctoritas* was abolished in 1919). Divorce was illegal, and yet courts regularly annulled marriages where the wife turned out not to be a virgin and they made no concessions if she had been raped. Wives were not permitted to have custody over their children in the absence of their father, adultery was considered a crime for women only, and unmarried women who worked or had property were expected to pay taxes but were not able to vote.[24]

The Code did bring some advantages to women's lives: fathers could no longer force their daughters over the age of twenty-one into an ar-ranged marriage, and girls and boys both enjoyed the same legal rights. Sons and daughters could inherit equally, and single women could make their own wills, engage in commerce, and own property. It came into effect in 1866, two years prior to the publication of the first edition of Gualberta Alaide Beccari's journal *La Donna*, and two years fol-lowing the publication of Anna Maria Mozzoni's pamphlet "La donna e i suoi rapporti sociali" (Woman and her social relationships, 1864), which challenged women's legal subordination to men. Arguably, the year 1910 marked the culmination of the work of the female emanci-pationists: Mozzoni had been largely responsible for the establishment of the National Committee for Women's Suffrage during this year, and Anna Kuliscioff had spearheaded a proposal, which was approved by the government in 1910, to establish a *cassa di maternità* that would provide a subsidy for the period of enforced absence from work for women. Money was amassed through an annual compulsory contribution of one or two lire a year depending on the age of the worker.[25] Regarding legislation passed in the new Italy relating to improvements in women's working conditions, in 1866 a law was introduced which sought to limit the working day of the *mondine* (the women rice workers). The law stipulated that work was not to begin until one hour after dawn and had to cease one hour before sunset, though it was widely ignored, even as late as the start of the new century.[26] Much later, in 1892, thanks to strikes held by women working in the textile and tobacco industries, in particular in Florence and Milan, the working day was reduced to ten hours in some factories. In 1902, largely due to Kuliscioff's efforts, a law was passed stipulating that a twelve-hour working day constituted the maximum number of hours that women could work. The law also granted unpaid maternity leave to women.

Returning to the topic of education, and concerning legislation passed in this field, on 3 October 1874, women were granted official permission by the government to enter the universities, and the Ministry of Education gave girls permission to attend *ginnasi-licei* (grammar schools) and the *istituti tecnici* (technical colleges) in 1883. Typically, middle-class girls who received state education in late-nineteenth-century Italy finished their schooling between the ages of twelve and sixteen years; the national curriculum for girls included arithmetic, Italian grammar, physics, biology, history, geography, geometry, religious education, art, pedagogy, French, calligraphy, and housework. Though Casati's law of 1859 – which introduced two years of compulsory primary schooling for girls as well as boys – did not explicitly ban girls from entering middle and upper schools for boys, debates about whether women should receive an education, what the curriculum should include, together with the existing prejudices surrounding mixed schools, presented girls with a psychological barrier to entry.[27] The first woman to graduate in the new Italy was a Jew of Russian origin named Ernestina Paper, who received a degree in medicine from the University of Pisa in 1877.[28] Between 1877 and 1900, 257 women graduated, whereas seven years previously there had only been thirty-eight women graduates.[29] In spite of these moves, before 1914, less than 4 per cent of university students were female, and the professions women could pursue were limited. "Acceptable" professions available to women included bookkeeping, secretarial work, working for a small business that accepted female members to its staff, charity work, working as a telegraph operator, and most commonly, working as a primary school teacher. Middle-class men typically trained to be physicians, lawyers, professors, and engineers. In terms of being granted the right to vote, although fascism gave women the vote in local elections in 1925, they could not exercise this right since there were no more local elections held. Women had to wait until 1946 until they could vote in local elections, and it was not until 1948 that they could vote in national elections.[30] The social, economic, and political condition of women in post–Unification Italy between 1870 and 1910 did improve thanks to the rise in female literacy, access to education, and the professions and better legislation protecting women at work. Nevertheless, as it will become apparent through a reading of Italian domestic fiction and journalism addressed to a female readership, women's everyday lives continued to be highly circumscribed and restricted when compared with men's.

One would come up against great difficulty if one were to set oneself the task of measuring, in a positivistic sense, the extent to which Italian women writers' domestic fiction and non-fiction from this period effected changes in legislation in education and the professions in favour of the condition of women and the growth and achievements of the emancipationist movement at the fin-de-siècle. The aim of this book lies elsewhere, for it seeks to demonstrate that the sympathy for ordinary women in late-nineteenth-century Italy that we glean through a reading of women writers' domestic fiction, and the themes with which the writers in question repeatedly dealt in their journalism addressed to women readers, held a great deal in common with the calls for changes in legislation – for example, improvements in women's working conditions and access to education – being made by the female emancipationist movement, particularly among moderates. The authors' public declarations that they did not support the emancipationist movement, which feature in a selection of their journalism and essays, are called into question by an examination of their contributions to journals for women during the late nineteenth century, as well as their correspondence with a few exceptional women in the public eye.[31] These reveal the same sympathy with and concern for women that is to be found in the domestic fiction, and they bear witness to the writers' feelings of solidarity for contemporary women writers, female performing artists, and their forebears. Read together, the writers' domestic fiction and journalism presents an implicit and sustained engagement with the construction of womanhood in the new Italy, one that is complicit with the discursive system it portrays, thereby challenging it subtly and implicitly.

Chapter 1 discusses the emergence of Italian women writers and readers of the new genre of domestic fiction in unified Italy. Chapter 2 examines the writers' conservative ideas on women's "proper" roles in a majority of their non-fiction writings while also revealing their engagement with the more liberal ideas with which the moderate emancipationists were concerned, such as women's access to education and the professions, and better working conditions for women in their contributions to journals for women. Subsequent chapters offer close readings of a selection of the writers' domestic fiction – their short stories and novels – to show how these point towards critiques of the doctrine of separate spheres of gender and women's confinement to the home, as well as women's limited access to education and the professions compared with men's. Chapter 3 examines the representation of public and private spheres in the fiction to argue that through the narratives' focus on female characters and the (lack of) spaces available to them within the "private" sphere of the home, the writers were raising awareness among women readers of their own restricted access to spaces outside the home. In Chapter 4, I analyse depictions of nervousness in the fiction to argue that the writers instilled in their women readers the notion of the female protagonists with whom they were identifying as sexually desiring subjects, whom they may have perceived as role models. In the final chapter, I look at depictions of women's relationships in the fiction to suggest that these pointed towards the writers' attempt to forge a sense of solidarity among middle-class women readers and writers. The texts I focus on have been selected according to date of publication, genre, and author: I refer to around thirty domestic short stories and novels, around ten non-fictional works, and thirty journalistic pieces that were written and published by the aforementioned writers during the period 1870 to 1910, and whose protagonists are middle-class young women and/or adolescent girls. Due to editorial constraints, it has neither been possible nor practical to refer to all of the domestic fiction published by the three authors during the period in question.

Chapter One

Italian Domestic Fiction,
Its Readers, and Its Writers

In this chapter, I address the emergence of women readers and writers in the new Italy and offer an analysis of the generic limitations of domestic fiction in the Italian context. Italian domestic fiction and journalism by women functioned as a type of conduct manual that taught women to deal with their predicaments and limitations. The genre shares certain characteristics with American domestic fiction from the 1820s to the 1870s insofar as it opposed radical demands for women's rights, presented day-to-day relationships among women who constituted the texture of their own lives, and employed an immediate, functional, and popular style of language. But where women writers of American domestic fiction sought to overturn the "male money system as the law of American life" by espousing a "cult of domesticity," that is, fulfilment for women in marriage and motherhood, Italian domestic fiction offers an implicit feminist intervention by subtly questioning women's prescribed roles as wives and mothers.[1] In contrast to the themes their male contemporaries addressed in their writings, Italian women writers illustrated a predominantly female world, one in which men formed the backdrop in a setting that was typically the home, in order to present slices of believable female characters' lives in a seemingly impartial way.

Women Readers and Writers in the New Italy

The emergence of the printing press in the second half of the fifteenth century, and the establishment of Venice as the European centre for publishing, provided favourable conditions for women who wrote poetry and religious and devotional writings for an ever-widening public.[2] In the middle of the sixteenth century, an anthology composed entirely of women poets was printed. Around the same time, however, the Council of Trent, which opened in 1545 and continued until 1563, produced a program of institutional and moral reform that imposed stricter control over women's sexuality and greater emphasis on the "rightness" of their subjection: women were to remain in the home and were given only the literacy required to teach their children.

In the aftermath of the French revolution, Silvio Pellico's 1819 review article in *Il Conciliatore* encouraged women not only to read but to write novels, arguing that the novel was best able to represent experiences that bore directly upon women's lives, and in 1822, Giovanni Pirotto launched a "Pleasant and Instructive Library for Gentlewomen" (Biblioteca amena ed istruttiva per le donne gentili), which specialized in translations of fashionable foreign novels for female readers. Several decades later, however, in a letter to Celestino Bianchi, Ruggiero Bonghi complained that Italian women – whom, in his opinion, should form the backbone of a modern public – do not read Italian books except for *strenne* (publications given to readers at Christmas time).[3] As Lucienne Kroha reminds us, during the Risorgimento, "the woman writer was perceived as nothing less than a trespasser invading a masculine domain unless she confined herself to pedagogical writing."[4] Yet while Caterina Franceschi-Ferrucci's pamphlets on the education of women put forward the new patriotic ideal of austerity and moral integrity, the 1850s also saw the publication of fiction by women, which targeted a female readership. These included works by the aforementioned Caterina Percoto from Friuli, and Luisa Saredo, born in Turin, who were both read and respected in their day by male critics and women readers.[5] Nonetheless, educators and intellectuals were keen for girls and young women to be taught an ideal model of femininity through their reading and thus recommended that women read and write conduct books, and read religious writings.[6] A recent study on Italian women journalists draws attention to the abundance of paintings and photographs of the woman reader from this period and depicts her as reading a variety of literary genres from clerical material to love letters and novels.[7]

Ian Watt's classic study *The Rise of the Novel* (1987) has shown that the emergence of the novel took place in France and England in the early eighteenth century, and novels by and about women in England and France began to appear in the late eighteenth century. The question of the rise of the novel has been debated, but there is little dispute that prose fiction took new directions in the eighteenth century and came to new prominence.[8] The first edition of Manzoni's historical novel *I promessi sposi* (The betrothed, 1827), established the arrival of the modern novel in Italy, which came almost a century after its French and English counterparts. This was due in part to the absence of a sympathetic cultural climate and of a national language, as well as low literacy levels.[9] By the end of the nineteenth century, the novel had a wide readership, yet it continued to be viewed with suspicion by members of the ruling class – priests, politicians, physicians, and intellectuals – who saw it as harmful to women's supposedly fragile minds and as bringing about social risks for women because of its associations with the exploration of themes of female desire, eroticism, and sexuality. Writing in his column "L'arte di vivere" (The art of living) in 1890, Il dottor Gigi refers to books that adolescent girls and young women "know they should not read and which get read precisely for this reason," defining these as "naturalistic or *verist* novels, however you wish to call them, but almost always pornographic or pessimistic, which get read bit by bit with the repugnance of doing something forbidden."[10] The pseudonymous author goes on to attribute the reading of novels as the cause of hysterical symptoms in adolescent girls:

> It is very often this state of continuous agitation of the spirit which develops from doing something wrong, the desire to do so and the fear of being found out, together with that genre of literature that creates *nervousness* in so many young women.[11]

Writing on novels by women in contemporary Italy in 1863, Carlo Cattaneo asserted that given women's supposedly natural preponderance for sentiment over reason, they were better able to offer "an exquisite analysis of sentiment, a delicate and highly refined knowledge of the human heart, a love for truth that defeats and surpasses every illusion."[12] In addition, Tommaseo's entry on the novel in the first dictionary in the new Italy defined this as "narrative prose focusing on the fortunes of one or more characters – responding to the taste of the masses but of poor literary value."[13] Read alongside Cattaneo's statement, and given that the novel was a foreign imported genre in the nineteenth century, it becomes clear that intellectuals perceived the novel as inferior for its appeal to a growing reading public, whose knowledge of classical literature (known only to the elite) was scarce or even non-existent.

Writing in the first issue of Beccari's emancipationist journal *La Donna* in 1868, Angelica Palli argued that women who wrote on education and literature were respectable, and that their literary endeavours were compatible with a woman's mission as wife and mother: "she can carry them out while being next to her children's cradle."[14] Italian women writers emerged onto the literary scene as never before around the mid- to late 1870s. Writing for a growing female readership largely comprising the middle and upper classes, women writers could be found in cities from Naples, Rome, and Milan to Venice, Florence, Turin, and Genova. Though they emerged around one hundred years after their British and French counterparts, undoubtedly they would have read and been influenced by previous generations of women writers in Europe whose works had been translated into Italian, such as Jane Austen (1775–1817), George Eliot (1819–1880), George Sand (1804–1876), and Ann Radcliffe (1764–1823). Angelo De Gubernatis's *Dizionario biografico degli scrittori italiani* (1879) records 180 women writers.[15] By the 1880s, conduct books, etiquette books, essays, and articles written by women had joined the growing number of female-authored novels and short stories available on the literary market. What marks the 1880s as particular with regards to literary production by women in Italy is the variety of literature available to women readers written by women journalists, editors and directors of journals, poets, and novelists. It was a literary production that, according to Antonia Arslan, constituted a kind of female subcultural *impegno* (ideological commitment) on behalf of women thinkers:

> If women are encouraged to "remain in the home," this takes place while reading, writing, forming groups, and *salotti* where female thought – which by now had firmly established itself – can develop itself and strengthen: the ignorant woman has gone out of fashion.[16]

In considering the circumscribed and restricted nature of women's everyday lives in late-nineteenth-century Italy within this legal, social, and cultural context, *some* (typically) middle-class women were able to exercise peculiar forms of discursive power from within the home. Thus, the woman writer emerged as never before in Italy as novelist and journalist writing for a growing readership made up of women and men. Her rise in popularity was facilitated by rapid industrialization and the expansion of the press, and contemporary male writers often held her in high regard. A review of La Marchesa Colombi's 1878 novel *In risaia* by the editor of *Il Giornale delle donne*, published during the same year the novel appeared, includes high praise of her work by the positivist scientist and popularizer Paolo Mantegazza:

> It really is wonderful. As art, I find the delicate and exquisite touch of a woman, a faithful and perfect picture of a world that so few know about, the psychological writer, painter and illustrator. Excellent Marchesa Colombi! Your book is also a novel about hygiene, and without wishing to be a pedant it touches upon social questions with the authority of a teacher.[17]

Neera, La Marchesa Colombi, and Serao shared similar socio-economic and cultural backgrounds with their female readers. Yet the writers' positions differed considerably from those of their readers: women writers had high public profiles, and their writings were widely distributed and open to criticism, debate, and dissent. Lucienne Kroha draws attention to the ambiguities of the period regarding the prescribed roles of women in Italian society and the serious woman writer, arguing that

> on the one hand, opportunities for self-expression were greater than they had ever been before and a variety of economic, political, social and literary forces were pushing women toward forms of consciousness that were profoundly threatening to the *status quo*. On the other hand, serious writing demanded a degree of self-exposure which not many women of the time were prepared to risk.[18]

Neera's *Il libro di mio figlio* (My son's book, 1891), which addresses a male readership, indeed illustrates her awareness of this difference in her status compared with the majority of women. In this, she describes women who endorsed their "proper" role as "humble souls," while referring to herself as a writer gifted with "richness, intelligence, knowledge" along with male writers and thinkers.[19] Neera's "anxiety of authorship" as a woman writer in late-nineteenth-century Italy becomes clear through a reading of her own views on women writers expressed in her non-fiction writings. In these, she consciously adopts a self-effacing role by appearing to have happened upon her career as a writer while carrying out her domestic duties. In her autobiography *Una giovinezza del secolo XIX* (A childhood in the nineteenth century, 1919), she confesses that "when someone enquires about the training I had to write the thirty or so volumes I have published, I reply: socks and shirts, shirts and socks."[20] In an article entitled "Le donne del secolo XVIII" (Women from the eighteenth century), published in *Il Giornale delle donne* on 16 March 1877, Neera even belittles Italian women writers, describing them as "lost and aggressive angels who dip the tip of their wings with ink,"[21] a comment that shares Aleramo's negative view of Italian women writers of this period, which she expresses in her 1906 autobiography *Una donna* (A woman): "All the writing by women in the country seemed deficient to me: long empty sentences without connection and conviction."[22] Serao reveals less humility about her status as a woman writer and is not ashamed to confess her ambition:

> I write everywhere and about everything with a unique audacity, I conquer my place through pushing and shoving, with an intense and ardent desire to get there ... I do not pay attention to the weaknesses of my sex and keep on going as if I were a young man.[23]

Notwithstanding divisions in professional status between women readers and writers, as well as differences of opinion on women's proper roles as wives and mothers in the new Italy among women writers, as I shall discuss in more depth in chapters 2 and 5, there prevailed a kind of covert, albeit not yet fully realized, solidarity among women readers and writers that cut across the writers' professional status and national reputations.[24] Certainly the wide circulation of fiction and non-fiction by women writers, which documented in minute detail the lives of the women readers reading their texts, contributed in some degree to the formation of a female solidarity, however unofficial, which ran in tandem with the more widely recognized solidarity among the female emancipationists in the public arena. Furthermore, there existed another burgeoning solidarity *à propos* of women writers and their female readers, one that was being forged, however accidentally, between the woman reader and the woman writer's (predominantly female) protagonist. Significantly, for the first time in Italy, middle-class women readers were reading about women like themselves who were depicted with sympathy and pity. As if to anticipate Luce Irigaray's assertion of the importance of female affiliation, and Hélène Cixous's idea that through writing women will create new identities for themselves and eventually new social institutions, women writers of domestic fiction – consciously or otherwise – were tapping into debates on the role of women in the new Italy by means of their recurring portrayals of female characters whose identities were predominantly shaped in relation to one another.[25] When she published "La donna e i suoi rapporti sociali" (Woman and her social relationships), Mozzoni was probably the first woman in the new Italy to invoke the lives and works of many women from history who had made an important contribution to society in a public document (she dedicated the story to her mother).

Furthermore, there is evidence in late-nineteenth-century women writers' texts of an attempt to present women from different generations together in writing. In her autobiographical novel *Una giovinezza del secolo XIX*, Neera invokes two generations of women, remarking that "there still exists a daguerreotype in which three young women, my mother and her two sisters, are portrayed sitting in line,"[26] and it is not by chance that Neera's and Serao's journalism in particular frequently document the lives and works of famous women, some of whom were women writers. The absence of an identifiable genealogy of women writers prior to the 1880s in Italy suggests that the roots of what Showalter calls a "female literary tradition" – one that laid the foundations for highly acclaimed future women writers of Italy, such as Aleramo, Annie Vivanti (1866–1942), and later, Ginzburg – were established in the late nineteenth century thanks to the favourable literary and cultural climate.

In *A History of Women's Writing*, Letizia Panizza and Sharon Wood ask the important question of what criteria justify separating women's writing in Italy from a history of Italian literature, and whether this is not simply another way to ghettoize women and what they do.[27] Responding to accusations of her "bad and highly imperfect use of language,"[28] Serao purportedly said in an interview with Ojetti in 1894:

> We four (I mean Verga, De Roberto, myself and Capuana to some extent), accused of incorrectness, have a public who follows us and who reads us: why should we die out in posterity? The novel is a recent art form [in Italy], and there are no historical arguments that go against this. We shall wait and see.[29]

The above passage is revealing of the fact that Serao saw herself as belonging to a "school" of predominantly male writers as opposed to being perceived as a "woman writer" in terms of belonging to a ghettoized group. The same is true of Neera, who in *Confessioni letterarie* (1903) also dismisses the notion that her writing belongs to a tradition of women's writing:

> I do not believe that this love of the minute, the intimate, the feminine comes from my being a woman, because other women writers do not have it and

it predominates in fact in all psychological writers, as I have already said, demonstrating that it is a consequence of temperament and not of sex.[30]

Narrating the Past and Literary Realism

Since this book emphasizes similarities between fiction and non-fiction writings in their narrative properties, it is important to consider briefly the nature of fiction. The word "fiction," which comes from the Latin word *fictio(-n)* from *fingere*, meaning to contrive or pretend, refers to prose literature figuring imaginary events and people. "Non-fiction" is purportedly its direct opposite. Nietzsche calls into question the notion of the literary fictitious as something that is not "real" or "true," something that is invented, as opposed to factual, by suggesting that "facts are precisely what there is not, only interpretations."[31] While acknowledging that the different forms of non-fiction writing (e.g., reportage, essay writing, travel writing, historical accounts) each have their own set of characteristics and narrative properties, generally speaking authors of non-fiction publicly take responsibility for their text, recounting and interpreting a series of empirically verifiable events in an apparently "objective" way. The writers of scholarly accounts and journalism, much like the writers of realist fiction, position themselves in their literary texts as outside the forces of events, as an apparently faithful interpreter and reporter. Yet writing (and, I would argue, any self-authored creative work) is always subjective, even while it may aspire towards objectivity, for non-fiction writing involves the subject as always already implicated in the text of which the purpose is to negotiate questions of politics and power. Though words can refer to facts, the language used to convey a fact in the context of a factual piece of writing has a particular ideological agenda. Thus, fiction and non-fiction writing share common narrative properties. All writing, be it fictional or non-fictional, is open to ideology and is structured around narrative cultural and metaphorical systems that predominate over facts, even while non-fiction writing seems to privilege the latter as an "objective" construction. In general terms, fiction refers to a literary work such as a novel, a short story, a play, or a poem that has been "invented" by its author: she or he adopts an ontological role that enables her or him to hide behind the guise of fiction.[32]

Literary texts can be used to understand social change and vice versa. They are bound up with other discourses and structures and are part of a history that is still in the process of being written. They are embedded within the social, political, and economic circumstances in which they are produced and consumed; they are circumstances that are not stable and are susceptible to being rewritten and transformed. From this perspective, literary texts are part of a circulation of social energies; they are both products of and influences on a particular culture or ideology in formation. Through a series of readings of nineteenth-century realist novels, Catherine Belsey has demonstrated that these texts perform the ideological function of interpellating their readers as subjects. In *Critical Practice* (1980), Belsey puts forward the view that realist novels offer themselves for interpretation on the principle that it is, above all, character that governs social action.[33] In drawing upon Louis Althusser's view of ideology as "interpellat[ing] individuals as subjects in the name of a Unique and Absolute Subject,"[34] Belsey shows how the reader of realist fiction is asked to read from the subject position of the omniscient narrator. She demonstrates how the reader is required to make sense of the text as if from within the subjective experience of one of the characters and is directly asked to take up the position of a subject. The ideological function of realist fiction contributes to the reader's belief that she or he is the centre of her or his own thoughts and actions and able to make sense of and determine her or his own life. In relation to realist fiction by women writers from late-nineteenth-century Italy, whose narratives repeatedly feature female characters as passively accepting their prescribed roles as wives and mothers or as spinsters, this presents an interesting paradox: the female protagonists are entirely conventional and recognizable to their female readers. While the protagonists may entertain thoughts of transgressing their desired role, and in some cases carry out these transgressions, the narratives conclude with their protagonists passively accepting their fates, thereby seemingly upholding the status quo.

This is the case in La Marchesa Colombi's *Prima morire* (Before dying, 1887), in which the protagonist Eva leaves her husband and daughter for a musician whom she soon abandons to return to her husband and daughter upon learning of her daughter's illness.[35] The same is true of Serao's short story "La virtù di Checchina" (Checchina's virtue, 1883), in which the protagonist accepts an assignation with the Marquis only to reject it for fear of bringing shame upon her and her husband's reputation.[36] Thus, on the one hand, late-nineteenth-century Italian women readers are interpellated into the narratives as subjects able to make sense of, and able to determine, their own lives, yet, on the other hand, the narratives' prevailing ideology is seemingly one that repeatedly upholds and perpetuates their roles in the new Italy as

wives and mothers.[37] Yet however conventional the subject matter of
individual narratives of domestic fiction may seem, by reading them it
becomes apparent that the same contemporary social issues with which
its female readership was intimately connected are addressed repeatedly, revealing sympathy on behalf of women writers for middle-class
women's predicaments.

Realism and Italian Women Writers

The publication of Capuana's *Giacinta* in 1879 marked the arrival of
naturalismo in Italy. This can be defined as the representation of a believable everyday "reality" that grew out of the French realist novel and
the naturalist school pioneered by Émile Zola through his portrayal
of the dark harshness of everyday life as we see, for example, in his
L'Assommoir (1877). Writing on the differences between *naturalismo* and
verismo, Gino Tellini argues that while naturalism analyses in a seemingly detached way the political and social struggles of the subjects it
describes, the narrator of *verismo*, rather than remaining outside the narration as a "detached" observer, is inside it as an embedded reporter,
as a voice that belonged to the environment she or he is describing.[38]
I do not find Tellini's distinction between the narrator of naturalism and
that of *verismo* to be convincing; as previously mentioned, the narrator,
in her or his role as observer and/or as reporter, always writes subjec-
tively, even while she or he may aspire towards objectivity. *Verismo* as
a literary school is commonly associated with Verga's short stories and
novels, which represent social critiques of the oppression, poverty, and
neglect of the south of Italy. The modes and concerns of the prevailing literary movements of *naturalismo* and *verismo* allowed – and even
required – women writers to present themselves as detached observers
of the events about which they wrote, thereby positioning themselves as
disengaged authors of the events they faithfully described. The female
narrator of domestic fiction set herself apart from what she described
by positioning herself as a reporter of things as they appeared to the eye
and the ear in everyday life; she thus had the apparent excuse of not
taking full ownership of the subject matter she described. Observing
the differences between Verga's and Serao's styles of writing, Wanda
De Nunzio Schilardi points out that whereas Verga

> does not need to intervene in his material on the hostile reality that he
> regards as immutable, on the contrary Serao ... intervenes frequently in

the first person to help the reader to observe, participate, feel moved and disapproving, but also to reassure him [sic] about the tensions and social revolts which appeared as though they had to devastate the constituted order.[39]

As I will discuss in the ensuing chapters, in Neera's and La Marchesa Colombi's domestic fiction and journalism for a female readership, their interaction with their readers is also apparent.

Neera's narrative fiction complies with the principles of *verismo*, with the important difference of focusing on female experience.[40] This is also the case in the domestic fiction by Serao and La Marchesa Colombi, as well as in the realist fiction that documents female experience among the lower classes, such as La Marchesa Colombi's *In risaia* (In the rice fields, 1878). Serao explores the exploitation of female workers peripherally through her frequent portrayal of servants who nevertheless remain at the margins of their respective narratives, and so, too, does Neera through her portrayal of the prostitute Falena in her short story of the same name (1893).[41] In Italian domestic fiction, the embedded reporter/narrator from *verismo* is internal to the events taking place in the fiction. This is given credibility by virtue of the writers' sustained attention to the representation of daily experience of middle-class women, which makes the fiction – partly influenced by the naturalists – unique. Women writers' use of language, notwithstanding its claims to objectivity and impersonality as realist, was, albeit in fictional form, the personal voice of certain women in spite of centuries of male-dominated literary discourse. The female narrator tells the story of "real" women from *her* point of view: as if to recover hundreds of years of a majority of silent female voices, an all-female world is being depicted in the texts.

While Verga's description of the eponymous heroine Nedda in his short story (1874) conveys her physical appearance in language as aspiring to be objective and detached from any emotional involvement with, or personal view of the character, Neera's pity of and sympathy for the female protagonist in her *Teresa* (1886), as well as her sympathy for the protagonist's mother, is apparent through her representation of their lives, which is given heightened credibility by virtue of her gender as female. Verga provides a matter-of-fact account of Nedda's appearance: "She was dark-skinned and poorly dressed, with that air of coarseness and timidity brought on by poverty and loneliness."[42] However, the reader gains insight into the eponymous protagonist's state of mind in Neera's *Teresa* through an account of Teresa's feelings upon having danced the previous night for the first time with a young man: "On awakening her first thought was of him; but instead of being a gay and happy thought it came almost like a pain, like a sharp thorn in her skin."[43] Women and men authors of realist fiction differed in their depictions of female characters: women writers emphasized the life cycles of female characters, which provided the plot and were crucial to the ways in which the stories were told. The language of writings by women from this period is often simple and direct; it is not the language of Verga's *contadini*, nor is it the language of D'Annunzio's aristocrats. Instead, women writers write feelingly about their protagonists' thoughts and emotions pertaining to their experiences, and they describe characters from different social groups through the personal voice of the female narrator, who empathizes with the characters' situations. As Ann Hallamore Caesar eloquently explains:

> Where *veristi* writers look to create the appearance of truth, *vraisemblance*, by giving readers the illusion that they are looking directly on the world without having recourse to an authorial lens, ... women writers ... develop an aura of truth by making very visible their own hand in the development of the narrative and by documenting it with letters, diaries and memoirs.[44]

Certainly, there are differences in the style of fiction and non-fictional language employed by the three writers whose works are the focus of this book: while La Marchesa Colombi's and Serao's use of language is a playful and ironic language that entertains, Neera's language is earnest, focused on describing the female psyche, and characterized by a moralizing tone. Women writers eschewed dialect and regionalisms and instead used standard Italian to talk about women's experiences of everyday life in late-nineteenth-century Italy. Referring to the language of women's journalism from the period, Silvia Franchini and Simonetta Soldani note the creation of

> a new type of writing, one which draws considerably upon less formal editorial forms: a rapid "imperfect" writing, rich in allusions to the writing of the daily press and current affairs, as well as of linguistic and syntactic forms that are more direct and closer to the spoken language.[45]

The same direct, rapid style of writing by women is also a feature of the writers' fictional works. As Lucienne Kroha argues, La Marchesa Colombi and Serao share a very modern and precocious awareness that literary language and structures are not mimetic and transparent. ... [Women writers] filter and *construct* images of reality rather than reflect reality directly: metafiction, parody, pastiche, authorial intrusion all testify to this awareness.[46]

A cogent example of this can be found in La Marchesa Colombi's short story "Impara l'arte e mettila da parte" (Learn a trade for a rainy day, 1877), in which the narrator takes the liberty to advise her readers not to search for the name of her protagonist (a professional artist) in the catalogue containing the names of artists who submitted their work to the Brera exhibition during that year: "Odda had finished a painting and had sent it to the exhibition in Brera. Not this year, though; I implore you, ladies, not to look her up in the catalogue, I do not want to advertise her name."[47]

Italian women writers follow the example of their British and French foremothers and counterparts such as Jane Austen, George Eliot, and Charlotte Brontë: "Parodic, duplicitous, ... all this female writing is both revisionary and revolutionary, even when it is produced by writers we usually think of as models of angelic resignation."[48] According to Anna Santoro, women's use of language in their writings from this period is even experimental:

> Experimentation, if one can call it this, is the continuous attempt that the woman writer makes to combine sentiment and technique, to keep her own voice present and to use (or to invent) a language whose official path was conquered with difficulty. La Marchesa Colombi's dry use of language as well as Neera's in *Teresa*, their grace and use of irony and of others, is a novelty in the literature of these years.[49]

Women writers such as La Marchesa Colombi and Neera were aware of this break with tradition in their style of writing, which was partially a consequence of the fact that many (including Neera) were, of necessity, self-taught. In La Marchesa Colombi's novel *Un matrimonio in provincia* (A small-town marriage, 1885), the narrator gently mocks the protagonist's father's enthusiasm for the classics, Latin, Greek, and the vernacular, pitting his knowledge and ability to recite these works to his daughters against their ignorance on their daily walks:

> He was the one who, from time to time, taught us to read, write and do arithmetic. And during our walks he gave us our literary education. At

least this is what he believed, because he told us the stories of the *Iliad*, the *Aeneid*, and *Jerusalem Delivered* ... Our poor dad came over all anxious and in a sweat, as if he had made those gestures himself.[50]

Similarly, Neera writes in her *Una giovinezza del secolo XIX* (1919) that "among the classics I found in my father's library, I read not even one; I judged them boring and cold."[51] While one must be cautious about making claims that there existed an Italian "women's writing" in the late nineteenth century, it is important to acknowledge the distinctions between female and male writers in terms of how they were received during a given time, their use of subject matter, the differences in their styles of writing and tone of language, and their very different experiences of everyday lives.

Chapter Two

Journalism, Essays, Conduct Books

I am not in favour of the emancipation of women; there, I am saying it outright. In my humble opinion I believe that women are sufficiently emancipated.

Neera, "La donna libera" (The free woman),
L'Illustrazione italiana, 2 April 1876

Women must not have political opinions ... at most they can be monarchists ... but they should not dare declare their political faith in public.

Serao, "La donna politica" (The woman politician),
Corriere di Roma, 6 April 1887

The day I see with my own eyes a female MP, a female doctor, a female lawyer under the beautiful sky of Italy will be the saddest day of my life.

La Marchesa Colombi, "La donna povera" (The poor woman),
L'Illustrazione italiana, 16 April 1876

These quotations illustrate how Neera, Serao, and La Marchesa Colombi positioned themselves in their non-fictional writings addressing a male readership as ideologically opposed to the ideals put forward by the female emancipationists.[1] In this chapter, I examine the writers' non-fictional works – journalism, essays, letters, and conduct books – some of which were distributed across the peninsula as well as abroad.[2] I argue that while putting forward conservative views on women's "proper" roles as wife and mother in the new Italy in their writings commissioned by journals and newspapers, as well as in their essays, whose intended readership was male (presumably in order to protect their reputations as women writers in the public eye), their contributions to journals for women and conduct literature are revealing of the writers' moderate emancipationist sympathies.[3] For, in these, the writers express a deep concern for, and sympathy with, the social and psychological pressures affecting ordinary women – in particular from the middle classes – in their daily lives (such as arranged marriages, women's legal subordination to men, their confinement to the private sphere of the home, and their limited access to education and the professions). These issues were equally central to the emancipationists' campaigns to "imagine a different society based on new social relations among its members, men and women."[4] From this evidence, it would seem that Serao, La Marchesa Colombi, and Neera belonged to what Beatrice Pisa has described as the group of moderate feminists: those who preferred women to be educated but only superficially, able to read but not a university graduate, a nurse but not a doctor, aware of their own moral rights but not of their legal ones, able to influence their husbands but not to vote themselves, able to vote in local but not in general elections.[5] Such positions and leanings, both ideological and moral, in journals for women, as well as in columns addressed to a female readership in newspapers intended to be read by men, were in part the inevitable effect of the writers' alignment with the editorial policy of the journal in question. Yet somewhat intriguingly, these writers – who were often at pains to declare themselves against the movement for female emancipation, particularly in their journalistic pieces intended for male readers – also actively sought to publish their writings, both fictional and non-fictional, in journals and columns for women in newspapers intended for a male readership.

My selection of journals and contributions to columns in newspapers for this chapter is based upon the following criteria: that the writers whose journalism I am concerned with contributed on a regular basis, and over an extended period of time, to the journals in question; that the journal has not been written about extensively by other scholars; that the selection draws upon publications which cut across regional divides and were distributed throughout the peninsula. As previously mentioned, there were differences of content and style of language among the three writers, and these differences will be considered at various points throughout the chapter. In addition, the chapter looks at how the writers' non-fiction developed over a forty-year period that saw changes in legislation in favour of women in education, and debates and campaigns for better working conditions thanks to Kuliscioff and Mozzoni.

Women Reading Newspapers

Assuming realist fiction can help us to understand the time in which these writings were set, representations of women reading newspapers in women writers' realist fiction in post-Unification Italy until the First World War are ambiguous: it is not clear to the reader whether female characters absorb the contents of the material they are presented as reading. In Neera's *Lydia* (1887), we learn that the eponymous protagonist, "Spent two full days sat next to her uncle's armchair reading *him* the *Revue*,"[6] while the narrator describes the male protagonist listening to the character Elvira from Capuana's *Giacinta* (1879), who is in the next room, apparently reading the newspaper.[7] Both the aforementioned female characters are marked as transgressive in their respective narratives: Elvira from *Giacinta* is dying of consumption, while Lydia commits suicide. Similarly, in Neera's *L'Indomani* (On the following day, 1890), while the female protagonist awaits the return of her husband from the club he regularly attends during the evenings, it is unclear to the reader whether Marta takes in the information she appears to be reading in the newspaper: "she did some needlework, leafed through the newspaper, yawned."[8] The narrator's use of the verb "leaf through" to describe her reading style indicates Marta's disengagement with the newspaper's contents, while her reaction to it is one of boredom and tiredness. La Marchesa Colombi represents her spinster-protagonist, Odda, from her 1877 short story "Impara l'arte e mettila da parte" (Learn a trade for a rainy day), as making a show of reading a newspaper: "[Odda] hardly had time to sit in an armchair and pretend to be reading a newspaper ..."[9] The question concerning whether women who read newspapers were regarded as "improper" is highlighted most poignantly in Serao's "Telegrafi dello Stato" (The state telegraph office [*women's section*], 1895), in which the narrator describes a telegraph operator's reaction when her boss walks into the room: "[Caterina] Borrelli folded up a literary paper called *The Butterfly*, which she was reading in secret, [and] put it in her pocket ..."[10] The depiction of women reading newspapers in realist fiction by women writers bears a close resemblance to the way in which La Marchesa Colombi, writing her column "Cronaca" in the journal *Museo di famiglia*, describes her female readers' occasional glances at political newspapers for news of society events: "she often sees them casting a glance of curiosity over the pages of the newspaper in search of novelty – of life."[11] Curiously, however, La Marchesa Colombi's own reading of newspapers is not treated as shameful: in the same journal, writing for the same column on 13 August 1876 in which she discusses politics, she cites having read the *Gazzetta di Torino* and *Il diritto*. Similarly, in the column she wrote for Neera's journal *Vita Intima*, called "Colore del tempo" (Sign of the times), assuming the role of intermediary between her female readers and the political newspapers with which she is familiar, on more than one occasion La Marchesa Colombi paraphrases news.[12]

Male characters, on the other hand, are depicted reading newspapers with an air of confidence and authority in women writers' realist fiction: we learn from Neera's *Teresa* (1886) how the tax collector would go to the bar in the square to read the newspapers, and in her *Fotografie matrimoniali* (Wedding photographs, 1898) how Gigi, "after having lit a cigar, takes a newspaper from the coffee table and reads it."[13] The reading of newspapers was widely considered to be an activity associated with men; women who read about current affairs were typically frowned upon for engaging in what was considered to be a male pursuit, and as such tended to be associated with the movement for emancipation.[14]

Columns by Women Writers in Newspapers and Journals

Periodicals for women in England and France were in circulation from the beginning of the eighteenth century, and although journalism in Italy took off from the early seventeenth century as elsewhere in Europe, it was not until the late eighteenth century that an Italian woman first started working on a periodical.[15] Elisabetta Caminer Turra (1751–1796) was the first woman to write for a journal in Italy in 1768, and she was later the director of the journal *Europa Letteraria*. The first journal for women in Italy, *La Toelette* (The toilette), came out in Florence in 1770, yet as Verina Jones has shown, Gioseffa Cornoldi Caminer's *La donna galante ed erudita* (The gallant and erudite woman), which appeared in Venice in 1786, was the first journal to address a predominantly female readership.[16] It published features on fashion and beauty, health and hygiene, marriage, family life, children's education, articles on literature and theatre, and *cicisbeismo* (the phenomenon whereby married women had a recognized male escort). The journal folded just before the start of the French Revolution. In 1804, Carolina Lattanzi (1771–1818) brought out the *Corriere delle dame* (Women's courier) in Milan. This was published on a weekly basis, and had 700 subscribers in 1811. The readers of the few journals for women that were circulating during this period were wealthy and cultured and from the upper-middle classes. As

Verina Jones points out, however, their husbands, who might be land-owners or members of the emerging entrepreneurial class, also read the journals, which contained the latest medical discoveries, practical advice on bringing up and educating children, as well as on breastfeeding.[17] Journals for women readers continued to be produced throughout the Restoration and, between 1848 and 1861, patriotic journals by women were founded.

The increase in women reading women's journals in post–Unification Italy was partly in response to the gradual rise in literacy rates following the opening up of schools to girls and the government's efforts to widen access to education to women and the lower classes during the period 1874–84. Women's journals tended to be financed and directed by men (which was still the case in Italy in the 1950s), presumably for economic reasons, although there were cases where women were founders and directors.[18] One could suppose that the contributors to these journals were predominantly female, although this is hard to determine since many authors, both male and female, wrote under pseudonyms. Neera and La Marchesa Colombi in particular, and, as previously mentioned, to a lesser degree Serao, all contributed to journals for women as well as to mainstream literary journals such as *Nuova Antologia* (New anthology), *Fanfulla della domenica* (Weekly literary supplement of Il Fanfulla), and newspapers. La Marchesa Colombi wrote for *Il Corriere della Sera* (Evening post) and *La Stampa* (The press), and Serao contributed to a variety of different newspapers. In the same year as La Marchesa Colombi was writing for the family journal *Museo di famiglia* (Family museum,1876), she began contributing to a column in her husband's newspaper *Il Corriere della Sera*, entitled Lettera aperta alle signore (An open letter to women), which she signed with the pseudonym "La Moda."[19] This addressed a female readership, and included discussions on fashion and good manners, the current debates concerning the "woman question," and widening access to education for girls. Serao also wrote a column in a national daily newspaper, *Corriere di Roma* (Rome's courier), between 1885 and 1886, which she founded together with her husband Edoardo Scarfoglio. Entitled "Per le signore" (For women), this column was featured regularly on the second or third page of a four-page newspaper and, as its title suggests, addressed a predominantly female middle-class readership in a newspaper aimed at a male readership. From a reading of Serao's entries, one finds descriptions of the monotony of women's daily lives, the lack of education open to women, the exploitation of child labour, the poor working conditions of telegraph workers, and declarations of sympathy for women who committed suicide due to false accusations of adulterous relations.[20] Curiously, in her column on 8 January 1886 about a woman doctor called Maria Farnè whose work she praises, Serao writes: "And I, old-fashioned, obstinately fighting female emancipation, enemy of all the rhetoric of political votes, of women lawyers, of women MPs and other similar wretched things, from my humble position as a female worker, I salute this strong sample of female workers."[21] Such columns sought to shift the emphasis from newspapers aimed at a male readership to include women, thereby calling into question the status of newspapers as objects of consumption for men alone and the stigma surrounding associations with women and the public sphere of work, knowledge, and political debate.

Many women wrote for women's journals during the period following Unification up until the onset of fascism. The three writers whose journalism is discussed here frequently contributed to literary and cultural journals, as well as to journals for women, over sustained periods of time (while La Marchesa Colombi's career as a journalist peaked during the period 1868 to 1875, both Neera's and Serao's journalistic production began in the late 1870s and lasted until their deaths). What follows is an examination of a selection of journals for women to which the writers in question contributed. Two of these were intended for families – *Museo di famiglia* and *Il Passatempo* (Pastime), which became *Il Giornale delle donne* (Women's daily paper) in 1872; one was intended for a female readership, to which Neera and La Marchesa Colombi contributed – *Vita Intima* (Intimate life); and, finally, I consider the emancipationists' journals *La Donna* (Woman) and *L'Italia femminile* (Feminine Italy), for which – somewhat surprisingly – all three writers, with the exception of La Marchesa Colombi in *L'Italia femminile*, were commissioned (and also actively sought) to write. The themes with which the emancipationist journals engaged bore a striking resemblance to those that are to be found from a reading of the domestic fiction by the aforementioned writers. For example, Serao's "Terno Secco" (Jackpot, 1887) is concerned with a private teacher's low pay and long working hours; her "Telegrafi dello Stato" deals with similar concerns in relation to young female workers from the lower and middle classes. Neera's *Teresa* (1886) highlights the authority figure of the father, and her short story "Falena" (1893) denounces the condition of prostitutes. La Marchesa Colombi depicts the isolation of spinsters through the figure of the aunt in *Un matrimonio in provincia* (A small-town marriage,

1885). While critics have for some time indicated a disjunction between the fiction of these writers and their journalism (in that the fiction may be read as more ideologically feminist than the journalism, which is generally perceived as conservative and supportive of the status quo), in the examples that now follow, I will show how this disjunction only holds when the writers are producing journalism addressed to a non-gender specific readership.

Journals for Women

Museo di famiglia (1861–79; Milan)

The first issue of *Museo di famiglia*, which came out in Milan in January 1861, offered to its female and male readers stories, poems, as well as features on history – such as the history of the names of calendar months, important dates from the Risorgimento successes – current affairs, science, and lifestyle. On the front cover, one finds the following inscription in the issue from 10 December 1861:

> The journal aims to offer enjoyable educational pieces which are edify-
> ing without being puerile, and which are suitable for young people and
> adults alike, and can be enjoyed during the long winter evenings and in
> the idleness of summer. We are delighted to present to Italian families a
> publication which is on a par with those of a similar kind which have been
> so successful abroad.[22]

The journal included illustrations of Italian cities, copies of famous paintings and statues, and portraits of famous men. One of its columns, "Illustri Donne Italiane" (Illustrious Italian women), was dedicated to the lives of great Italian women. The journal came out every Thursday, and typically contained sixteen pages. Readers could have a subscription, although prices varied according to the reader's location. La Marchesa Colombi, writing several times for *Museo di famiglia*, addressed a female readership. In the first instalment of her column, "Cronaca" (Chronicle), which she wrote for the best part of 1876, she included news on current events, art and culture, theatre and fashion, lifestyle, and gossip. As with her column "Lettera aperta alle signore" (Open letter to the ladies) in *Il Corriere della Sera*, she writes for women readers alone. She introduces herself somewhat histrionically: "I simply cannot enter into a relationship with my kind readers without a formal presentation. And when I have explained that my name is *la marchesa colombi*, they will know that I was Parini's contemporary ... and that's enough."[23] La Marchesa Colombi's style of writing is characterized by a self-conscious playfulness, dry humour, and ironic understatements. She complies with – whilst at the same time going against – dominant discourses and traditional models. The following excerpt, taken from the same article for La Marchesa Colombi's column, illustrates this point:

> *Museo di famiglia* – serious, instructive, had until yesterday kept itself away from the chaos of city life, to avoid the shoves from the crowd, the flirtatiousness of elegant people, the street brawls and the gossip in the salons ... And as a tribute to its twenty years, *Museo*, or a person on its behalf, made me a proposal and said: "Do you, Marchesa, who have been afflicted in your home by so much tittle-tattle ... feel able to talk about news, art, theatres, fashions, and about that part of human life that could be of interest to women, avoiding tittle-tattle, and the frollicks of your times ... and of ours, and the pedantries of your age?" I consulted my mind. It seemed to me as though I could still take on that job, and so I did. (*Museo di famiglia*, 1 June 1876)[24]

As well as containing humour, the passage is an example of what Antonella Gramone describes as La Marchesa Colombi's "pre-narratological tendency" in her presentation and deconstruction of the role of the author and the author's authority; following Roland Barthes, Gramone argues that far from being "dead," the author "is able to write and interrogate herself on her function and on her relationship with her readers, for whom she is able to fill in the gaps in the empty spaces."[25]

There is, in fact, a striking similarity in La Marchesa Colombi's justification for writing her column here with the preface to her conduct book *La gente per bene*, published a year later in 1877. In her introduction, she addresses both female and male readers as a 143-year-old Marchesa Colombi, in which she tells her readers that the editor of the volume approached her thus: "You, Marchesa, who have lived for many, many years among fashionable society, who have been able to observe the customs over three or four generations, should write a book, which deals precisely with social conventions and mores." Drawing attention to her respect for women readers, La Marchesa Colombi continues: "Now, the type of book that I would be willing to write should have women as its natural critics."[26] Such playful and innovative devices not only offered La Marchesa Colombi a way of entertaining her readers, they also allowed her to distance herself from her readers as a woman writer in a profession consisting for the most part of men. In addition, they gave her a legitimate strategy for winning over the many male readers who were likely to have been familiar with her column "Lettera aperta alle signore" in *Il Corriere della Sera*, as well as "Cronaca" in *Museo di famiglia*. Her writing style here, as indeed elsewhere, is characterized by a colloquial and ironic language that seeks to inform and entertain. In her entry from 29 June 1876, she apologizes if she is boring her readers: "But I fear my chronicle will seem too long."[27] In the entry of 10 September 1876, she includes a reference to her ignorance of Latin, explaining in a rather tongue-in-cheek fashion: "Me, I know no Latin except for the Our Father."[28]

Whether La Marchesa Colombi refers to writing from a beach or a poolside (fictitious or otherwise), she offered her female readers a vicarious experience, metaphorically transporting them to places where many of them would not have been permitted to go. In an article entitled "Esposizione di Filadelfia: Il Padiglione delle donne" (Exposition in Philadelphia: The women's pavilion), published on 1 June 1876, La Marchesa Colombi writes enthusiastically about the opportunities available to women in America compared with Italy: "Everyone knows that in America the fairer sex is also the stronger sex. There, women are fighting and taking on all the work that the men do. No wonder they did not want to take part in the exposition!" Moreover, writing in her column "Cronaca" on 22 October 1876, she somewhat provocatively puts forward her views on politics and foreign affairs, and makes fun of men, who, during election time, seem to be obsessed with voting, drawing attention to women's exclusion from the event.[29] In her "Cronaca" from 31 May in the same year, La Marchesa Colombi had congratulated the prima donna Erminia Frezzolini on her marriage. Here, she wryly draws attention to the fact that the singer "has finished her career as an artist" (ha finita la sua carriera d'artista), and that "now she will begin that of a wife" (comincia ora quella di sposa), implying that it is a pity the singer could not practise her profession and be a wife contemporaneously.[30] Indeed, La Marchesa Colombi's critique is recast several months later by Beccari, who, writing in her journal *La Donna*, congratulates the poet-improviser Giannina Milli on her marriage, explaining wearily in her article that "she has renounced her post as history and geography teacher and as director of the teachers' training college in Rome."[31]

Neera also contributed regularly to *Museo di famiglia*, from July 1875 onwards, to a column entitled "Conversazioni con mia figlia" (Conversations with my daughter), in which she sets up a fictional dialogue between herself and her thirteen-year-old daughter named Maria. Through the mother, Neera reveals a strikingly modern view with regard to women who work. In response to the daughter's comment that she would be very unhappy if she were forced to go out to work, the mother replies in a gently provocative yet resigned fashion: "The person who works acquires a greater right to life."[32] Adhering to the social norms of the day, the mother educates her daughter in *buone maniere* (good manners). Though the mother–daughter relationship is a hierarchical one, it is also mutually respectful and caring: in her entry on 22 July 1875, the mother adopts the term "mia cara fanciulla" (my dear girl) to teach her daughter the value of work, and presents her thinking over the advice she has given by referring to her daughter with a diminutive, commenting in the first person: "In her tiny head my words crowded together a little" (Nella sua testolina le mie parole si accozzavano un poco). The emotional closeness between mother and daughter in Neera's fiction challenges Freud's notion of the mother as having been symbolically rejected by the daughter who, in the Elektra complex, identifies with the authority of the father. Rather, it anticipates Julia Kristeva's maternal semiotic pre-Oedipal *chora*,[33] in which the subject is envisaged as a speaking being, and Luce Irigaray's celebration of the maternal and the mother–daughter bond. La Marchesa Colombi's and Neera's collaborations on *Museo di famiglia* had a twofold effect: they played a significant role in shoring up the journal's reputation and appeal to an expanding middle-class female readership, and they contributed to enhancing the writers' reputations and furthering their careers as professional women in the public eye.

Il Passatempo (1869–72; Turin); *Il Giornale delle donne*
(1872–1938; Turin)

Directed by Americo Vespucci, *Il Giornale delle donne* began as *Il Passatempo: Letture amene per le famiglie* in 1869. It was published bimonthly. As with *Museo di famiglia*, readers could subscribe annually, every six months, or every three months to the journal. It aimed to promote women's culture, defend her rights, and declared that it would *"Avoid political and religious matters"* (*sfugg[ire] dalle questioni politiche e religiose*).[34] Despite its moderate intentions, the journal engaged with contemporary debates on the role of women; for example, their access to education, their entrance to the professions, and the question of the vote and divorce were all treated on many occasions. The journal published La Marchesa Colombi's inauguration speech (also featured in the emancipationist journal *La Donna* on 29 January 1871), which was delivered at the opening ceremony of the school Gaetana Agnesi and at the conferences she took part in with Mozzoni in the early 1870s. It, too, contained news of developments in education in favour of women – for example, it included an announcement in the issue of 17 August 1879 of the Minister of Education's plans to extend the number of years of study for girls in the high schools from two to four years, and it outlined his plans to include the teaching of foreign languages in the curriculum. In the same issue, there was news of a woman from Naples who had gained a degree in Literature and Philosophy from the University of Naples. The journal's front-page illustrations evoke such themes: a mother is depicted reading a book entitled *Donne illustri* (Illustrious women) to her daughter. The figures are surrounded by objects associated with received notions of femininity and the education of women: flowers, ribbons, scissors, a quill pen, a stool, sheet music, a piano, a globe, and books are all featured in the picture. At the bottom of the page the words "Education," "Hobbies," and "Morality" are printed.

La Marchesa Colombi, Neera, and Serao all contributed to the journal during their careers. La Marchesa Colombi's collaboration began in 1870 with a column entitled "Il piccolo corriere" (The little newspaper). This featured short stories, reviews, correspondence, and poetry. An article written by Serao entitled "Poesia casareccia" (Home-grown poetry) depicted sympathetic portrayals of the stereotypical late-nineteenth-century middle-class young woman, widow, aristocratic woman, and grandmother, but presented the spinster in an unfavourable light. This angered the journal's readers as well as its editor.[35] Subsequently, no further articles appeared by her in this particular journal. This represents yet another example of how the journal shared the same concerns and sympathies towards unmarried women with that of the more radical *La Donna*. Twenty years later, writing in her conduct manual *Saper vivere* (1900), Serao speaks favourably and sympathetically of spinsters, recommending that unmarried women move beyond the feelings of disappointment at not having found a husband and enjoy the freedoms of a single lifestyle from age forty onwards: "From the age of forty onwards … one can go out alone; travel alone; live alone or with a faithful female friend who finds herself in a similar situation; receive guests alone; all that without being laughed at ... One can come and go, discuss, write, leave, return, without having to answer to anyone."[36]

Neera contributed to the journal between 1877 and 1882. She wrote for women readers, addressing them with the polite form *voi* (adopting the publication's official mode for addressing its readers), and referring to them as "my ladies."[37] Recalling La Marchesa Colombi's linguistic playfulness, at times Neera's use of language teetered on sarcasm: in her article "Lui: pensieri di una mamma" (Him: thoughts of a mother), in which she explores a mother's angst at having to leave her son at school, she fantasizes about the possibility of keeping him at home and educating him herself. Recalling La Marchesa Colombi's entry in her column for *Museo di famiglia* from 10 September 1876, she writes:

> And Latin? And Latin? Madam teacher, do you know how to translate Marco Tullio Cicerone? And mathematics? Would you happen to know what lorgorithms, integral and differential calculations are? ... Ah! no, unfortunately I know nothing about lorgorithms, nor calculations, and not even Marco Tullio Cicerone. I see that one has to resign oneself to this fact.[38]

Typically, however, her writing style is earnest, its tone moralizing. Her articles for *Il Giornale delle donne* included "Le donne del secoloXVIII" (Women from the eighteenth century), in which she writes about the lives of women such as Marie Antoniette, Madame de Staël, and Napoleon Bonaparte's wife: an informative piece in which Neera sets out to educate her women readers about exceptional women from the past in the public eye. Neera eulogizes a woman writer from the seventeenth century, Maria Rabuton Marchesa di Sevigné, whom she describes as "a rare and delicate feminine mind," "a woman of great spirit," who possessed "a certain ingenuous grace."[39] In a later article, "Le donne milanesi: cherchez la femme" (Milanese women: cherchez la femme, 1881), anticipating her realist novels *Teresa* and *Lydia* (1887), and *L'Indomani* (1889), Neera examines the life cycle of the young woman from adolescence, to marriage, to motherhood, focusing in particular on Milanese women.[40] What is striking is Neera's apparent endorsement of women who lead an active life as opposed to one in which women spend their days cooped up in the home carrying out domestic chores:

> In the other provinces of Italy, also in many main cities, women lead such a solitary and monotonous housewifely life between spending time with

their husbands and making stockings; they are quite rightly surprised by Milanese women's vertiginous running from a shop to a theatre, from one house to another, from a book to hats specifically for women, from a concert to a conference, always quick, swift and darting around.[41]

In the following passage, which in many respects bespeaks the themes of La Marchesa Colombi's *Un matrimonio in provincia* (A small-town marriage), Neera sympathizes with adolescent Milanese girls, using the euphemism "è un po' malata" (she is a little ill) to describe young girls of thirteen or fourteen years beginning their menstrual cycle:

> Her years as a young girl are quite hard, poor thing! ... Later she starts to become emancipated ... She disappears between the ages of thirteen and fourteen ... She is a little ill; she is too tall to go out and about all day; often her dress has become short, and while waiting to have another one made she stays at home helping her mother to peel potatoes ... Many of these are good girls, deep down; they get married early, they have babies which they often breastfeed, they become fat and no longer care about what they wear.[42]

Neera's final contribution to *Il Giornale delle donne* is in the form of a letter addressed to Eduardo De Albertis. Published on 5 August 1881, it is Neera's indictment in response to his damning review of her novel *Il castigo* (1881), in which the female protagonist, who is married, has an adulterous affair with a younger man.[43] Neera defends her work, using sarcastically vituperative language and a forthright tone. More significantly, she berates De Albertis for his lack of sympathy for women, who, she argues, do not have the same freedoms as men, in particular in matters concerning sexual desire:

> So, you don't like my *Castigo*? ... If I am allowing myself to write this letter to you it is because, moving beyond the intrinsic merit of the book (I say merit by way of expression, you know), you wanted to attack the genre ... You, Mr De-Albertis, are your own master of wanting *books that are read out loud in the family*, but if the entire literature from Homer to Virgil, from Aristotle to Shakespeare, from Balzac to Dumas, had been restricted to this theme, the repertoire would be quite limited – you would be pleased, I understand, but tastes vary ... Laura is one of the most human types immaginable ... Certainly she is not likeable, but have you given any thought to the sad life that she led until her thirties? ... Do you know what

it means to always be deceived and disappointed, to live surrounded by love without being in love ... *Ah! You men are always fine, and satisfied, happy, well-balanced in mind and spirit, you find it noble, courageous and honest to deride and insult wretched women, to whom love was forbidden their whole lives; you call them hysterical spinsters, and they wonder why an author listens attentively and understands their secret agony. And you know, I understand how you cannot find a single feeling of sympathy for this ill and embittered woman – you judge her too easily from your fortunate position as a man.*[44]

Even while the journal's self-declared objective was to steer clear of questions concerning politics and religion, it explicitly followed developments in the law, which favoured women's access to education and the professions during this period. Furthermore, the journal encouraged the collaboration of women writers whose contributions invited an open dialogue with the journal's expanding number of women readers – readers who are most likely to have been familiar with the writers' realist fiction in which similar themes are addressed.

Vita Intima (1890–1; Milan)

Neera founded and edited her own weekly journal, *Vita Intima*, in Milan between 1890 and 1891. In a letter to Giovanni Verga, dated 14 June 1890, Neera invites the writer to contribute to the journal, which, interestingly, she does not confess is her own. Describing the journal, Neera writes: "It is not literary, nor artistic, in the usual sense. It is addressed to women, to all women, *even those who do not have a literary education but can read.*"[45] Neera also elicited contributions from Luigi Capuana, Serao, Federico De Roberto, and Roberto Bracco. She aimed to produce a journal that could be read by women who read novels, whom she sought to interest in comment and analysis and current affairs. In a letter to Angiolo Orvieto dated 22 May 1890, Neera emphasized that, as the director, she would remain anonymous:

At the end of the month a journal will appear in Milan under my auspices (annonymous), not a literary journal in the true sense, but rather a journal about humankind, *causeries*, gossip, dedicated principally *to women who do not all (thanks be to God) concern themselves with literature* and who also want to read something ... designed to offer a variety of articles to women who stay at home, where one talks about everything that one would normally talk about in a *salon* among friends.[46]

Thus, Neera's intentions were not dissimilar to those of La Marchesa Colombi, whose "Cronaca" in *Museo di famiglia* brought news of events, lifestyle, theatre reviews, and which sought to inform its readers about the lives of famous singers and actresses. La Marchesa Colombi wrote a regular column in Neera's journal entitled "Colore del tempo" (Sign of the time) from June 1890 to January 1891, which, like "Cronaca," included comment and analysis on current debates, cultural events, concerts, opera and theatre performances, society life, the latest fashions, and focused on depicting outdoor spaces rather than issues pertaining to the domestic sphere of the home. The aforementioned matters were generally discussed in articles by Neera, although La Marchesa Colombi's regular article, "Il governo della casa" (Running the home), was also concerned with domestic issues. Neera also wrote a feature column entitled "Farfalle nere" (Black butterflies), which she signed with the pseudonym La Vanessa Atalanta.[47] It contained reflections on woman's nature and on love, and her conduct manual *Il libro di mio figlio* (My son's book), published by Galli in 1891, also appeared first in her journal. In terms of the journal's layout, typically, La Marchesa Colombi's column "Colore del tempo" featured on the first page of the journal and was followed by an article by Neera on feminine behaviour (one article was on women's hands, for instance, while another discussed devout women). In one of her early articles, which she signed with her name, Neera gave her traditionalist views on the ideal woman: "Dear ideal woman ... you must be: beautiful and modest, religious and solemn, devoted to your home and to sweet affections!"[48]

One of the most intriguing regular contributions to the journal was the aforementioned column on mental and physical health, "L'arte di vivere" (The art of living), signed by "Il dottor Gigi." Il dottor Gigi kept up a regular correspondence with his (or her) readers, offering advice on topics such as breastfeeding, the different stages of a woman's life (such as adolescence and motherhood), nervous illnesses, and how to live a healthy and balanced lifestyle.[49] The journal engaged with the lives, trials, and tribulations of its women readers on a level that was new to them. The following extract illustrates the thoroughness with which Il dottor Gigi discusses the different stages of girls' and young women's lives, which recalls many of the themes that are explored in domestic fiction:

Then when one thinks of the enormous separation between every stage of women's lives, for which the adolescent has needs and feelings which are profoundly different from the young girl's, puberty has roles which are so different from those of the adolescent, the wife such a new life compared with that of the adolescent, the mother so different from all, a special dictionary of hygiene for women would seem essential ... I would take the female type, the mother; I would initiate her little by little in the secrets of how to give her female child a physical education. We would take her as a newborn, and we would accompany her together across all the stages of life: infancy, childhood, adolescence, fatherhood, motherhood, critical age, old age, we would study her in her relationships within the home, with men, with her surroundings, with the world in which we live.[50]

Thus, the aim of the journal was to steer clear of features on fashion, recommendations for home improvements, and recipes. The editorial board was made up of female and male writers such as La Marchesa Colombi, Bracco (who signed his column "Corriere da Napoli" with the pseudonym "baby"), and De Roberto, and the journal's contributors included Capuana, Contessa Lara, Annie Vivanti, Bruno Sperani (pseudonym for Beatrice Speraz), and Anna Vertua Gentile. It came out every Tuesday until 29 December 1891, when it ceased to appear with no explanation.[51] The same recognition of the disadvantages of being a woman in late-nineteenth-century Italy is evident in Neera's letter to De Albertis published in *Il Giornale delle donne*, and recurs in her opening address in *Vita Intima*. The tone of the piece is personal, intimate and informal, and aims to forge a close and honest relationship with its female readers, as well as to deny the commercial nature of the transaction. In addition, whereas Neera addresses her female readers in *Il Giornale delle donne* with the formal *voi*, here she uses the informal *tu* form, which at the time was unusual:

For you who reads. *Vita Intima* salutes you, gracious reader. – It is born and wants to live above all for you; she wants to become your most trusted friend, asking you only for a little affection in exchange. The men have their newspapers that they read along the streets, in cafés, in clubs, in theatres, a little everywhere and at any time; serious newspapers, packed with boring politics, at which you cast a glance with a little grimace.[52]

Neera's recognition of women's social and psychological oppression, which is illustrated most famously in her novel *Teresa*, is also acknowledged in the literary journal *Fanfulla della domenica* on 15 April 1888: "People have called me unjust, pessimist, a supporter of my sex when in works written with the most ardent love for my neighbour, I have dared to defend women, pure women, fallen women ... that is to say, the oppressed."[53]

On the surface, Neera's journal presented traditional views on women's roles. Yet its incarnation also permitted her to address the women readers of her realist fiction on discursive matters such as female subjectivity, personal hygiene, debates on women's access to education, current affairs, and contemporary culture, in a more autonomous way than in her aforementioned contributions to journals for women, and in her collaboration with Mantegazza. Through her own journal, Neera was able to establish and foster relations with like-minded middle-class women, the majority of whom were wives and mothers whose lives revolved around the domestic sphere, home, and family, and whose access, production, and consumption of intellectual stimuli was, on the whole, circumscribed.

La Donna (1868–92; Padua; Venice; Bologna) and
L'Italia femminile (1899–1904; Milan)

Mozzoni wrote frequently for the first official publication supporting the emancipation of women, *La Donna*, which was founded, run, and financed by Beccari. The journal began in Padua and ran from 1868 to 1890. In 1871, it expanded the number of its pages and transferred to Venice, where it became bimonthly and changed its identity as a "moral and educational periodical" to an "educational periodical." In 1877, it transferred again, this time to Bologna, where it remained until 1891. The journal was suspended between 1891 and 1892, apparently because of a dearth of contributions, and because Beccari had become involved on a new journal entitled *Mamma*. The last copy of *La Donna* that Beatrice Pisa has been able to find dates from October 1892, and the *Annuario della stampa italiana* (Italian newspaper yearbook) from 1895 does not mention it.[54] The journal was unique insofar as it represented the only publication to be run by women, for women, although men also contributed to the journal on occasion. Mantegazza, for example, published an article entitled "Un idillio sull'Abetone" (An idyll on the Abetone) on 10 December 1875. *La Donna* explicitly stated its mission to promote solidarity between women both on a national and international level, "to maintain lively relations with our sisters from other countries ... to unite all thinking and reasoning women from around the world."[55] (Though the term "solidarietà" is absent from Tommaseo's and Bellini's

Dizionario della lingua italiana [1861–79], Aleramo uses it in *Una donna* to claim that "a secular female solidarity did not exist then.")[56] The journal's distribution was low – in 1890, the periodical guide reported that each issue had a print run of merely 500 copies.[57] Its readers were educationalists, teachers, and female workers from the upper and middle classes, and contributors to the journal were not paid.

The journal presented itself as political rather than literary – it published neither serialized novels nor short stories, and it avoided any inclusion of "frivolous" topics, such as fashion, lifestyle, or suggestions for home furnishings. It did, on occasion, publish poems with a serious message.[58] There were pieces on educational reforms, reports on the opening of new schools for girls, announcements of the first women graduates, the publication of figures of women's poor salaries, reports on the pitiable working conditions of women workers, debates on the proposal for legislation on prostitution, articles on the way in which women who did not marry were estranged from, and perceived with shame by their community, and pieces on the Civil Code. The journal followed with interest developments in favour of women's rights in America. An announcement on this topic appeared in the issue of 10 May 1872: "Our readers are well aware that at the University of Michigan, as in all universities in the United States of America, women are admitted to study Law and Medicine like men and in perfect equality with them."[59] La Marchesa Colombi's collaboration on the journal lasted from 1870 to 1873. On 29 January 1871, the journal published her aforementioned inaugural lecture that had appeared in *Il Passatempo* during the same year. Serao contributed to the journal with an article published on 20 November 1879 entitled "Domenica," in which the writer describes a typical Sunday in Naples, and is as unfavourable towards spinsters as she is in her earlier piece, "Poesia casareccia" (Home-grown poetry), from *Il Giornale delle donne*: "A little hope returns to the dried up hearts of mature spinsters; they cover their yellowing faces with a little pink net veil, they try to forget the distant past, ah! And they smile at the future."[60]

Serao and Neera also contributed to Aleramo's journal *L'Italia femminile*. This came out weekly on a Sunday, and, like *Il Giornale delle donne*, it was sold abroad. Neera published a short story entitled "Equilibrio" on the front page of the issue of 22 January 1899 in which she describes a wife's regret at not being a mother. In the same issue, the editorial board awarded Neera a "Medallion," praising her "intelligence" and "good manners": "She is a gentlewoman, in the best meaning of the word. She talks very little, and never about herself, but she thinks a lot; which one can see from her very dark, beautiful eyes … It is a true pleasure to have her as a collaborator."[61] Serao contributed a short story entitled "La cravatta del rimorso" (The sorry cravat), which appeared on the journal's front page on 22 October 1899. Her story depicts with irony a man's remorse at having betrayed his fiancé on a business trip to Rome from Naples only to discover that in his absence she has become engaged to another man.

Despite what could be described as Serao's and Neera's implied nod to the emancipationist movement through their contributions to journals such as *La Donna* and *L'Italia femminile*, their readers openly challenged their conservatism concerning women's "proper" roles that they put forward in journals and newspapers targeted at a male readership. For example, emancipationists published open letters in response to Neera's and Serao's conservative views on women's roles published in other articles in newspapers. On 10 October 1883, Emilia Mariani published an "Open Letter to Matilde Serao" in *La Donna* in response to an article on women lawyers in *Capitan Fracassa*, in which Serao had argued that women should not be allowed to practise law.[62] Similarly, in *L'Italia femminile*, in response to an article Neera published in *Il Corriere della Sera*, in which she had argued that women should not be brought up to work alongside men but instead should be mothers and wives, Adele Maiani Nulli had published an "Open Letter to Neera." Though paying tribute to Neera as an "intellectual," Maiani Nulli argues:

> And what if one does not find a husband? And what if one does find one, in the name of that very article of our Civil Code which says: 'the woman in certain cases is obliged to contribute to maintaining the family,' how can she do it if not being a factory worker? She doesn't have the necessary background to approach a profession, or to get a job.[63]

La Marchesa Colombi's, Neera's and Serao's collaboration on emancipationist journals is certainly intriguing. By commissioning women writers who publicly declared themselves against the movement for female emancipation, the journals' ideological positionings were overtly tempered. In addition, the women writers' collaborations opened up a dialogue between their emancipationist contributors and readers, and, perhaps more significantly, between emancipationists and women writers whose views on women's roles were frequently presented as conservative elsewhere.

Conduct Books, Essays, Letters

"Proper" behaviour, or behaving "well," was valued highly in late-nineteenth-century Italy, and this was particularly the case as far as women were concerned. One of the many ways of behaving properly in society was to demonstrate a sufficient degree of modesty (*pudore*) – a psychological attribute of social behaviour that one may associate with embarrassment, shame, or awkwardness. Writing on the history of modesty in Italy between Unification and the Second World War, Bruno Wanrooij draws attention to the fact that conduct books were also written for men after Unification: women writers were just as interested in imposing modesty on men as they were interested in imposing it on women.[64] In line with their implied fashioning of self-respecting, intelligent, dignified, and heteronormative women who invite men's respect and courtship, La Marchesa Colombi's and Serao's conduct books included advice to male readers, encouraging them to treat women respectfully. Serao begins her conduct book *Saper vivere* (1900) by addressing a male readership,[65] and La Marchesa Colombi advises men against reading a newspaper at the dinner table or following a woman on the street in her *La gente per bene* (People in polite society, 1877).[66] Similar advice to men on treating women with due respect is tactfully put forward by Neera. In her collection of aphorisms, *Farfalle nere e farfalle bianche* (Black butterflies and white butterflies), she offers advice to men, such as "Respect is without doubt a major expression of love coming from a man," and "Some men, ignorant of the value of compassion, spoil the little they can give to fallen women. They seem to me like those who, having only a piece of bread left, give it to a dog."[67] Similar comments on treating women with respect, which are aimed at a predominantly male readership, are evident from a reading of Neera's aforementioned *Il libro di mio figlio*, *L'Amor platonico* (Platonic love, 1897), and *Battaglie per un'idea* (Fighting for an idea, 1898). Yet modesty was impressed predominantly upon women in the new Italy. The first dictionary in the newly unified state, *Dizionario della lingua italiana* (1861–79), included a long entry on *pudore* and contained the following description:

> *Pudore*: A feeling that informs the spirit of something morally improper; it is an exterior sign of such feeling. *Pudore* in man is instinctive; and it seems certain animals also have it; and the kindest and most loveable among them show the most signs of it, and those who do not seem to have it disgust us more. In man it has a moral origin; it is the good sense of decency.[68]

The importance of women's *pudore* in late-nineteenth-century Italy is also illustrated in the many conduct books or *galatei*, published mainly by women. Among the most popular of these were La Marchesa Colombi's *La gente per bene* (1877), Neera's *Dizionario d'igiene per le famiglie* (1881), which she co-authored with Mantegazza, and Serao's *Saper vivere: norme di buone creanze* (Knowing how to live: Norms for good manners, 1901).[69] The manuals addressed a general readership and offered advice – predominantly to women, but also to men – on courtship, the family, young women's first attendances at public occasions such as balls and the theatre, and advice on how to dress. Neera's entries in *Dizionario d'igiene* primarily offered advice to mothers on how to bring up their daughters, and provided meditations on breastfeeding, love, weakness, pain, emancipation, youth, pregnancy, reading, nervousness, and tiredness.[70] Neera had wanted to include entries on the following topics: menstruation, the experience of having intercourse with one's husband on one's wedding night, and lust, yet Mantegazza had objected on the grounds that the book would not have been read "by that great majority of mothers who believe ignorance is synonymous with virtue and silence is a very good preventive."[71]

In La Marchesa Colombi's conduct manual, the author makes the point – albeit wryly – of appearing modest to her readers: in addition to posing as the 143-year-old wife of the character il Marchese Colombi from Paolo Ferrari's satirical play *La satira e Parini* (Satire and Parini, 1856), in her chapter on brides under the heading "honeymoons," in which she speaks favourably of the joys of travelling as a married couple, she apologizes in advance for causing offence to any readers who may have held more conservative views on travelling with one's husband for the first time.[72] The book had an immediate success, and by 1902 there had been twenty-seven editions. The kind of advice La Marchesa Colombi offered to young girls included respecting one's elders; behaving with sangfroid in relation to one's marriage prospects; being careful not to intimidate one's mother with newly acquired knowledge; when receiving guests, being sure not to invite their peers to go into a separate room or to stand on a balcony thereby exposing themselves in public and offending their mothers; and not wearing a low-cut dress to the theatre. The author reveals that there are more benefits to being a "signorina matura," which included being able to write with more freedom and to read a quantity of things that a few years before were forbidden to her.[73] La Marchesa Colombi's advice to spinsters is consoling and encouraging, and focuses on the advantages

of spinsterhood.[74] While her conduct manual was ideologically conservative, certain uncommon stylistic features in the text, such as the
occasional playful self-ironic remark about her age, and the tongue-in-
cheek statement about men being more intelligent than women, render
it entertaining and engaging to her readers, almost undermining its
conservativism.[75]

Neera's and Serao's advice to spinsters and writings on spinsterhood
is similarly encouraging. In her *Saper vivere* (1900), Serao also speaks favourably of spinsterhood, recommending to unmarried women to move
beyond the feelings of disappointment at not having found a husband,
and to enjoy the freedoms of a single lifestyle from age forty onwards.
In addition, Neera appeals to her readers to be sympathetic towards
spinsters in the aforementioned collection of essays *L'Amor platonico*:

> If we then consider the old spinsters, these evanescent figures who are
> aunts, cousins, teachers, faithful and devout servants who have sewn
> around us many many metres of cloth, who have made many many stock-
> ings for other people's children, and who still blush if someone mistakes
> them for a married woman, how many shy and ardent women, all mel-
> ancholy, all marked by destiny's painful and sometimes ironic stigmata![76]

For women readers, such conduct manuals functioned to boost their
readers' morale, to restore in them a sense of self-respect and dignity,
and to console them. For instance, Neera's entry on "Emancipazione"
in her *Dizionario d'igiene* puts forward the view that women's designated role as wives and mothers makes them better off than men, of
whom "great things" are expected in education and the professions:

> For the majority of them, studying is a chain that they have to drag with
> them their whole lives at their work desk ... Women who are in charge of
> their home, their time, among tranquil occupations, in the sweet work of
> the family – with their embroidery, with their books, in the corner at the
> happy hearth, on the window sill – women with their privileges, their
> rights, don't they seem happier to you than men?[77]

The writers' recommendations for good conduct reveal a concern with
fashioning and upholding a heteronormative, albeit modern, model
of femininity that commanded men's respect, and that showed
women to be dignified, intelligent, well-turned-out, and self-respecting.

La Marchesa Colombi remarks upon young girls' intelligence being superior to that of men's.[78] She also advises young women who receive marriage proposals to be decisive, pragmatic, and forthright in the manner in which they give their reply.[79] Serao's advice to young women of age eighteen in her *Saper vivere* is similarly concerned with ensuring that women can "take extreme care of [their] demeanour in public: a reserved demeanour, but gracious: courteous but not overly familiar: a lively conversation, – if it is lively – but not excessive: moderately jokey, not sulkiness: the right level of seriousness, though not sad."[80]

In the aforementioned essay *Battaglie per un'idea*, while Neera puts forward a generally conservative view concerning women's role, she includes passages with themes that bear a striking resemblance to the ideas presented nearly forty years previously by Mozzoni in her "La donna e i suoi rapporti sociali" (Woman and her social relationships, 1864). Mozzoni draws attention in her essay to the numerous literary texts dedicated to women, in which women are perceived as objects of desire rather than independent, intelligent subjects.[81] Similarly, in *Battaglie per un'idea*, Neera is quick to point out to her predominantly male readership that women should not be objectified: "It is not true that women are gracious little animals who are brought into the world for the pleasure of the stronger sex ... Women's virtue is not sufficiently appreciated; it is not sufficiently appreciated, strangely enough, by those who are most interested in having it, that is, by men."[82] Earlier on in her essay, Neera draws attention to the women who inspire, console, and comfort artistic men of high repute, arguing that without these women there would be no such literary and artistic works:

> Without women we would not have our masterpieces, Shakespeare and Goethe would not have written, nor would Raphael have painted. Why? Behind every man's glory is a woman, in every flourishing household one finds the work of a woman, in every happy childhood one finds woman, in every charitable passion, woman, in every generous and heroic action, woman, always a woman: inspirer, consoler, friend, guardian, sacred ark of future generations, and one dares to say that she has nothing to do, that she has not done anything and that she will only do something when she studies Latin.[83]

This quote bears a striking similarity to the mantra adopted by second-wave feminism that behind every successful man there is a woman.

Curiously, Virginia Woolf ponders the same thought several decades later in her book *A Room of One's Own* (1929):

> Why are women ... so much more interesting to men than men are to women? A very curious fact it seemed, and my mind wandered to picture the lives of men who spend their time in writing books about women; whether they were old or young, married or unmarried, red-nosed or hump-backed – anyhow it was flattering, vaguely, to feel oneself the object of such attention.[84]

Mozzoni argues that women have agency as wives, but only if their marriages are based on love, otherwise, argues Mozzoni, wives become slaves.[85] This idea shares something in common with those put forward by Neera in her *Battaglie per un'idea* on marriage. Here, she argues that women and men are equally disadvantaged in their prospects of finding love in marriage, and that when men marry, they have a lot more life experience than women: "Men marry in conditions of absolute advantage over women. They are older, freer and strong, they know life, you know."[86] Neera's and Mozzoni's views on the education of women, and their reactions to positivists' claim that women are intellectually inferior to men, are also strikingly similar. Mozzoni presents the view in her essay that women must be educated, and that it is no longer possible or practical to deny women access to knowledge.[87] Neera takes issue with positivists' theory that because women's brains weigh less than men's, one can deduce that women are intellectually inferior to men:

> It is said that women's brains weigh less, but then it is also said that women weigh less, so the particularity of the brain's weight is excluded and only a smaller general weight remains ... But perhaps men who weigh sixty or seventy kilograms are considered inferior to those who reach one hundred kilograms? ... And doesn't the brain of many animals not weigh more than that of a man?[88]

On the subject of women's limited access to education, in her *Battaglie per un'idea* Neera highlights men's advantages over women through receiving an education both at school and in the home: "Still more difficult than for men is girls' judicious choice, since they will have learned great and beautiful things at school and at home, but certainly not knowledge about men, a knowledge that I refuse can ever be given to women if not after marriage."[89] Another point that Mozzoni raises in her treatise, and which Neera also criticizes in her *Battaglie*, concerns the perception in society that men are considered to be strong, whereas women are perceived as being weak.[90] In her discussion on affect, Neera argues that "sensitivity to pain is equal among the two sexes, and that they only vary due to external or accidental causes."[91] Neera observes how men are permitted to express themselves when experiencing physical pain (arguably, the reverse is true nowadays), whereas women have been conditioned to suffer in silence:

> Has one not thought that women, in the dentist's surgery, under the hands of that operating surgeon who is invariably young, with whom she is in such immediate contact that their breaths get entwined – with the waiting room nearby where female friends, rivals, perhaps an admirer, await – have a million reasons to repress an ugly and irritating cry? ... Out of coquetry or out of shyness, women remain silent, and then, educated or not, knows that men are inclined to find her weakness, to mock her, and among the forms of her *pudore* there is also this: to hide her physical sufferance.[92]

Mozzoni also raises the issue of the importance of the establishment of organizations for women and run by women, to address the inequalities in the law, and to instil and foster solidarity among women.[93] Even while Neera, La Marchesa Colombi, and Serao do not explicitly address the notion of female solidarity in their non-fiction writings, through a reading of their correspondence, an unarticulated solidarity among women becomes evident. When corresponding with male writers, the contents of the letters by women writers tends to focus on work, which is particularly evident in the correspondence between Neera with Orvieto, Marinetti, Croce, Capuana, and with Serao and Hérelle. On the contrary, in correspondence with women – such as in Serao's case with the actress Eleonora Duse (1858–1924) – the tone is less formal, and the women writers are more open about their feelings, views, and attitudes towards work. In one of Serao's letters to her friend, the writer Olga Ossani, who wrote with the pseudonym Febea, Serao excuses herself for not yet having sent her the chapter she had promised by explaining that she had been busy juggling housework and commitments on other projects:

> Sorry if I have not yet sent you the chapter. I think I will be able to send it this week. It is always the same story. With the house in chaos, *Fracassa* without collaborators, people visiting and an obstinate cold which is

disturbing my brain, come the evening, I haven't been able to concentrate my mind on this blessed chapter, which I would like to be good.[94]

As well as Febea, Serao also corresponded with Ida Baccini and Sibilla Aleramo, and Neera corresponded with the writer Vittoria Aganoor.[95] Following Neera's death, Serao dedicated a lengthy obituary to Neera whom she addresses as her "sorella in arte" (sister in art), paying homage to her life and works and praising these highly.[96] In a similar fashion, in *Una giovinezza del secolo XIX* (1919), reminiscing about the past, Neera includes a quotation from an article written by Serao upon Aganoor's death, in which Serao recalls her days as a young writer.[97]

Further evidence of the beginnings of a female solidarity, or nascent sisterhood among women in the public eye that becomes clear from a reading of women writers' epistolary writings is to be found in the contents of the letters of Serao and La Marchesa Colombi, both of whom speak highly of famous female actresses and singers. In a letter to Giovanni Marano, La Marchesa Colombi praises highly the work of the actress Sarah Bernhardt (1844–1923) and the singer Adelina Patti (1843–1919):

I was better and I could bear the exertions of the end of carnival, the last dances, and now the evenings of Sara Bernart [*sic*]. You cannot immagine the charming beauty and artistic talent of this woman. Only Patti inspired a similar admiration in me; but this woman is much more beautiful and elegant, and I am more enthusiastic about her.[98]

In addition, Serao corresponded regularly with the actress Eleonora Duse with whom she was a great friend, and whom she held in very high regard.[99]

Neera, La Marchesa Colombi, Serao: Moderate Emancipationists?

As Silvia Franchini has argued, if women who read newspapers tended to be associated with the movement for female emancipation, was it not the case that women writers such as Neera, La Marchesa Colombi and Serao were emancipationists? The authors' declarations that they did not support the movement for female emancipation (in particular Neera's and Serao's), which feature in a selection of their journalism and essays, are called into question by an examination of their contributions to journals for women during the late nineteenth century, as well as their correspondence with a few exceptional women in the public eye. As we shall see in the ensuing chapters, these reveal the same sympathy with and concern for women that is to be found in domestic fiction, which becomes apparent and bears witness to the writers' mutual admiration for and support among women in the public eye. Discussing Serao's writings in her introduction to *L'Invenzione del reale* (Inventing the real, 2004), Wanda De Nunzio Schilardi draws attention to the fluid relationship between discourses of literature, journalism, and politics during the late nineteenth century in Italy, identifying a symbiotic connection between these forms of writing.[100] De Nunzio Schilardi points out the significant role Serao's narrative and journalism played in addressing and engaging with current affairs, which could also be applied to the domestic fiction and journalism by Neera and La Marchesa Colombi.[101] Nonetheless, and as we shall see in the following chapters, it was ultimately through the guise of domestic fiction that the writers were able to implicitly address and engage with the burning social and political issues of the day regarding the woman question. Whether the writers were aware of their engagement with the issues with which the emancipationists' were concerned is a question that will remain unanswered. Certainly there is evidence to suggest that the emancipationists read the writers' fiction as critical of women's prescribed roles. A review of "Checchina's Virtue" (1883) by Serao, written by a contributor named "Gardenia," which appeared in *La Donna* on 15 July 1884, contained the following citation:

And with what mastery the author depicts that disparity of upbringing, tastes, habits, that notwithstanding the principles of equality professed by us, separate and will always separate the various classes in society! And how well drawn is the portrait of the shy and ignorant woman, enclosed in the home, under the tyrannous yoke of marital despotism and superstition, which condemn to inertia the most noble of her faculties, they abbandon her without support to the exhausting struggles between the miserliness of a coarse and selfish husband and the innate love of beauty and material being, which naturally if the right occasion presents itself, shakes, allures and conquers the frozen soul from a passive life, uniquely devoted to those material housewifely occupations: which, whilst they require a lot of care and attention, leave faint traces, in fact they resemble Penelope's cloth, nor being able to demonstrate their worth in money in the eyes of some, don't have any value ... But what surprises us is that the warning comes from her; from she, who in many very well-known writings, has publicly declared herself opposed to women who ask to apply their intelligence to a wider field; to women who aspire to be not humble handmaids or contemptuous slaves, vilified by the despotic will of a master; but collaborators and partners of men in the path of life. What surprises us is that whilst Signora Serao wants to regard this moral and intellectual elevation as an extensible privilege only to the select few great minds, she then chooses as subjects of her literary works the miserable lot of women who are humble, simple, shy, oppressed and poor-in-spirit. *Does she not think that by so doing she serves her adversaries more than if she wrote a treatise backing their theories?*[102]

Gardenia draws attention to the themes of the lack of education for women; the ideology of separate spheres for women and men, and women's confinement to the home; the authority of the protagonist's husband and the oppression he represents in Serao's story. The reviewer's rhetorical question at the end of the piece points towards her belief that Serao's fictional presentation of female oppression through literary realism represents a more powerful indictment of women's condition than any theoretical piece on the subject. Some years later, a review of Neera's *Teresa*, written by the emancipationist Virginia Olper Monis, appeared in the same journal. The reviewer's reading of Neera's text emphasizes the author's sympathetic portrayal of her protagonist whose psychological development, according to the reviewer, is representative of "everywoman." Olper Monis argues that Neera's portrayals of her protagonist writing her initials intertwined with those of the man she loves on the wall of her bedroom, her ignorance of being in a physical and emotional relationship with a man, and the superficiality with which male characters are drawn, all point towards her implied critique of women's experiences of growing up in late-nineteenth-century Italy.[103]

In her pamphlet "Woman and Her Social Relationships," Mozzoni suggests that since women had never officially been given the opportunity to discuss the legislation to which they have been subjected, they fought for better legislation and better rights for women through journalism.[104] Indeed, as Emmanuelle Genevois has pointed out, in particular for women, collaboration on newspapers was a means of gaining social visibility.[105] Genevois describes La Marchesa Colombi's "journalistic two faces" through her collaboration on the emancipationist's journal *La Donna* and her association with the more moderate magazine *Il Giornale delle donne*.[106] Writing on Neera in his introduction to her novel *Teresa*, Baldacci puts forward the view that while Neera tends to present herself as "antifeminist" in her non-fiction, her novels such as *Teresa* represent documents of the feminist spirit.[107] Similarly, in his essay on Serao, Giuliano Manacorda raises the point with regards to her journalism and fiction, suggesting that her fiction is revealing of a concern in Serao for women's social, psychological, and economic condition.[108] Serao's biographer, Anna Banti, puts forward the view that Serao's conservatism on the role of women was not her own, but was influenced by that of her husband and her colleagues, D'Annunzio, Michetti, Lodi.[109] Nancy Harrowitz draws on the work of Angela Dworkin to argue the same point, which could also be applied to La Marchesa Colombi and Neera:

> Some of the criteria that Dworkin applies to Right-wing women in order to understand their political allegiances can, I believe, be applied to Serao as well. As the lone female figure on the journalistic front in Italy at the end of the century, she was surrounded by domineering male figures such as Gabriele D'Annunzio and Edoardo Scarfoglio. One could speculate that it might have been easier for Serao to pretend she was "one of the boys" than to explore in depth her connection to other women and to the female condition.[110]

Whether these three writers upheld the moderate ideologies of the movement for female emancipation is, I think, superfluous. Certainly none of them defined themselves as emancipationists, and all three, in particular Serao and Neera, contrary to what some critics have argued, were careful not to align themselves with the movement. Yet, as we have seen through a reading of their journalism and other non-fiction writings, their writings reveal striking paradoxes regarding their views on women's roles in late-nineteenth-century Italy.

These writers ought to be appreciated precisely for their ability to negotiate their positions as professional writers during a time in which women who partook in debates in the public sphere were frowned upon. While Croce perceived and admired Neera first and foremost as a moralist, it is equally important not to disregard her contribution to the emancipationist journal *La Donna*, as well as her contribution to Sibilla Aleramo's *L'Italia femminile*. Neera set up and ran her own journal for the female reader; she collaborated with Mantegazza to publish *Dizionario d'igiene*, which enabled her to write about subjects which, as a woman writer, she would undoubtedly have been frowned upon for writing about alone; she contributed frequently to journals that had a predominantly female readership, so as to offer sympathy to spinsters, to young girls experiencing bodily changes in adolescence, and to newly married women; she corresponded with other women writers whom she held in great esteem, including La Marchesa Colombi and Serao; and she wrote of similar concerns put forward by Mozzoni's "Woman and Her Social Relationships" in her *Battaglie per un'idea*. Even while Serao spoke out against the vote for women and positioned herself outside the movement for female emancipation, she was the first woman journalist to set up and run her own daily newspaper, *Il Giorno*, which addressed itself explicitly to a growing female readership. Moreover, along with La Marchesa Colombi, who wrote the column, "Lettera aperta alle signore" in her husband's newspaper *Il Corriere della Sera*, Serao was one of the first women journalists to address a female readership in a daily newspaper in her columns "Per le signore" and "Api, Mosconi e Vespe" (Bees, flies, and wasps). Nor should it be forgotten that while La Marchesa Colombi presented herself as upholding the status quo in her conduct book *La gente per bene*, she travelled the country delivering lectures on the importance of teaching girls literature in schools with Mozzoni, and all the writers prescribed work as a cure to symptoms of so-called hysteria. These factors challenge the notion of these writers as supporters of the status quo in their journalism and non-fiction works, which in fact reveal contradictions in the writers' views on the woman question.

Finally, one must not disregard the influence these writers had in determining the direction of journalism. While La Marchesa Colombi and Serao tended to write about society and social problems in their journalism, Neera's pieces focused on the female psyche and problems directly affecting women, such as hygiene and health. Writing on the contribution both La Marchesa Colombi and Serao made in their journalism to debates on social problems, such as underpaid, exploited female workers, and women's confinement to the home, Francesco De Nicola recognizes that the writers made a considerable contribution to the growth of civilization in Italy, even sowing seeds that others later would reap the benefits of.[111] Franchini highlights the contribution women journalists made to the "democratization" of cultural products, works of art, history and geography through their journalism, a democratization which, she argues, helped to educate readers and spread knowledge.[112] La Marchesa Colombi, Serao, and Neera, through their non-fiction writings, were actively involved, albeit on the margins of literary and intellectual circles, in the formation and establishment of a new model of womanhood, one that sought to fashion women in all social classes as dignified, self-respecting, and epistemic.

Chapter Three

Gendering Private and Public Spheres

[My mother] rarely talked to me about her childhood, but from what she did say I formed a picture far less interesting than the one my father's memories conjured up.[1]

Sibilla Aleramo, *Una donna* (1906)

During the Risorgimento, a few exceptional women from Milan and Naples participated in debates on the "woman question" in the public sphere by publishing articles and delivering speeches on women's legal and social position. The majority of middle-class women, however, conformed to the desired roles of wife and mother, remaining within the private, domestic sphere of the home. As Ann Hallamore Caesar observes:

[After] unification ... women found themselves slowly squeezed out of the public domain and relegated to a separate sphere. With rare exceptions, one of the most notable being Gualberta Alaide Beccari's emancipationist journal *La Donna*, the growing women's press, and women writers themselves, accepted and internalized their exclusion from politics by rejecting it, along with economics, as unutterably boring and a feature of the alienating world of men.[2]

The doctrine of the separate spheres assigned to women and men outside the home in late nineteenth-century Italy is poignantly illustrated in Neera's *L'Indomani* (1890) when the protagonist, Marta, accompanies her husband to the street from their front door, but goes no further: "She followed him across the courtyard until they reached the street door; when he was at the end of the street, she turned back. Marta re-entered her home momentarily happy, feeling dignified in her position as a wife and lady of the house, ready to carry out the domestic duties."[3] Adopting an essentialist viewpoint, Cesare Balbo in his book *Delle speranze d'Italia* (On the hopes of Italy, 1844) celebrates the home "whose care is assigned by 'natural order' to women."[4] In light of this remark, it is perhaps not surprising that women who sought public recognition of any kind were considered to be a threat to the identity of the new Italy. Women's "proper" place in the home was strengthened by Pisanelli's Code of 1866, which excluded women from all areas of political activity, reinforcing the gender stereotype of the domestic interior as female and private. Paradoxically, however, by the 1880s, the middle-class woman writer and reader had become commonplace both in the public and the private spheres.[5]

This chapter explores how the domestic fiction by Neera, Serao, and La Marchesa Colombi articulated the implementation of the middle-class doctrineof separate spheres based on gender and class in the new Italy. It focuses in particular on how middle-class female and male characters are represented both inside and outside the home, examining the various arenas described and prescribed (e.g., domestic, urban, and rural spaces), as well as those who occupied them. I demonstrate that even if the writers' depictions of architecture, cities, towns, and countryside that are based on culturally embedded patriarchal principles are faithfully represented in their domestic fiction, while appearing to endorse these principles, the authors simultaneously render visible women's confinement to, and restricted movement within, yet also outside, the private sphere of the home. The three authors have in common an interest in depicting indoor and outdoor spaces that were accessible to women in late nineteenth-century Italy, yet they were circumscribed. Heralding Virginia Woolf's assertion in her 1929 book *A Room of One's Own* that if women are to write they need a room of their own, I show how in Italian domestic fiction the home is presented symbolically as the locus from where women writers – albeit not necessarily consciously – begin an ideological critique of women's confinement to it.

The Private and the Public in the New Italy

Recent work carried out on the construction of space according to gender and class in the humanities and social sciences has posited categories of public and private as pertaining to the male and female genders respectively, and as being understood in terms of an ideology of separate spheres.[6] While these are potentially useful terms for studying the public and the private in the nineteenth century – a period in which domestic space was delineated according to social and economic hierarchies – some scholars have argued that it is perhaps more productive to think of these as shifting spheres rather than as mutually exclusive categories.[7] In her book *Questioni di cittadinanza: donne e diritti sociali nell'Italia liberale* (1995), Annarita Buttafuoco posits that the movement between the spheres produced a certain dynamic whereby those women with the greater stake in the domestic realm were able to exercise peculiar forms of discursive power. Buttafuoco "rejects the classic division between the public and private spheres and instead posits a continual interchange between them: it is this interchange that inspired Italian women to redefine the meaning of citizenship."[8] Jürgen Habermas, in his *The Structural Transformation of the Public Sphere* (1969), was the first to challenge this binary distinction.[9] Habermas defined the public sphere as the *salons*, theatres, and clubs, in which private people exercised their reason and criticized public authority. For Habermas, the public sphere is a masculinist gender construct, an intermediary space between the intimate sphere of the family and the official sphere of the state, a space free from prejudice and separate from the government in which authority is held up to public scrutiny and where the common good of the people is debated; the public sphere is a forum in which members of the public (artists, writers, intellectuals, clerics, politicians) can meet with one another to debate rationally the affairs of state. Women writers fall into this category, yet Habermas fails to account for the emergence of women, including performing artists such as actresses, singers, dancers, as well as politically active women, into the public sphere.[10] Although the body politic of late-nineteenth-century Italy emphasized women's desired roles as mother and wife, concomitantly Italy also experienced women's emergence into what Habermas terms the "intermediary space," which expressed alternative forms of power and enabled women of the time to engage in the public sphere in particular ways.

Whilst I would agree in principle with Habermas's definition of the public sphere as an intermediary space, it was by no means unmediated by issues of gender, social class, and ethnicity, nor indeed was the private sphere unmediated. Linda Colley argues that the ideology of the separate spheres for women and men in late-eighteenth-century Britain was being increasingly prescribed in theory while it was being broken down in practice as women writers, artists, and thinkers emerged into the intermediary space.[11] A similar phenomenon was taking place in the new Italy: while middle-class women were being confined to the private sphere of the home, at the same time, some exceptional, questioning, and educated (often self-taught) women were emerging into Habermas's public sphere of political debate, as readers, writers, and political activists. This constituted an unusual, creative and industrious mix, blending domestic, consumer and cultural agents as never before.

As I argue in this chapter, the writers' representations of the public and the private in late-nineteenth-century Italy in their domestic fiction depicted social spaces (of gender, class, and ethnicity) based on imitation of the observed world. It was the writers' faithful depictions, and their apparent endorsement of the organization of space structured upon the binary of the separate spheres, that facilitated their own emergence into the public sphere, and that enabled them to write about the private, which by its very nature keeps the observer at bay. Moreover, as this chapter also seeks to demonstrate, the writers' depiction of a predominantly female world was ultimately ambiguous, for it potentially constituted a critique of women's confinement to the home compared with men. Nancy Armstrong's *Desire and Domestic Fiction* (1987) linked the history of sexuality to the history of the novel to argue that fiction and non-fictional works written by and for women in eighteenth- and nineteenth-century England antedated the way of life they represented.[12] Italian domestic fiction was doing something very different: adopting a verist approach, the fiction presented a slice of life, as a photographic image of everyday life from a middle-class woman's point of view. As I show in this chapter, in domestic fiction the public sphere of knowledge and debate is represented as being inhabited only by men. Cecilia Dau Novelli has remarked that within the late-nineteenth-century home in Italy, the divisions between public and private arenas were becoming more marked: "The 'private' areas comprised of the bedroom and the kitchen, while the public rooms were the dinning room, the *salotto*, the study."[13] La Marchesa Colombi, Neera, and Serao represent these marked divisions between public and private within the home in their domestic fiction as gendered: the majority of rooms that made up the middle-class home are presented as a woman's territory, while others are shared by both genders. Only the study – signifying the world of the affairs of state and public discourse – is reserved for the men of the household.

As previously mentioned, realist fiction is a highly visual form of literature concerned with the "faithful" depiction of things, objects, rooms, and environments. Peter Brooks describes the process of realism as "Removing housetops in order to see the private lives played out beneath them," and draws upon Wallace Stevens's *Notes towards a Supreme Fiction* (1942), whom he suggests argues that fictions arise from the need to build a space or even a shelter for ourselves in an alien world.[14] We can apply Stevens's idea to how realist fiction by women writers from late-nineteenth-century Italy functioned in allowing them access to the public sphere: their fiction produced a photographic image of a world that was familiar, not alien to them, and which facilitated their entry into the rather alien world of literary circles for the first time.[15] Thus, women writers participated in public debate and the affairs of the state in an apparently apolitical way by virtue of their depiction of an almost exclusively all-female world in which middle-class women had little or no access to the public sphere, were confined to the home, had limited access to education, and were required to remain in the home as wives and mothers. The public sphere in domestic fiction is presented as the world of men, which implicitly stands for self-development, experience, and freedom, while the private realm is illustrated as the world of women, which stands for confinement, oppression, and ignorance. As with the maintenance of the status quo, the dichotomy is a constantly recurring topos in the fiction. Yet through a reading of different ways in which women and men occupy spaces inside and outside the home in late-nineteenth-century Italy, time and again, the line between a presentation of the separate spheres and a critique of them becomes blurred.

The Private Sphere: The Italian Middle-Class Home

The confines of the home were the boundaries of [the woman's] kingdom. This was where she exercised a gentle and improving sway over her husband and forged the next generation ...[16]

While I by no means wish to infer that women exercised sway over their husbands and forged the next generation in the late-nineteenth-century Italian home, as the above citation claims for their British counterparts, it is useful insofar as it illustrates a degree of power held by women in the late-eighteenth-century home. Such control, as becomes apparent through a reading of the domestic fiction by La Marchesa Colombi,

Neera, and Serao, was similar to that held by women in the late-nineteenth-century Italian home. Yet the home is also written about with ambivalence by the writers, who, on the one hand, describe it as a place of shelter and protection from the outside world for women, and, on the other, see it as confining. For example, the home is presented as a place of safety, shelter, and comfort in Serao's "Terno Secco" (Jackpot, 1887), where mother and daughter console one another at the thought of being evicted from their home.[17]

Middle-class young girls between ages fourteen and sixteen typically left school to take up their "proper" role in the home to learn how to be good homemakers, which is indeed the fate of Neera's eponymous protagonist, Teresa, in her novel. As we gather from a reading of Neera's autobiography *Una giovinezza del secolo XIX* (A childhood from the nineteenth century, 1919), Teresa's occupation of the home in adolescence recalls the author's own experience of leaving school at age fourteen to take up her designated role as homemaker:

> At the age of fourteen, having finished classes, I left school ...
>
> I then began my domestic existence – methodical, like the rules of a convent: I got up at eight o'clock, tidied my room and the *salotto* (where no-one ever entered), and sat down at my work desk at around ten, from where I did not move until four, with one aunt on one side and another aunt on the other.[18]

The importance of adolescent girls' occupation of the home in late-nineteenth-century Italy in order that they could learn how to manage it in preparation for when they would become wives and mothers is presented in a similar way in La Marchesa Colombi's *Un matrimonio in provincia* (A small-town marriage, 1885). The stepmother tells her husband: "[G]irls don't have to be professors. Now is the time for them to learn to keep a house in order, to sew, iron, cook, and be good housewives."[19] The depiction of the Scognamigli girls' confinement to the home in Serao's "Terno Secco" represents the most extreme case: the girls do their shopping from the ground floor of the palazzo where they live so as not to be seen by anyone.[20] While in each of the aforementioned cases the scenarios would presumably have been interpreted by women readers as entirely natural, taken together, the depictions begin to appear as critiques of the ideology of the separate spheres and young adolescent girls' confinement to the home. This becomes even more apparent through a consideration of the language used to describe the girls' transition from being outside and attending school to being in the home on a full-time basis. That La Marchesa Colombi gives the stepmother (who is not a particularly sympathetic character) the lines illustrated above is perhaps revealing of the author's sympathy towards adolescent girls; furthermore, in the aforementioned citation Neera recalls her monastic existence as an adolescent as "methodical, like the rules of a convent." Neera draws similarities between her home life and how she imagines life in a convent, adhering to strict rules and timetables. The impression she gives of her memory of home life is negative, and in *Teresa* (1886) she shows sympathy for her protagonist who is suddenly expected to carry out the duties of a housewife in adolescence. The home as a place of confinement for adolescent girls becomes strikingly apparent in Neera's *Teresa* when the protagonist, who is on a visit to her aunt's, experiences temporary respite from her domestic existence as she runs through the rooms of her aunt's house while visiting her. The shift in the protagonist's state of mind is striking: Teresa is "so completely happy that if they had told her to fly she would have tried it at once."[21] The theme of flight is used as a motif of escape and desire for evasion. Interestingly, and perhaps somewhat paradoxically, La Marchesa Colombi, writing in her conduct book *La gente per bene* (1878), recommends to young women hoping to get married not to come across in society as annoyed with their duties in the home.[22]

Emilia Nevers's conduct book *Il galateo della borghesia: norme per trattar bene* (Bourgeois etiquette: Rules for good manners, 1877) contains the phrase, "Tell me how you live and I will tell you who you are."[23] The citation properly illustrates the interchangeability of the terms "woman" and "home" during this period in the new Italy, and is exemplified in the domestic fiction. In Neera's *L'Indomani* (1890), in describing Marta's relationship to the home, the narrator poses the rhetorical question: "Should her home not be her kingdom, her horizon, everything?"[24] The narrator's use of the noun "kingdom" is revealing of the power and status married women adopted in the home. As Marta's kingdom, the home represents the apex of her experience of womanhood. The home is indeed presented as a metaphor for motherhood, and it is a place where wives are expected to provide their husbands and children with protection, shelter, and stability. We see from La Marchesa Colombi's *Prima morire* (Before dying, 1881) that once a woman marries, her attachment to, and responsibility within the home intensifies. Leonardo tells his new wife, Mercede: "You represent me now; you carry my name, you are my family, and it will be up to you to play hostess."[25]

So fundamental is a wife's and mother's governing of the home that in La Marchesa Colombi's *Prima morire*, Eva's impromptu departure from her home to be with her lover brings about her husband's mental breakdown and her daughter's illness, and this in turn forces Eva to sacrifice her relationship with Augusto and to return home to carry out her duties and responsibilities as a wife and mother.

Women who did not conform to their proper role in the home are presented in domestic fiction as being ostracized by their community, yet not without a certain degree of sympathy. Calliope from Neera's *Teresa*, who lives alone, encaged behind iron bars, is perceived by the townsfolk as an "eccentric misanthrope who made faces like a little urchin behind the iron grating on the ground floor."[26] Her access to rooms within the home appears even more limited than married women's, and recalls the representation of the aunt in La Marchesa Colombi's *A Small-Town Marriage* (1885) who lives in a similarly confined space in a corner of the kitchen. The protagonist, Denza, describes her aunt as "a little old spinster as dried up as a herring, who slept in the kitchen where, in order to hide her bed, she had put up a screen behind which she spent her life in the dark."[27]

Adolescent girls and married women remain in the home for longer periods of time throughout the day compared with adolescent boys and young married (or single) men, who spend more time outside of it. As we learn from Neera's *Teresa*, adolescent boys were permitted to play on the streets,[28] and in La Marchesa Colombi's *A Small-Town Marriage*, Mazzucchetti confesses to Denza that he and three friends play at being the Musketeers.[29] In her conduct book *La gente per bene* (1877), addressing middle-class adolescent girls, La Marchesa Colombi invites them "in a place where [they] have never been ... in a young man's room," the study.[30] In Neera's *Teresa*, Signor Caccia has a study which is used by his son in order to carry out his homework. Totò from Serao's "Checchina's Virtue" (1883) also has a study. Both tax collector and doctor respectively receive clients in their offices, which are designated as public, and as spaces that were occupied by women and men, assuming he had female clients; the women of the household in Neera's *Teresa* enter the study with a feeling of awkwardness and discomfort, and people only enter it for a particular purpose.[31] Located at the opposite end of the house to the study in Neera's *Teresa* is the women's room – the sitting room where women sew, do the laundry, and manage the daily accounts. The women's room (*gineceo*) is a safe-haven for women, a place men rarely entered, or if they did, they did so uncomfortably out of anxiety that they would threaten to disturb the silent intimacy between mother and daughter: "Signor Caccia avoided this room, and if he appeared by chance, the mother-daughter intimacy was immediately suspended."[32] By contrast, if a single man lives on his own he is not ostracized from his community in the same way as a spinster is. Don Giovanni Boccabadati from Neera's *Teresa* can participate in social events with relative ease, and Eva's lover in La Marchesa Colombi's *Prima morire*, who lives alone in a dismal attic room, is a fairly well-respected member of his community.

The Salotto

The late-nineteenth-century Italian *salotto* in the middle-class home was the "public face of family life,"[33] the place in which members of the household could receive and entertain visitors. This is illustrated in La Marchesa Colombi's *A Small-Town Marriage* when the protagonist's father remarries and the *salotto* takes on a more functional role in order that his wife can receive guests. Indeed, for the first-person narrator/ protagonist the *salotto* becomes what Philippe Hamon defines as a "small theatre" where gossipers and chatterers could conduct multiple conversations.[34] Denza and her sister's reaction to the arrival of guests in their newly functioning *salotto* reveals their isolation in, and confinement to, the home, as well as their ignorance of the outside world. The prospect of having invited guests in their house fills them with excitement, and prompts them, along with their aunt, to perceive events that take place in there as spectacle:

> [The visits] were great fun for us. We would run into the living room and sit openmouthed to hear what was being said. Even Auntie, carried away by this new state of affairs, put on a dress that was softer, blacker, and more clinging than usual and a dazzling white bonnet with a pretty starched frill that framed her face and came to sit in the living room, smiling quietly with her hands folded in her lap.[35]

Paradoxically, the *salotto* is also presented as a private and intimate space used predominantly by women. This model concurs with Mariuccia Salvati's argument in relation to the late-nineteenth-century *salotto* in which she argues that the layout of the *salotto* becomes more and more enclosed, intimate, and domestic, and the space is less public and more private.[36] In Neera's *Teresa*, the protagonist and her mother spend the majority of their time there carrying out their domestic duties. So, too, does Marta from *L'Indomani*, which is by the same author. Marta spends her evenings in her *salotto* waiting for her husband's return from the *circolo*; this is typical particularly during the winter evenings. It is also apparent from a reading of La Marchesa Colombi's short story "Serate d'Inverno" (Winter evenings, 1879), in which, introducing her collection of short stories by the same title, the author reveals her motive for having written the collection: "They're the dread of half the world, those long, long winter evenings that last from seven until ten, at least three hours ... There are an infinite number of people who pass their evenings as we passed ours ... These lonely and bored people, in that time of loneliness and boredom, are open to indulgence, as were my brothers and I during our long family evenings."[37] Men are seldom represented in domestic fiction as entering or occupying the *salotto*; if they enter it, they do so for a particular reason. For example, in Neera's *Teresa*, the protagonist's brother enters the *salotto* many times to distract his sister from her domestic chores by dancing a waltz with her.[38] As we see from Serao's "O Giovannino, o la morte" (Giovannino, or death, 1888), and Neera's *Teresa*, young men typically spend time in the *salotto* in order to become acquainted with their fiancés. Furthermore, women and men occupy the *salotto* differently: while women sit in upright positions on hard, functional chairs, men sprawl on armchairs and fall asleep on sofas. Serao's "Checchina's Virtue," for example, depicts the female protagonist sitting on the sofa in the *salotto*, "her bust erect," while her husband falls asleep in an armchair.[39] Similarly, in La Marchesa Colombi's "Serate d'Inverno," the first-person narrator recalls how "[The] eighty-year-old patriarch would nap in a large chair next to the fireplace."[40] The depiction echoes Neera's own experience of the double standards of comportment in the *salotto* according to one's gender when she recalls of an evening, "having finished [lunch], my father stretched out on the sofa where he seemed melancholy having a nap and my aunts, who were sat next to the wall, immobile, their heads held rigid and upright like great statues, mentally recited their orations."[41]

Salvati argues that as the form and function of the *salotto* changed over the nineteenth century, the display of objects as metaphors signifying a family's social position became more visible.[42] The narrator's inventory of the late-nineteenth-century Italian *salotto*'s material contents measured a family's wealth, and there is evidence in the texts of families owning a staple collection of furniture that consisted of a sofa, four armchairs, eight chairs, and a round table. This is the case in La

Marchesa Colombi's *A Small-Town Marriage* in Denza's house, which contains the same objects that the stepmother brings by chance to the house when she moves there. The *salotto* in Serao's "Terno Secco" also contains a sofa, four seats, and a round marble table. As we learn from Neera's *L'Indomani*, flowers, embroidery, and stools referred to in a number of the texts also make up the contents of a typical *salotto*. The glass-covered glove box positioned in the centre of the table in the *salotto* from La Marchesa Colombi's *A Small-Town Marriage*, together with two embroidered napkin rings, a red velvet cigar case, and a dark leather case lined with deep blue satin which reveals a silver bowl and a small silver plate are held up as symbols of the family's wealth and social class, and are all objects associated at the time with women and domesticity. The stepmother from La Marchesa Colombi's *A Small-Town Marriage* insists upon storing provisions of food (flour, potatoes, nuts, apples, and rice) in the *salotto* to give visitors an impression of the family's abundance and wealth. In the more private, intimate *salotto* from Neera's *Teresa*, in which the only visitor welcomed is Teresa's sister's fiancé, objects such as unsewn socks, balls, bundles, used games, and baskets fill the room. The primary luxury object is a thick, solid painting. The presentation of the *salotto* in domestic fiction as a room primarily associated with women, and as a room that women were expected to manage and govern is, at first glance, entirely conventional. Yet its recurring topos as a place where women were required to work and entertain, and in which they were not permitted to relax (at least in company), points towards a subtle critique on behalf of women writers of the limitations and restrictions imposed on women, and is suggestive of a sympathy held on behalf of the writers for women's confinement to the home in the new Italy.

Bedrooms and Kitchens

The different ways in which women and men occupied the rooms of the late-nineteenth-century home are also apparent through a reading of the authors' presentations of bedrooms and kitchens in Italian domestic fiction. Although men share the bedroom with their wives, given the focus on female characters in the narratives, we rarely have insight into male characters being in bedrooms, and men are never illustrated in the domestic fiction as occupying the kitchen; literary and cultural conventions permitted male writers to describe women on their own, but this was not acceptable in the inverse. In Neera's *L'Indomani*, Marta experiences anxiety when she awakes the morning after her wedding day to find she is lying in bed with a man she barely knows. Her new bedroom is described methodically, and in minute detail:

> Three large windows illuminated it making the sun's rays penetrate across a rich drapery of flowery material against a deep blue sky. The same material was hanging from the very tall and wide bed, half covered with a light blue silk quilt, on the edge of which fell, carefully ironed, the lace cover. On the dressing table lay another lace adornment, which was wound around a light blue ribbon, and which acted as a mat for a shining bright crystal set. On the mirrors and picture frames, there was not an atom of dust to be seen.[43]

The windows and mirrors create the illusion that the bedroom is larger than it actually is, and the emphasis on the cleanliness of the room is striking. A shining crystal set tells us something of Marta's social status. Neera provides a similarly detailed description of the marital bedroom in her novel *Teresa*. Other than the bed, upon which there is a yellow silk blanket with large green flowers, the furnishings inside Signora Soave's room, which are representative of the objects that were included in the bedroom, consisted of two walnut chests of drawers, a *prie dieu* covered with books, a knee rest, a small greenish mirror, curtains at the window, two pictures representing the marriage of the Virgin Mary framed in black wood, and a small wax baby boy under a glass bell.[44]

A less affluent bedroom is depicted in Serao's "Terno Secco," whose space is taken up by a large iron Neapolitan bed, a chest of drawers, a small and ugly dressing table, a clothes stand, and several chairs.[45] In contrast to the kitchen, which is the domain of servants and maids, the bedroom is conceived of as a private, middle class, and quite bare place. The kitchen and the bedroom have in common an identity as places where women can share their thoughts and feelings with one another, where they can discuss their experiences of motherhood, where mothers counsel their daughters on being good wives and mothers, and where servants and *signore* can confide in one another. In Neera's *L'Indomani*, while in her daughter's bedroom, Signora Merelli tells Marta of how she gave birth to her first child exactly nine months after getting married and how she has been pregnant ever since. Neera gives Signora Merelli the following lines, which are revealing of the author's sympathy for women's experiences of childbirth: "Three whole days with aches and then a pain, a pain ... the Lord has given us women an awful role. Men have all the good things!"[46] Marta's mother and Marta have a discussion at the end of the novel in Marta's bedroom about how young girls are brought up to believe in the myth of romantic love, and the bedroom is also the place where Marta comes to accept her role as wife and mother. In Neera's *Teresa*, the protagonist and her friend discuss romantic love and marriage in the kitchen while Teresa carries out her duties as homemaker, and in *L'Indomani*, for want of anything better to do, Marta whiles away her time in the kitchen talking to her servant: "She would often come now to see Apollonia; sitting on that little chair, she would follow the good woman's movements for hours."[47] A similar depiction of women from different social backgrounds spending time together is to be found in Serao's "Jackpot" with regard to the maid and her signora. As we see from a reading of Serao's "Checchina's Virtue," however, relations between servants and signore are not always amicable. On a number of occasions, Checchina, feeling preoccupied by something, enters the kitchen where Susanna is working only to be met with the maid's silence: "For half an hour [Checchina] was annihilated by desolation, while in the kitchen Susanna scraped the table with a large knife in order to remove the grease."[48]

The bedroom has a similar function to the kitchen in that it is also presented as a place where young girls and middle-class women release pent-up emotions. In Neera's *L'Indomani*, the narrator describes how "on more than one occasion, without any apparent reason [Marta] had run to hide herself in her room to cry."[49] In La Marchesa Colombi's *A Small-Town Marriage*, while Denza comforts her baby stepbrother, who is in pain because he is teething, embracing him as if he were the young man with whom she is in love, she is scolded by her stepmother, and she runs into her room in order to allow herself to cry.[50] Similarly, the protagonist from La Marchesa Colombi's short story "Racconto alla vecchia maniera" (Story from old times, 1888), upon hearing of the forthcoming marriage of the man with whom she had been in love for the past three years (during which time she had sewn her wedding trousseau), out of a sense of *pudore*, waits until she returns home to shut herself away in her bedroom in order to cry.[51] The relative freedom women could experience within the bedroom is apparent when, after having danced with joy in her guest room on a visit to her aunt's, Teresa, though rejoicing in her new-found freedom at being away from her domestic tasks, remains conscious she may be seen by other members of the household, and, upon entering the courtyard, carries herself as a serious and composed young woman.[52] Similarly, upon seeing Orlandi unexpectedly at a masked ball, only when Teresa is in her bedroom can she reflect on the evening.[53] In La Marchesa Colombi's "Impara l'arte e mettila da parte" (Learn a trade for a rainy day, 1877), when Odda discovers her love for Fulvio is unrequited, "She got up as a sob stuck in her throat, went quickly to her room, and gave herself over to desperate crying."[54]

Indeed, at night, the relative privacy of the bedroom provides a space for adolescent girls and married women to let their minds wander without being caught off guard. This is apparent in Serao's "Checchina's Virtue." While the protagonist's husband sleeps, snoring profoundly, Checchina visualizes the route to the Marquis's apartment, to which she has been invited, unbeknown to her husband and friends: "[B]etween those glacial sheets, again Checchina felt growing inside her, alive and strong, the desire to go to that apartment in via Santi Apostoli ... In the solitude of the night, her ardent eyes fixed in the shadows, wide open with insomnia, she felt full of courage. She no longer feared this big man ..."[55] In her "Giovannino, or death," feeling angry at the interest her betrothed takes in her stepmother's "shameful" occupation as a pawnbroker, the protagonist excuses herself in saying she is tired and wishes to go to bed, where, "she could no longer sleep ... At night she would turn the oil lamp back on, walk around her bedroom, write, and then she would tear up the letters full of torment which came out of her pen addressed to Giovannino."[56] Here, the bedroom is described as a relatively private space that provided adolescent girls with the opportunity to write. In Neera's *Teresa*, the protagonist writes the letter "E" for Egidio Orlandi, which she entwines with the letter "T" for Teresa on her bedroom door next to her bed where no one can see it, and with religious adoration she kisses it every night.[57] The bedroom is also a place in which middle-class adolescent girls can express themselves physically. After having danced for the first time with a young man, in her bed that same night Teresa remembers the sound of organ music and imagines herself dancing to it, and, while acting out the dance, moves in her bed.[58]

In Neera's *Teresa*, we gain insight into men's bedrooms, and the differences that characterize these in relation to marital bedrooms and adolescent girls' rooms. As a symbol of the men's world of self-development, experience, and freedom, Carlo's room is bare, white, light, and airy compared with Teresa's dark and sparse room:

In Carlino's room both windows were thrown wide open, letting a bold and cheerful light poke into every corner from floor to ceiling. The practically bare white walls reflected the sunbeams in the brightness of the splendid morning.[59]

Having arrived home from university, Carlo casually leans against the wall in his bedroom, smoking a cigar. His suitcase, a metaphor for his relative freedom and his temporary stay, is open, and its contents are scattered on the floor. His bedroom is unfamiliar territory for Teresa and represents an exotic, exciting place. Not only is it unfamiliar to her, so, too, are the objects within it – what they represent and describe. The omniscient narrator reveals how Teresa would creep up into her brother's room when it was empty, how she would read in a cursory fashion the books in which relationships between women and men were discussed, and would open his drawers to stroke and put his ties in order.[60] Indeed, even Carlino's presence in the home dictates the relations members of the household have with the space they inhabit, for when Carlo goes to his room in order to study it is a sign that the other members of the household must be silent.[61] The bedroom is thus represented as a place where adolescent girls and married women can have an outlet for self-expression in private, away from their humdrum domestic chores, to fantasize and dream. Paradoxically, at the same time, they are somewhat inhibited in their room, and are required to move within it in a constricted way compared with men. The kitchen, on the other hand, is presented as a public, all-female place of work where women from different social backgrounds and of different generations gossip and share their experiences away from the company of men.

The Study

In domestic fiction the study is presented as a place inhabited by men and associated with access to knowledge. In the context of late-nineteenth-century Italy, this presentation is not entirely representative of the status quo; indeed, the writers' presentation of the study could be construed as critiquing what appears to be an absence of studies inhabited by women. We glimpse an impression of Serao's study thanks to the writer Ugo Ojetti's description of this in his interview with her: "I see books all around, well-placed and nicely bound, placed on long tables, inside closed cupboards and on revolving shelves." Ojetti is careful to balance his presentation of Serao as a bluestocking with her identity as a mother; in the sentence that follows, he remarks: "From the room nearby comes a happy sound of children's voices."[62] In La Marchesa

Colombi's *Prima morire* (Before dying), in a letter to his friend, Leonardo describes the study where he teaches his pupils: "It is an extensive, airy, unadorned room, with a large square table in the middle, a desk for me, and a few very high chairs which can be adjusted to the children's height."[63] The study's interior furnishings recall those described in the study in Neera's *Teresa*. As a room in which Teresa's father, a tax collector, receives clients, the study is located just inside the front door of the house, to the left of the vestibule, and down two little steps, to ensure that guests do not pass through the more private rooms of the home. The study contains two bookcases, one of which "contrasted with another slightly worm-eaten one with broken glass, half-filled with neatly ordered old books."[64] Few people enter the study, and those who do are never without a reason. Teresa's brother is obliged to learn Latin grammar there for two hours each day when he returns home from school. The bookcase, situated opposite the desk where he sits, contains copies of *La Divina Commedia* (1308–21), *L'Orlando Furioso* (1516), *La Gerusalemme liberate* (1518), several dictionaries, the historical novels *Niccolò de' Lapi* (1802) by Massimo d'Azeglio, *Cimitero della Maddalena* (1800) by Jean-Batiste Regnault-Warin, *Le Notti* by Edward Young (1742–45), and finally, *Storia d'Italia dal 1789 al 1814* by Carlo Botta (1824). There are also *strenne* (publications given to readers at Christmas time), almanacs, and two or three books by Sir Walter Scott – indications of the kind of books owned by typical middle-class families. In La Marchesa Colombi's "Serate d'Inverno," the first-person narrator reveals that in her house the bookcase, which belonged to her father to whom she wryly refers as "our dear head of household," contained scientific works, as well as plays by Goldoni and Alfieri, which, as soon as the girls had finished their schooling and returned home, was put under lock and key.[65]

Denza's father in La Marchesa Colombi's *A Small-Town Marriage* has an office at home from where he works as a notary. All we learn of the study from the first-person narrator is that "his office was not exactly besieged by clients. [Papa] kept a young apprentice and was able to take care of everything with his help."[66] When the father receives guests, he is expected to do so in his study. The presence of a study in middle-class provincial homes was common (we learn that the Bonelli cousins' father also has one). It seems that the rules governing whether family members could enter the study were such that other than the head of the household, only young boys and married women could gain access. When Denza and her sister visit the Bonelli cousins, the stepmother goes into the cousins' father's office while the girls congregate in the *salotto*. In Neera's *Teresa*, only the tax collector's wife can enter the study to clean it. Checchina, from Serao's "Checchina's Virtue," also has access to her husband's office, for she reveals to her friend that he has headed writing paper in there. It seems that there were no rules governing what men could and could not do in their studies – when Checchina enters her husband's office to check if he is there she finds him "sleeping, snoring over a thick book, with his mouth half-closed and contorted."[67] This depiction arguably presents a subtle critique of the study as a male pretension to knowledge and work. The recurring presentations in domestic fiction of the study as an all-male place from which women are excluded are highly suggestive of the social structures outside the texts. They are represented in similar ways by the authors, and constitute an implied critique of the ideology of the separate spheres and women's limited access to education and the professions.

Thresholds: Doorways and Staircases

Following John E. Crowley, threshold spaces are transitional devices that give space for the negotiation of passing through from the public outside arena into the privacy offered within the dwelling.[68] Italian domestic fiction depicts women as less likely to be standing in doorways than men, who loiter in them for no apparent reason, or who guard an entrance to a *palazzo*. In *L'Indomani*, the pharmacist, Toniolo, stands smugley on the doorstep and stares at women who pass by: "he would get some air at the entrance to his pharmacy, with his thumbs in the pockets of his waistcoat, following the women who passed by with long and intense stares."[69] In "Checchina's Virtue" by Serao, the eponymous protagonist is deterred from entering the Marquis's apartment because of the presence of the doorman, who looks threatening: "on the threshold, blocking half of the entry, the porter was leaning against the wall. He was big and tall. His vulgar face was hairy with grey whiskers, he wore a red wool scarf around his neck and, angled a bit oddly, a cap with a visor. He was smoking a pipe, and looking in the air."[70] Educated young men are depicted loitering in doorways. In La Marchesa Colombi's *A Small-Town Marriage*, Denza sees Mazzucchetti waiting in front of their door.[71] This scene recalls one of the many occasions in Neera's *Teresa* in which Orlandi is lingering, either in the piazza or at Teresa's window. It indeed echoes a scene in Serao's "Checchina's Virtue" where the narrator, recounting the number of times Checchina had seen the Marquis on holiday in Frascati, cites "a Wednesday, in the afternoon, she was sewing behind the glass panels of her balcony, replacing the cuffs of an old shirt that belonged to her husband, and the Marquis, passing in the street, saluted her."[72] Similarly, in La Marchesa Colombi's short story "Cara Speranza," (Dear hope, 1888), the protagonist-servant Amalia, a twenty-seven year old ex-worker from the rice fields, whose appearance revealed that "Life in the rice fields had left their mark on Amalia's entire being," met her betrothed, a gardener, through speaking to him through the kitchen window.[73]

Unmarried, young, middle-class women are not depicted standing in entrances, whereas married women are occasionally. There is a scene in Serao's "Terno Secco" in which a married woman, who is also the owner of her *palazzo*, takes pleasure in bargaining with the grocer on her doorstep in the landing: "One of her greatest amusements, whilst she was a lady who could send her cook to the market every morning, was to make the vendors come up on the landing and discuss the price of a kilo of peaches for an hour."[74] In the same story, servants and young girls from the lower classes are depicted lingering at entrances and walking up and down stairs.[75] Tommasina, the maid who is pregnant, is described climbing the stairs in the following way: "slowly, slowly she ascended the three floors, staggering, panting, half-closing her eyes in pain."[76] In Neera's *Teresa*, when arriving at and leaving her assignation with Orlandi at the window for the first time, Teresa's state of mind determines how she walks on the stairs. On her way to the meeting she feels anxious, whereas upon returning to her room, feeling excited, "she went up the stairs slowly, carefully, but no longer fearfully, amazed by her feeling of strength."[77]

What is said through or at doorways typically signifies a possibility, a hypothesis, or a threat, or it details an unhappy event, a change in circumstance, a premonition, or something forbidden. In "Giovannino, or death," during an argument with her stepmother, through a gap in the doorway the protagonist warns her stepmother with the words of the title of the story, which indeed come true: Chiarina chooses death when she sees her betrothed and her stepmother passionately embracing one another. The adolescent protagonist in Neera's novel *Teresa* is told by her mother upon opening her mother's bedroom door to give her news about the town's flood: "'Tonight you'll have another little baby brother or sister … something you'll understand later …' Teresina leaned against the door frame, frozen, her throat constricted by unexpected disturbance."[78] Teresa, who is on the cusp of womanhood, remains in the corridor, anxiously contemplating the changes taking place around and within her. Later in the novel, upon returning from mass, Teresa is the last to enter her house, at which point her admirer surreptitiously passes her a note inviting her to meet him that night at the window.[79] Perhaps the most significant threshold the protagonist crosses is at the end of the novel when Teresa finally leaves home to join Orlandi, who is ill, in Milan: "As Teresa was leaving the room after showing her ticket, her friend grabbed her for a last embrace. She wanted to tell her something, but emotion made her mute."[80] In their discussions of Neera's *Teresa*, Silvia Valisa and Lucienne Kroha interpret the ambiguity of Teresa's departure differently: whereas Valisa perceives Teresa as "[having finally] achiev[ed] the status of seeker, that is of a subject fully equipped with both epistemological models and with the intellectual and physical awareness that comes with them," Kroha views Teresa's choice as an act of submission: "At this point in her life Teresa has no more family ties: one cannot help but note that she is once more going to minister to a sick and worn out man, after having nursed her father for so many years. Rebellion, Neera seems to be suggesting, is futile, since woman's lot is always the same in the end." I am inclined to agree with the latter.[81]

The presentation of doorways and stairways in Italian domestic fiction illustrates the different ways in which women and men related to, and behaved in, such places in the observed world outside the texts. Whereas men could confidently stand in entrances, it is unlikely that a middle-class woman would be found at a doorway unless she was married. Unlike the home and its rooms, entrances and staircases are depicted as sites of exchanges, possibilities, and shifts in the narrative's turn of events and relations between characters. Encounters with the other gender occur, boundaries are traversed, and new possibilities are offered up.

Thresholds: Balconies and Windows

Balconies and windows are similarly constructed as places of possibilities and encounters in Italian domestic fiction. In her conduct manual *La gente per bene*, La Marchesa Colombi describes the unsophisticated custom of offering daughters of female visitors the chance to stand on one's balcony to find a husband:

> The custom of certain young ladies to invite daughters of visitors into another room, or to go with them on the balcony, is terribly provincial ...

Besides, to go out onto the balcony because they are young ladies, whilst the women remain in the living room, is as if to say: "Since we have not yet found a buyer, let's go and show ourselves off; who knows?"[82]

From this passage, it would seem that La Marchesa Colombi disapproved of young girls exhibiting themselves on balconies, a practice which in the context of late-nineteenth-century Italy was closely linked to prostitution. Yet, in her novel *A Small-Town Marriage*, and in works of domestic fiction by other women writers, the depiction of adolescent girls standing on balconies is a recurring motif. On more than one occasion, the first-person protagonist-narrator describes how her suitor would see her standing on the balcony of her cousin's house,[83] and in Neera's *Teresa*, we recall how the girls who stand on a balcony are watched by Orlandi and his colleagues from their office window: "[T]wo beautiful girls, egregious flirts, who constantly tempted them from their balcony."[84]

Windows are also represented as public spaces that adolescent girls use to their advantage in order to increase their chances of finding a husband. Indeed, we might take Orlandi's remark to Teresa in Neera's novel as evidence of how young men could court young women: "I never see you in town ... Not even at the window."[85] It would appear that windows have the same function as balconies insofar as they offer young women the possibility to look outside of their familiar surroundings in the home. In addition, people outside look at them. The many hours Teresa spends staring out of the window indicates the boredom she feels within the home, and is suggestive of the pleasure she derives from her role as voyeuse: "At the window, Teresina followed the wheelbarrow with her eyes, and when she couldn't see it anymore she stood there looking down the long street with its rows of houses."[86] The reader is also given an idea of the geographical positioning of the houses along the street of San Francesco through Teresa's looking out and the omniscient narrator's access to her thoughts. An interesting gender role reversal occurs at the end of the novel when Teresa leaves her house: the town's philanderer, Don Giovanni Boccabadati, looks out of the window and watches her leave, which recalls a scene at the beginning in which, while Teresa stares out of her window, the narrator describes how one morning Boccabadati "left elegantly dressed, carrying a little travelling bag of Russian leather."[87]

Women and men are represented differently when looking out of windows. When women look out of windows, they do so with curiosity, while men look out of windows with their eyes glazed, as if what they see is not of interest or is simply familiar to them. In Neera's *L'Indomani*, when the pharmacist shows Marta and Alberto into the bedroom of his new fiancé, the narrator describes a rare moment of male intimacy between the friends who both look distractedly out of the window.[88] Similarly, in La Marchesa Colombi's epistolary novel *Prima morire*, in a letter to her former lover, Eva, having returned to her husband, writes that she has seen her husband "on more than one occasion standing still behind the glass separating the balcony and the *salotto*, watching [her ex-lover's] window."[89] When men are represented near windows, they are generally depicted in transit (walking past them) or meeting the women they court. In Neera's *Teresa*, when the eponymous protagonist stays with her aunt, Teresa's admirer passes under her window five or six times in a day. In Orlandi's letter to Teresa, in which he requests a meeting with her, he informs her: "This evening between ten and eleven I'll walk by until you have the goodness to open the ground-floor window," and the window is the place where subsequent assignations between Orlandi and Teresa occur.[90] Teresa is indeed forbidden to sit at or even go near the window when her father learns about her relationship with Orlandi. Finally, the changes in seasons from winter to spring catalyse a change in young girls' and married women's relationships with what is outside of the home. Windows are opened and daily life outside merges with that of the home and vice versa, giving women a greater sense of freedom and connection with the outdoors:

> Spring brought no change in the family's monotonous routine, except that windows were opened and rays of new light, the sound of footsteps, the murmur of voices, entered from the street.
>
> Windows in other houses also opened, revealing freshly starched muslin curtains. Pots of flowers kept inside from the cold reappeared on windowsills, dry geraniums, dusty verbena.[91]

Balconies, windows, doorways, and entrances are depicted in Italian domestic fiction as public spaces that offer possibilities for women to encounter the opposite gender and to exchange information with men. "Proper" behaviour of married women and adolescent girls in these spaces is highly circumscribed compared with that of men and adolescent boys.

The Public Sphere: The Outdoors

In the countryside as in the city, at the baths as elsewhere, a young woman must never go out on her own, not least find herself in a place unfrequented by colonies of occasional holidaymakers.

La Marchesa Colombi, *La gente per bene* (1877)

Through a reading of Italian domestic fiction, it becomes apparent that social mores required unmarried middle-class women to be accompanied when among townsfolk in the street, and that their behaviour outside the home was equally, if not more, circumscribed when inside certain rooms. Paola from La Marchesa Colombi's "Una Vocazione" (A vocation, 1884) illustrates the separate spheres of young women and men and women's confinement to the home when she tells her sister: "I am twenty-two, I know how to take care of myself, and you do, too; and we go out so little that it shouldn't bother [Dad] to accompany us; no one comes to the house."[92] In *A Small-Town Marriage* by the same author, Denza and her sister take it in turns to stroll along the main street with their father and his new wife and baby. Denza is embarrassed to be in the company of townsfolk and feels vulnerable and self-conscious, as if somewhat harassed by the people who are watching her: "I had often overheard snatches of the observations uttered by the men who watched me in the street: 'A handsome young woman ... Beautiful face ... Lovely big eyes ... Fresh as a rose.'"[93] A similar scene occurs in Neera's *Teresa*, in which the eponymous protagonist turns heads in the streets as she travels through them in a carriage accompanied by her aunt, earning the quiet approval of the mayor's wife and the doctor's sister. In contrast to Denza, Teresa perceives her ability to turn heads as empowering:

> ... crossing the street was a triumph. Luzzi, who was smoking a cigar at the café, raised his hat with such a flourish that she blushed. Next to him, Don Giovanni Boccabadati, indolent and distracted, also looked at her through half-closed eyes. The pharmacist came to the doorway and craned his neck to see. Near the church two women, the mayor's wife and Doctor Tavecchia's sister, smiled kindly.[94]

The code of conduct for adolescent girls is more relaxed in rural places. For instance, in La Marchesa Colombi's *A Small-Town Marriage*, when

Denza's father takes her and her sister on their daily walks – sometimes three times a day, during which he would educate them by retelling literary classics, such as *The Aeneid* (29–19 BC) – Denza would take note of her surroundings, looking at people and things.[95] Indeed, Denza is dismayed when her father remarries and she and her sister are excluded from the evening walks, for she can no longer observe the townsfolk: "The only time when we had ever seen any civilized, well-dressed people was in fact when we crossed the city after supper on our way to the market arcade."[96] The freedom the young girls have through the country walks is denied them once the stepmother moves in with the family and decides the girls need to learn to be good homemakers. As the first-person narrator-protagonist comments wryly, "Even the long walks on the main roads, white with snow or dust, were given up, and we embarked on a completely different life," poignantly illustrating the separate spheres assigned to women and men.[97]

The Passeggiata *and the Streets*

The *passeggiata* (the Italian stroll around the centre of town) provided an opportunity for adolescent girls to leave the home and seek respite from their domestic work. Writing in *La Donna* on 20 November 1879, Serao depicts a typical Sunday on the Via Toledo in Naples:

> In the morning there is the stroll up and down the street on the Via Toledo, where, *by chance*, one can meet and greet whoever one likes at least twenty times; there are other walks, little trips, meeting places, visits, late nights out – and among the limited number of national holidays, Sundays take first place.[98]

There were, of course, restrictions concerning how young women could behave. Serao, writing in her conduct book *Saper vivere* (1900), points out that a lady never kisses her friend in the street. In La Marchesa Colombi's *A Small-Town Marriage*, Denza observes certain modes of behaviour during a *passeggiatina*, including the custom for men to walk behind women and for fathers to accompany their daughters.[99] There was a common expression in circulation at the time to describe respectable young women who went out into the streets, which we discover is *fare la signora* (to act the lady), so performative is the experience of being out of the home for adolescent girls and on show to the general public.[100] Being in the town centre provides an opportunity not only for men to stare at women, but also for women to stare at men, thus draw-ing attention to a female 'desiring' gaze. Amusingly, when Denza is told her admirer has a large frame in *A Small-Town Marriage*, she looks only at the larger men in the street: "On the street I looked attentively at all the plump men, and it seemed to me that I had always hated thin ones."[101] Denza reveals how self-conscious she feels at being "on show" to the public, as if performing to strangers:

> I walked very awkwardly, with my feet sticking out beneath my skirt and my wrists, red from the cold, showing between my gloves and the ends of my sleeves. For a while I didn't dare say anything, thinking that Maria was probably ashamed to be seen with me, since she said nothing and behaved in a rather haughty way that I had never seen before.[102]

The street as the ultimate Foucauldian panopticon for all to see and all to be seen is apparent in Neera's *Teresa* when the narrator informs the reader that the townsfolk know about Teresa's affair with Or-landi: "Everyone had seen Orlandi on Via di San Francesco and had guessed why."[103] Through the domestic fiction, we learn that the *passeg-giata della domenica* (the Sunday stroll) was a national pastime. Serao's "Checchina's Virtue" contains a reference to "the beautiful ladies of Frascati" who would stroll on Sundays in the piazza where the mu-nicipal band would play.[104] Denza's experience of being in the streets becomes much less circumscribed when the maid is put in charge of accompanying her and her sister to mass: "There was no one to accom-pany us to mass and, as much as our stepmother and Papa objected to 'the practice of leaving the girls in the care of a servant who was more or less their own age, and less educated,' for once they had to give in and send us to mass with the servant."[105] Denza waits until they are in the streets to suggest that they attend mass at her admirer's church, and they run through the streets in order to arrive at the church on time. Their subversion is twofold in that as well as transgressing "proper behaviour" expected of adolescent girls by running through streets, they also deceive their father: "She didn't argue. We agreed to instruct the servant not to tell anyone, and we set off in a hurry, because the church was quite far away."[106]

The rules were somewhat different for married women, who could walk in the streets alone. In Neera's *L'Indomani*, we read that Marta returns of her own volition several times to the spot where she and her husband had crossed paths with Giuditta, her husband's former lover. In Serao's "Checchina's Virtue," Isolina and Checchina, both of whom are married, walk the streets of Rome alone by day. Certainly there were limitations to this unwritten rule: if married women were out of the home during the day, it was generally assumed that they had a purpose, typically of a domestic nature. When Checchina is on her way to the Marquis's home for the second time in "Checchina's Virtue," she meets a mutual friend of her husband by chance and tells him she is on her way to the dry cleaner's on Via San Marcello to collect a dress.[107] In the same sequence, when Isolina and Checchina cross one another's paths by chance and stop to converse, Isolina drags her friend off the street into a doorway and out of sight in order to question her as to why she is in an unfamiliar area.[108] Servants and spinsters could also walk the streets alone and could linger to talk to acquaintances without being looked upon with suspicion. In Serao's "Jackpot," when the maid Tommasina does not return with the coffee she has been sent to buy, the mother tells her daughter: "They will have held her up in the street to talk to her about her hitting the jackpot."[109] Moreover, Tommasina would get up every morning at six o'clock to walk to work. It appears that the rules as to when in the day it was appropriate for married women, servants, and spinsters to leave the home differed. In Serao's "Checchina's Virtue," when the protagonist insists upon leaving the house to supposedly visit Isolina one late afternoon as it is getting dark (in fact, she intends to visit the Marquis), Susanna, Checchina's maid, makes the following statement before telling her mistress (to her dismay) that she will accompany her: "It's not right for an honest woman to walk by herself at this hour. So many evil-minded people are about. Besides, it's just the right time to be taken for one of them."[110]

The Countryside

In her conduct book *La gente per bene*, La Marchesa Colombi gives the following advice to young men: "To follow a lady or a young lady in the street, to stroll beneath her windows ... are impertinences unworthy of a gentleman."[111] Men move through urban and rural spaces swiftly and with confidence, as if to express ownership of them. The reader is introduced to Orlandi in Neera's *Teresa* as he arrives heroically from Parma by boat, after battling with the flood and struggling fiercely with his oars; later, we meet him riding a horse-drawn cart and travelling at high speed.[112] The great extent to which young men travel is illustrated when the driver of a carriage says to Teresa and her aunt: "You meet [Orlandi] everywhere. Here today, tomorrow in Mantova. Mornings dashing through the countryside in the sulky evenings in Parma or Cremona."[113] This recalls a scene in La Marchesa Colombi's short story "Learn a Trade for a Rainy Day" where the protagonist, Odda, tells her male companion, "You're ... well travelled ... in a month you'll be smoking in London or Paris or Paraguay."[114] In Neera's *Teresa*, the grocer, Caramella, who lives on the outskirts of town where he owns an allotment, slowly meanders up and down the streets with his wheelbarrow full of cooking apples and pears. Men have the right to travel abroad, and for long periods of time. In Neera's *Teresa*, Orlandi and Teresa's brother (once he goes to university) are seldom in town, and in La Marchesa Colombi's *A Small-Town Marriage*, the protagonist's sweetheart goes on an educational tour to Paris, London, Belgium, and Holland. Thus, through a consideration of the domestic fiction from late-nineteenth-century Italy, it becomes clear that women and men were expected to behave differently outside the home as well.

Public Buildings, Cafés, and Nightlife

In Italian domestic fiction servants and spinsters are often depicted as more pious than adolescent girls, who typically perceive the act of attending church as an opportunity to have respite from their monotonous domestic work or to interact socially with members of the opposite gender. In "Checchina's Virtue" by Serao, Susanna, the maid, expresses her frustration at being forced to remain at home to prepare for the Marquis's visit since she would prefer to attend mass: "Already that morning she had been unable to attend mass at the church of Sant'Andrea delle Fratte, and Susanna was implacable when she couldn't hear mass."[115] As if proposing a female secularism, adolescent girls attend mass with an aunt or a servant not because they are devout but because they wish to pray for the return of their beloved (as in the case of Denza in La Marchesa Colombi's *A Small-Town Marriage*) or because they seek respite from the home (as in the case of Chiarina in Serao's "Giovannino, or death"). When the man Denza pines for is away on a European tour, she confesses: "Even though I wasn't usually religious, that year I went out every morning at seven with my aunt, who was observing the nine days of Christmas at San Marco ... In the dark church I would kneel in contrition and, staring with beseeching eyes at the faraway light of the candles on the altar, I would whisper fervently, 'Oh, Jesus, let him come back!'"[116] Similarly, we read of how attendance at mass provides an opportunity for Denza and Mazzuc-chetti to express their mutual desire for one another. The first-person narrator confesses the following:

> On the very first evening, a few minutes after I had come in ... I raised my eyes, my heart beating wildly ...
>
> He looked at me straight in the eyes and went on watching me intently, tirelessly, all through the service ...
>
> The next evening, and on every one thereafter, he returned at the same time ... he would stand in the same place, and give me the same long, in-tense looks. On the second evening, however, something else happened. At the moment of the benediction – as ... everybody bowed their heads in reverence – I slowly raised mine and looked at Onorato.
>
> He had had the same idea and was looking at me.
>
> In that deep, solemn silence, our eyes – as though isolated and alone, over those bent heads, in that heady scent of incense, that mysterious light, that place of prayer – met in one ardent look of love: a long merging of souls, an embrace, a kiss.[117]

A similar scene occurs in "Racconto alla vecchia maniera" by the same author, between Mario Pedrazzi and Carmela during a religious festival when they first meet.[118]

In Neera's *Teresa*, attendance at mass for adolescent girls and married women also gives them an alibi to gather their energies for the strenu-ous housework that awaits them at home as they listen to the sermon which rocks them to sleep, as if it were a lullaby:

> The women very carefully moved their chairs so they could rest their feet on the chairs in front of them ... Everyone got comfortable, extending el-bows for more room ...
>
> The curate ... perhaps knew he wouldn't be listened to. And seeing those nodding heads gradually falling onto chests, conquered by sleep; seeing the endless row of yawns, those benumbed bodies rigidly immobile, he, the good curate, rushed the words drowning in his throat, breaking off the conclusion until his sermon was reduced to an indistinct murmur, sweet as a lullaby – sweeter and more lulling than ever on that dreary November day propitious for sleep.[119]

Neera subtly mocks the protocol of attending religious rituals in late-nineteenth-century Italy by likening the sermon to a sweet and gentle lullaby that sends the women to sleep. In La Marchesa Colombi's *A Small-Town Marriage*, we learn that it was typical in the provinces for young men to stand in the church next to the door. This enabled them to see the young women entering and exiting the church while simultaneously appearing "gentlemanly" by giving up their seats. The narrator has her own ideas about their motives: Mazzucchetti is standing next to the door, "as young men do, perhaps to show that they are there against their will and that they're impatient to leave."[120] It is not only young men who engage in such "clandestine" behaviour. From a reading of "Una Vocazione" by the same author, we learn that La Marchesa Colombi makes a mockery of Signor Cantinelli, who eyes up the women coming out of church in order to find an apparently devout wife: "Certain of the validity of his beliefs, he started eyeing up the women he met, especially at the entrance to the church, to be sure to come up against a God-fearing bride."[121]

In Neera's essay *Il libro di mio figlio* (1891), we are told that women sit on one side of the church and men sit on the other.[122] Lucetta Scaraffia, in *Women and Faith* (1999), observes how the implementation of the separate spheres of gender in late-nineteenth-century Italy went hand in hand with a process of an exclusively masculine de-Christianization. The separation between women and men became even more pronounced with apparently devout women and either unbelieving men or men who participated lukewarmly in church.[123] Scaraffia's assertion is not borne out by our writers, for although women participated in religious ceremonies, this was, for many, more out of an obligation to do so than out of a fervent belief in God. In "Checchina's Virtue" by Serao, we learn through the maid, Susanna, that Checchina's husband, a physician, does not believe in God. Serao makes a point of drawing attention to his hypocrisy: "The master of the house doesn't believe, because he knows what's inside men, and because he sees so many Christians die an evil death ... But, you know, these men are all the same: when they're well they laugh at religion and sin like so many damned souls, and later, when they fall ill, they call out for God and the Madonna."[124]

The ideology of the separate spheres of gender was also apparent in theatres throughout Italy in the late nineteenth century. In Serao's conduct manual *Saper vivere*, we learn that the experience of going to the theatre was as much (if not more) about meeting new people, being seen, and being able to see others as it was about watching what was taking place on the stage.[125] This is articulated in La Marchesa Colombi's short story "In provincia" (In the provinces, 1879), in which the narrator describes the theatre event as the principal arena of socialization among the genders in the provinces: "From time to time there is a play: and everywhere the same people meet, meet again, look at one another, get to know one another, study one another, get to know one another, and they see families and hearts from the inside in the same way as a glove turned inside out."[126] In Neera's *Teresa*, the judge's wife persuades Teresa's father to allow her to attend the opera, arguing that "Teresina was now grown up and if they wanted her to marry they had to let her be seen."[127] Upon arrival at the theatre, Teresa is conscious of being watched: "When she looked around and saw ... all those heads below, and so many others above ... she felt everyone was looking at her."[128] The experience of going to the theatre for young men was different. In the same novel, we learn that Carlo had been to the theatre where he had watched from the gallery. As La Marchesa Colombi's "Racconto alla vecchia maniera" indeed illustrates, men in particular were preoccupied with looking at women rather than taking an interest in the theatre production: "[Mario] had started to pass many times a day under Carmela's window, watch her in the street, from afar, because, naturally, she didn't go out alone, and watch her with the binoculars the whole evening, when he happened to see her at the theatre."[129] In her advice on introductions and presentations at theatres, Serao counsels: "Before presenting a gentleman to a lady – since *never, never* should a lady be presented to a gentleman – ... whether in her box ... or in a public meeting place, at all costs you must ask permission."[130] Furthermore, in her conduct book *La gente per bene*, La Marchesa Colombi announces: "Women who consider themselves obliged to take turns to change places after each act, as if they were part of the performance, are provincial."[131] Interestingly, in *A Small-Town Marriage*, when Denza goes to the theatre for the first time she confesses that she and her cousins behaved in such a provincial way: "We changed seats between each act so that we could each sit for a while at the railing that ran along two sides of the box, where we could see and be seen better."[132] Expressing one's emotions in public was considered to be inappropriate behaviour for adolescent girls. The experience of watching the performance of Verdi's *Rigoletto* for Teresa in Neera's novel moves her to tears: "Gilda's tragic end with the cynical duke in the background softly singing struck her deeply. She had to shrink back in the darkness to hide her tears."[133]

In the section on thresholds, we saw how women come into contact with the outdoors with the arrival of spring. Spring is also the time of year for the opera season. For middle-class married women, an outing to the opera or theatre was seen as a welcome distraction from the monotony and drudgery of their daily existence. In La Marchesa Colombi's *A Small-Town Marriage*, Denza's visit to the opera illustrates how inexperienced adolescent girls were when it came to relating to adolescent boys and the ways in which they were physically separated from them. As if to confirm moralists' and intellectuals' fears of the so-called harmful effects that romantic stories had on the susceptible minds of adolescent girls, after watching Gounod's *Faust* (during which, according to her cousin, Denza attracts the attention of Mazzucchetti), Denza's whole outlook on life changes: "From that evening on I began to live with my mind far removed from the household and my everyday tasks. And having a new focus in my life, so different from the thoughts that had absorbed me until then, did wonders to dispel the gloom of that house and to lighten the burden of my chores."[134] Yet another example of the lack of experience that young girls had with relating to young men is demonstrated in Neera's *Teresa* where upon entering the unfamiliar dance hall for the first time, and never having danced before, the eponymous protagonist expresses her anxiety: "She saw no one and looked at nothing. Like a sleepwalker she went to the darkest corner, where there was a humble, forgotten little chair in the window space hung with a white blanket disguised as a drape."[135]

Teresa's ignorance of dancing is exemplified when she dances for the first time with Cecchino:

> Teresina fell again into darkness. She was no longer conscious of herself, turning, turning …
>
> She was dying, but didn't have the courage to admit it. She was intoxicated by the movement, the leaping music, the warmth of that body next to hers, the strong smell of jasmine emanating from her partner's hair …
>
> The second, third time she danced with Cecchino she was less fearful, but her excitement had increased.[136]

So rare is the occurrence of adolescent girls' participation in public events that it brings out feelings of anxiety, fear, and, on occasion, sadness. At the village dance at Marciaria in Neera's *Teresa*, the eponymous protagonist is anxious at the prospect of dancing with a young man for the first time. Likewise, in La Marchesa Colombi's *A Small-Town Marriage*, Denza alters her behaviour when she sees Mazzucchetti while with her family at the Café Cavour – rather than face the shame of being seen by Mazzucchetti while sharing three servings of ice cream among five people (and asking for two extra plates), she makes up the excuse that she has a headache.[137] The same is true for married women and spinsters. In Neera's *L'Indomani*, while at Signor Merelli's wedding reception, Marta, not used to being surrounded by her husband's friends and their wives, privately grows unhappy in her isolation while watching her husband increasingly enjoying himself in the company of the other guests: "Marta looked on with the lethargic impassiveness of dreaming, finding herself ever more isolated and sad."[138]

The motif of sleep, which we saw from the example of Teresa's experience at the dance in Neera's *Teresa*, recurs here. Not knowing how to relate to their respective situations, it is as if the female protagonists consciously remove themselves from the events as a means of coping with them. In Neera's *Teresa*, feeling ecstatic about having met Orlandi unexpectedly at the ball, Teresa imagines what it would be like to walk the streets at midnight alone and begins to run, forgetting that she is with her father and sisters:

> It was the first time she had been on the street at that hour. And in that state of exaltation caused by suddenly meeting Orlandi, she would have liked to walk alone in the dark, in the cool air, in silence ...
>
> Without realizing it, she began to run again, deluding herself that she was in control, feeling one of the most inebriating joys of her life in this deception.
>
> But the tax collector's voice called in falsetto: "Teresina!" and the enchantment vanished. Father, mother, family, decorum, habit, all the chains of her existence took their place again.[139]

In *Saper vivere*, Serao lists the advantages of being a spinster, which include "coming, going, conversing, writing, leaving, returning, without having to answer to anyone."[140] Thus, as a thirty-year-old spinster, Teresa can go out of her own accord and wherever she pleases: "She was now more than thirty years old and no one paid attention to her anymore ... She walked out of town ... she was overcome by so many sweet and sad emotions – so vivid, so intense – that that evening walk signalled the most beautiful time of her day."[141] At the end of the novel, she leaves her home and goes to Milan of her own volition in order to nurse Orlandi.

Men, on the other hand, are depicted as being relaxed and confident in public places. It was customary for married men to spend their evenings together in cafés, which, as we learn from La Marchesa Colombi's

"Serate d'inverno" (Winter evenings, 1879), were places in which men would discuss not only politics but also the latest gossip:

> The young men have related the latest news gathered at the *café* or at the club; who's gotten married, who is on the brink of it, who has died, who is in love, what new developments are in store in Manzoni's new *manifesto*; who was the most brilliant lady in attendance at La Scala; what the fans are planning for the leading lady's benefit performance.[142]

In Neera's *Teresa*, each evening from seven o'clock until ten o'clock Teresa's father would go to the local café in the square to read newspapers and take in his "dose" of politics. His return home would signal the "decisive moment" for the members of the household in that it would indicate their bedtime.[143] Thus, Teresa and her siblings would only see their father at meal times. This recalls Neera's *L'Indomani*, in which on more than one occasion the narrator remarks upon the infrequency with which Marta and her husband see one another and how even when they are in each other's company, Marta feels estranged from her husband.[144] The narrator from La Marchesa Colombi's "Serate d'Inverno" calls attention to how women and men occupy separate spheres during the evenings, referring to the

> infinite number of families, whose Dad [*sic*] is out for one reason, whose brothers are out for another, and the ladies pass their evenings at home amongst themselves. Then there are the others, in which the Mom [*sic*] is still young, or believes herself to be so, and goes to the theatre, circulates in public society; and the young ladies who are not meant to frequent the theatre, are not meant to see the ballet, are not meant to hear things in conversation, they stay at home alone.[145]

The repetition of La Marchesa Colombi's use of the expression "are not meant" is suggestive of her underlying critique of these social mores. In Neera's *L'Indomani*, Marta's husband spends hours at the home of his friend, the pharmacist, on evenings after dinner. On one occasion, Marta accompanies him but feels bored and isolated in the company of Alberto's friends (of whom she is jealous), who discuss politics and current affairs such as Italy's colonization of Africa.[146] Italian domestic fiction indicates that bachelors would also spend their evenings at cafés. In La Marchesa Colombi's *Prima morire* (1881), for example, Augusto writes to his friend: "One evening I entered the café out of habit."[147]

During the day, a young unmarried girl or a married woman, if accompanied by a married man, can enter a café. Denza from *A Small-Town Marriage*, referring to her family, tells us that "the few times that we went out for ice cream we went to a modest, less frequented café, and we went in through the back door into an empty room."[148] Yet as the above examples from the texts illustrate, the "proper'" behaviour of women in public places was highly regulated when compared with men, who had more freedom and were consequently more confident and self-assured outside the home. This was also the case in relation to middle-class adolescent girls and boys, where "all tidy girls have ... a set routine during their day" and carry out their domestic work within the home, while adolescent boys partake of physical and cultural activities away from the home, occupied by "theatres ... lunches, horse-riding lessons, cycling, ice-skating, swimming ..."[149]

Sympathy for Women and Young Girls

By homing in on the female protagonists' thoughts and feelings, and through the use of a realistic mode of representation based on a predominantly female-observed world, the narrators distance themselves from the male characters as if to indicate that their sympathies lie with the female protagonists' daily experiences. The writers invoke their readers to do the same through the technique of interpellation. The writers' decisions (in the majority of cases) not to describe men's thoughts and feelings may be a reflection of the fact that women writers felt less comfortable writing about men, whose psychologies they knew less about. In calling this to the reader's attention, through the writing of a social history of women's experiences in late-nineteenth-century Italy in the guise of fiction, the writers suggest that words like "feeling," "emotion," "tenderness," "sentiment," and "character" are coded terms that belong to a cultural milieu, a particular temperament, and not to the gender of the protagonist. The following assertion by Armstrong regarding domestic fiction in the British context can, I think, be applied to domestic fiction in Italy:

> Domestic fiction mapped out a domain of discourse as it invested common forms of social behaviour with the emotional values of women. Consequently, these stories ... offered their readers a way of indulging, with a kind of impunity, in fantasies of political power that were the more acceptable because they were played out within a domestic framework

where legitimate monogamy – and thus the subordination of female to male – would ultimately be affirmed. In this way, domestic fiction could represent an alternative form of political power without appearing to contest the distribution of power that it represented as historically given.[150]

The domestic fiction by La Marchesa Colombi, Neera, and Serao concentrates on a representation of women's everyday lives, yet this is not to the exclusion of men, whose world is represented as being outside the home and associated with self-development, experience, and relative freedom. The female world that is presented to us in this fiction reveals the behaviour expected of adolescent girls and married women, both inside and outside the home. Adolescent girls' and married women's ignorance of, and anxiety about, being in public places and their inability to read the conventional codes of sociability are recurring motifs. The similarities between the authors' depictions are striking. Through the omniscient narrator's access to the psyches of female characters, we learn how women fantasize about an imaginary utopian space, in order to escape the drudgery of their everyday lives. Neera in particular positions the character of Teresa in active (albeit imaginary) roles, either as voyeuse or running through the streets at night. In La Marchesa Colombi's *A Small-Town Marriage*, Denza describes the effect of being in love and of having that love reciprocated in the absence of descriptions of events, the passing of time and seasons, the weather, and everyday life in Novara. Her love would have been perceived with suspicion by late nineteenth- and twentieth-century readers (and present-day readers as well), and considered unfounded and based on fantasy. Herein lies the story's irony in Denza's words: "Having gotten over the doubts that had tormented me and the anxiety about meeting him, blissful in the sense of security and trust that his love gave me – I was too absorbed in my new happiness to even notice the irritations of my life at home, which had made me want to get married in the past."[151] In Neera's *Teresa*, when Teresa's friend La Pretora tells her that Don Giovanni Boccabadati had left his house to travel in search of a job one morning, Teresa fantasizes about the prospect of being able to leave one's house without warning: "Teresina ... thought it would be nice to fly like Don Giovanni on a nice April morning, with a little travelling bag, fly away through the world into the unknown, fly through green and flowering country, over blue lakes, over fantastic mountains."[152] Once again, the flight imagery here is strong, and recalls the scene in the novel mentioned earlier in which Teresa visits her aunt, illustrating her unconscious desire to experience the world of men. In Serao's "Giovannino, or death," Chiarina looks forward to getting married to Giovannino so that she can have her own house: "Oh if only the day when she would be able to leave the house where she had suffered so much would come soon."[153] Men's inner thoughts are less frequently represented. In some cases, although not in the domestic fiction, we do have access to men's inner thoughts and feelings. For example, in La Marchesa Colombi's *Prima morire*, in a letter to Leonardo, Augusto compares the feeling of falling in love to the collapsing of a building.[154] In Neera's *Teresa*, the narrator depicts men as being unaffected emotionally – all we learn of the male protagonist's feelings for Teresa is that "[h]is love for the girl was not a chivalric or heroic passion. Perhaps he would not risk his life, but he sincerely loved her. He would have loved her just the same if she had been a man, or even as an old woman, because what he loved in her above all was her affectionate goodness, her smiling sweetness, her simplicity."[155]

If realism is "a kind of literature and art … that attempt[s] as much as possible to reproduce the look and feel of the real thing,"[156] if it "builds upon a presentation of things as they appear to the eye and the ear in everyday life,"[157] then La Marchesa Colombi, Neera, and Serao faithfully illustrate scenes from everyday life in their domestic fiction, from the perspective of middle-class women in late-nineteenth-century Italy. In so doing, they reveal sympathy towards women's experiences on the part of female authors: whereas men could move around inside and outside the home relatively freely, women's behaviour in public and private places was circumscribed and limited. The frequency with which such depictions are presented in domestic fiction points towards a subtle critique of the ideology of the separate spheres of gender being implemented by the hegemony of late-nineteenth-century Italy.

Chapter Four

Freeing Negative Emotions

Is there a difference between a feeling and an emotion? In 1884, William James wrote that an emotion is a mental awareness of a visceral change, suggesting that feelings, or affects, are visceral, psychosomatic, and immediate, whereas emotions are the conscious reverberations of feelings and the cognitive thoughts that accompany them (though these are not necessarily rational).[1] According to historian Alberto Banti, emotions are not simply bodily feelings, they are moral judgments. Whereas passions are associated with religious and philosophical discourses, emotions are essentially secular and have their origins in the eighteenth century.[2] Barbara H. Rosenwein has recently coined the phrase "emotional communities," which she suggests are tied together by personal friendships, shared texts, or institutional affiliations. An "emotional community" is

> a group in which people have a common stake, interests, values and goals. Thus it is often a social community. But it is also possibly a "textual community," created and reinforced by ideologies, teachings, and common presuppositions. With their very vocabulary, texts offer exemplars of emotions belittled and valorized ... Emotional communities are not constituted by one or two emotions but rather by constellations – or sets – of emotions. Their characteristic styles depend not only on the emotions that they emphasize – and how and in what contexts they do so – but also by the ones that they demote to the tangential or do not recognize at all.[3]

As Rosenwein points out, the aforementioned distinction between emotions and feelings is not universal since in many cultures the two words cover approximately the same lexical field. In France, love is not an *émotion* but a *sentiment*, which is more subtle and of longer duration than an *émotion*, which is short term and violent. The same can apply in Italy for the terms *emozione* and *sentimento*, but they can also be virtually equivalent – much as the English word "feeling" tracks approximately the same lexical field as "emotion."[4] For Rosenwein the term "emotion" is a constructed term that was coined by the scientific community around 1800 and that refers to affective reactions of all sorts, intensities, and durations. In this chapter I refer to the terms "feelings" and "emotions" interchangeably.

Writing an entry on nervousness in the *Dizionario d'igiene per le famiglie* (Dictionary of hygiene for families, 1881), Neera suggests that its symptoms are brought on by the accelerated speed of life in early post-Unification Italy and women's hopes for emancipation:

> Nervousness takes on all forms, affects all the organs, it exalts and depresses; it takes people in the prime of their strength and prostrates them with terrible convulsions; it takes away their ability to walk, work, think, it makes them powerless, and as a crowning torture it leaves them with a profound awareness of their misfortune.[5]

There is also an entry on "hysteria," written by co-author Paolo Mantegazza, in which symptoms of convulsive fits appear in striking similarity to those described by Neera. Mantegazza presents hysteria as not being limited to women and says that a cure was not to be found in marriage.[6] Rarely does Neera use the term "hysteria" in her writings.[7] Her recommended cure for nervousness in women is that they should resign themselves to maternal and caring roles and not take on so-called masculine roles in the public sphere as proto-feminist writers, politicians, and intellectuals.

Symptoms of "hysteria" were manifestations of women's repressed sexualities and their confinement to the home in late-nineteenth-century Italy, and, as has been frequently argued, if feminism calls into question constraints on sexual identities, then the "hysteric" may be considered a proto-feminist.[8] In this chapter I argue that women writers such as Neera, La Marchesa Colombi, and Serao consciously dissociated themselves from the discourse of hysteria in their domestic fiction and journalism, which was addressed to a female readership, to endorse instead a discourse of nervousness. Through a reading of domestic fiction, which functioned like conduct books in teaching women to deal with their limitations and avoid internment,

I demonstrate how feelings of nervousness on the part of female protagonists were a vehicle for their subsequent discovery and freedom through the fiction of their auto-eroticism and (predominantly) heterosexual desires. By examining particular moments in the domestic fiction by Neera, La Marchesa Colombi, and Serao, in which the reader is given access to the female protagonists' innermost thoughts and feelings (and in some cases their "nervousness"), I argue that the narrators' detailed descriptions of the female protagonists' bodies and the inner workings of their minds during moments of anxiety sought to counter and readdress notions of female sexuality as threatening and unfathomable to the body politic. Describing the restricted spaces in which middle-class women lived and exposing their feelings, anxieties, and desires was (and is) in itself an act of liberation. I demonstrate here that women writers in late-nineteenth-century Italy show an *explicit* commitment to an exploration of female bodily concerns and states of mind that was new and quite striking at the time. Thus, through their depictions of female affects and states of mind in domestic fiction, women writers were proposing a new model of womanhood, one that sanctioned, albeit in a covert fashion, the expression of a female sexual desire. But before we examine the aforementioned, let us first look at how men's negative states of mind are portrayed in Italian domestic fiction.

Men's Emotional Suffering

In realist fiction by late-nineteenth-century Italian women writers, men are portrayed as having been taught by society to sublimate their feelings of grief into their chosen professions. As a musician, Augusto in La Marchesa Colombi's *Prima morire* (1881) channels his feelings of love for Eva, who is a married woman with a daughter, in composing an opera,[9] and Eva's husband, who works as a businessman, upon discovering that his wife has deserted him for Augusto, directs his negative feelings into his work. The male protagonist, Giovanni, from La Marchesa Colombi's *Il tramonto di un ideale* (The fading of an ideal, 1882), who from time to time remembers his betrothed, Rachele, whom he left behind in his native town, has a similar experience while training to become a lawyer in Milan.

Female protagonists in domestic fiction are also portrayed through their domestic work (which is, of course, unpaid) in coping with disappointments in love. Denza from La Marchesa Colombi's *A Small-Town Marriage* (1885) adopts a "masculine" approach to controlling her emotions upon being told by her cousin that the man she loves is marrying another woman. Like Augusto and Eva's husband in *Prima morire*, Denza channels her feelings of longing and desperation into her domestic chores. Yet, whereas the male characters' sublimation is enacted in the public sphere of work, the expression of Denza's grief is restricted to the private sphere of the home, a place where she lives and works, and one that she associates with her early feelings of love for the male protagonist: "[T]here were the inevitable household chores, which helped me to overcome, if not my pain, at least its outward manifestations!"[10] La Matta, the servant in La Marchesa Colombi's *Il tramonto di un ideale* presents another example of a woman who channels her feelings of disappointment in love into her (paid) work, after suffering rejection from her former master. Here the narrator implies that La Matta uses work as a means of alleviating her suffering. Indeed, work is prescribed as the antidote to suffering nervousness by the writer of the regular column "L'arte di vivere" (The art of living) in Neera's journal *Vita Intima* (1890–1).[11]

While the narrator of domestic fiction presents the male protagonists' innermost feelings about disappointments in love, there is no mention of their *thoughts* concerning their predicaments (i.e., their emotions). In Serao's short story "Checchina's Virtue" (1883), even as the narrator reveals the female protagonist's private thoughts about her frustration at not being able to afford a new dress for her illicit assignation with the Marquis of Aragon, the reader is given no information about the Marquis's viewpoint; indeed, the narrator's gaze barely even fixes itself upon him. On the few occasions when the Marquis is mentioned in the narrative, any reference to his innermost thoughts and feelings is lacking, and the narrator is concerned only with describing the male character's outer appearance.[12] In La Marchesa Colombi's novel *Il tramonto di un ideale*, though female and male emotional suffering is presented on a par before the male protagonist leaves his native village for the city to train to become a lawyer,[13] the differences in the ways in which women and men respond to emotional setbacks concerning love are highlighted at the end of the novel when the male protagonist returns to his betrothed twelve years later. The narrator describes Rachele's feelings of distress, both during and after Giovanni's visit, at their realization that it is by now too late for them to maintain their promise to one another. Giovanni is merely reported as having thought rationally about their situation at length, and his feelings are not presented. Thus, the notion that rational thought is superior to emotion is posited, and normative responses on behalf of "rational" men, in contrast to supposedly "irrational" women, are presented. In Capuana's *Giacinta* (1879), Andrea, upon learning of Giacinta's death, sobs with his head between his hands while clutching her portrait. There is no mention in the narrative of his feelings in response to the event, even if it is clear that these are communicated through his actions.[14] The absence in realist fiction of textual descriptions of male characters' innermost thoughts about their feelings is curious and is perhaps indicative of an unspoken prohibition on displays of suffering by men in the "extratextual" world (i.e., in everyday life beyond text) or of a certain holding back on the part of male writers. The following passage from Serao's *Il castigo* (Punishment, 1893) exemplifies this. The male protagonist laments his being male and reveals his resentment towards women, for whom displays of suffering are in his view more socially acceptable:

> Oh, the great thing, the great avantages, of being a man! How fortunate: it is a pity I cannot appreciate it! You are a woman, that is true, but it is women's fate to suffer; and all their faculties are made for this condition, but man is made to be happy, and nothing in him is suited to pain; you are a woman, you can despair, I am a man and I cannot and must not; you are a woman, you can cry; I cannot and must not cry. A man, right: what a great advantage! I suffer like a thousand women all together and I can neither cry out, nor wring my hands, nor tear my hair out.[15]

The passage is suggestive of Serao's sympathy towards men in the late nineteenth century. Neera, several years later in her collection of essays *L'amor platonico* (1897), also reveals sympathy towards men, whose emotions are hidden due to a prevailing sense of male *pudore*:

> The belief that men are less susceptible than women when it comes to sentimental affects is an error of superficial experience. Without doubt we must remember that between men and women (not wishing to offend the campaigners for equality) there is a huge abyss, that not all men are as I say, but many, I repeat, are, and much more so than one would suppose. The only difference is that men's sentimental life is more hidden and shorter; more hidden due to a particular masculine *pudore* which makes them resistent to confiding their feelings, which is almost imposed on them by the inevitable and uncouth company of other men.[16]

La Marchesa Colombi makes reference to there being a specifically male *pudore* in her realist short story "Teste alate" from her collection *Serate d'inverno* (1879). When Gustavo is about to confide in the first-person male narrator, the latter confesses the following: "Had I followed my instincts I would have held Gustavo close to my heart, I would have cried with him. But for that silly restraint which makes us blush from our best feelings, and hold in the manifestations of them, I limited myself to clasping his hands."[17] Serao's realist novel *Cuore infermo* (1881) includes a passage in which the narrator describes how the male protagonist, upon reflecting on how his wife-to-be does not show signs of passion towards him, expresses his frustration and desire to convey his emotions: "He would have liked to burst into cries, sobs, to curse, shout, thrust his nails into his chest and tear it to pieces, roll around on the floor like a man possessed, to drive out that torment, that hatred."[18] Since the birth of opera in the late sixteenth century, there was of course one place in every Italian city and town where the expression of men's emotional suffering was accepted and even expected: on stage, in the theatre auditorium. Interestingly, male characters in realist fiction by women writers are depicted experiencing hysterical symptoms, which is indicative of women writers' sympathies for men and also exemplifies how attention to the effects of social conventions cuts across both genders. Men's expressions of emotions here are similarly represented in tragic operas from the same period, such as Puccini's *La bohème* (first performed in 1896). In Serao's *Il castigo*, the male protagonist suffers "a violent contraction"[19] when reminded of his mistress, for whom he is fighting a duel, and Augusto from La Marchesa Colombi's *Prima morire* suffers insanity and emotional torment out of love for Eva "in a continuous alternation, between absolute prostration and a violent delirium … produced by a great moral dislike."[20]

Women's Emotional Suffering

In Italian domestic fiction, women's suffering is shown to be acceptable, even expected. Unlike the one-dimensional way in which male characters are presented when experiencing disappointment in love, in La Marchesa Colombi's *A Small-Town Marriage* (1885), the first-person narrator-protagonist reveals somewhat candidly the psychosomatic symptoms she experiences when her cousin, Maria, informs Denza of her lover's new relationship. Denza turns cold and trembles, as if in close proximity to death:

> I felt myself turning cold, and I was shaking like a leaf and could say nothing more. I felt that every link that had bound me to life had suddenly

broken, and that after such a cataclysm my life was over and there was nothing for me to do but die ... My chest heaved with sobs, and my throat ached. I held back for a minute, and then I abandoned myself in her arms – sobbing in despair, saying that I wanted to die, or become a nun, that I couldn't go out anymore, because everybody who saw me would laugh, and I would die of shame.[21]

A similar depiction of female suffering out of love occurs in Neera's *L'Indomani* (1890). Here, the narrator describes the protagonist's dismay as she experiences the emotional detachment of her husband, for whom she privately feels romantic love, having just written to her mother about her supposedly blissful experience of being married:

Alberto entered and they didn't even exchange a kiss; he was serenely cold, she distracted, paralysed by the reality of the false sensations she had endured previously. Marta's whole body felt the effects of this pathological state. She was thin, her eyes lifeless; she suffered from long low moods; already many times without an apparent reason, she had run to hide herself in her bedroom to cry.[22]

The omniscient narrator's description of Marta's depressed state of mind reveals the character's emotions within a narrative fiction that purportedly sought to represent its characters and events in an impartial way. Access to the female protagonist's psyche by means of the female narrator presented the protagonist in a sympathetic light, far more so than her male counterpart. Readers were thus invited to feel sympathy for the female characters' predicaments.

The language used by women writers of domestic fiction to describe female characters' states of mind represents a departure from the scientism of naturalist writing; it gives rise to the female protagonists' thoughts and feelings pertaining to their experiences, and describes characters from different social groups through the "impersonal" voice of the female narrator, who shows sympathy for the characters' situations. This is apparent not only in the different ways in which writers of domestic fiction present their female protagonists' physical responses to hitherto inexperienced situations which cause anxiety, but also in their depictions of the protagonist's emotional response to a given situation. The female protagonists in La Marchesa Colombi's *A Small-Town Marriage* (1885) and Neera's *Teresa* (1886) respond emotionally to the action on stage when they attend the opera. In La Marchesa Colombi's novel, the first-person narrator describes her enthusiasm upon learning that in Gounod's *Faust* the hero falls in love with the heroine, and she begins to identify with the heroine vicariously and to fantasize that she is in the heroine's shoes:

> Then the performance really began to interest me. How did he fall in love? Oh, how eagerly I waited for that moment! When Faust bent amorously towards Marguerite, murmuring sweet nothings to her in the softest of voices, I felt as though I were consumed with love, just as though he had murmured these things to me ... I didn't understand much of the plot, but the love scenes remained engraved in my mind.[23]

The narrator's emotive, personal, and colloquial style through the use of interjections such as "oh" and the inclusion of exclamation marks, convey the expressivity of the protagonist's emotional reaction to the prospect of watching the love scene; the narrator's choice of adverb "eagerly" and strong verbal ending ("I felt as though I were consumed") to describe her feelings gives the reader access to the protagonist's thought processes. The female protagonist's emotional and vicarious involvement in the scene is demonstrated in her use of the phrase "murmuring sweet nothings to [the heroine] in the softest of voices" to illustrate Denza's wish fulfilment, which is also presented through the breathlessness of Denza's short sentences. Similarly, in Neera's *Teresa*, the third-person narrator describes the protagonist's excitement about watching Verdi's *Rigoletto* (first performed in 1851):

> Teresina was enraptured. The beauty of art revealed itself to her heart already open to love. She anxiously followed the development of the dramatic action. The kidnapping of Gilda frightened her, she cried with Rigoletto, she had disrespect and scorn for the courtesans, and waited excitedly for Gilda's return to the stage.[24]

The repetition of verbs in short succession here draws the protagonist into following the action, and they are modified by emotionally and psychologically charged terms such as "enraptured" and "anxiously" to convey the protagonist's responses, which are indeed those which composers and librettists sought to elicit from female and male audience members watching tragic opera. The insight offered into Teresa's state of mind invites the reader to perceive the protagonist as an agent, one who feels and reacts viscerally. Yet any visible signs of emotion in response to the love story need to be hidden from public view: the narrator shows how reacting to Gilda's death – perhaps out of a sense of *pudore* – Teresa "had to shrink back in the darkness to hide her tears."[25] The large extent to which women's lives were bounded and shaped by a pervasive sense of *pudore* is also depicted in La Marchesa Colombi's short story "Una Vocazione" (A vocation, 1884). In this, the sisters Paola and Bianca, upon being informed by their father about his forthcoming marriage to his second wife, feel a sense of embarrassment and shame rather than happiness for their father: "When [he] had disappeared, the girls hurried on with their needlework, embarrassed by that idea between them, feeling offended in their delicate *pudore* as young women, and not daring to talk about it."[26] Paola experiences a psychosomatic reaction to her father's news – "Her hands trembled, and her breathing became short and difficult. She felt the need for an outlet for the bitterness she felt accumulating in her heart minute by minute"[27] – and enters a convent before her stepmother gives birth out of a strong sense of *pudore*; "the idea of being at home at that moment made her shudder."[28]

Descriptions of female characters' thoughts and feelings in realist fiction by male writers are curiously absent. In Flaubert's *Madame Bovary* (1856), when Emma attends a performance of the opera *Lucia di Lammermoor* (1835) by Donizetti with her husband, there is no mention of Emma's thoughts and feelings about it. Indeed, Emma is portrayed as being markedly uninterested by the opera, in particular by the mad scene.[29] Any interest she might have had is lost with the arrival of her former lover, which causes her to distance herself further from the action on stage as she remembers the times she spent with her lover: "From that moment she listened no more. The wedding chorus, the scene between Ashton and his manservant, the great duet in D major, for her it all happened at a distance, as though the instruments had been muted and the stage set farther back."[30] In contrast to the vicarious reactions of the protagonists to watching Romantic opera in Neera's and La Marchesa Colombi's novels, Emma Bovary – unhappy in her marriage and disillusioned in love – is presented as being disengaged from the opera. Describing Emma's response to the action on stage, the narrator's style of language is scientifically descriptive:

> Emma found herself back in the books of her youth, in the land of Sir Walter Scott ... Remembering the novel, she could understand the libretto

without difficulty, and as she followed the plot, sentence by sentence, elusive thoughts came back to her, to be dispersed immediately by the thunder of the music ... Gravely Lucy entered upon her cavatina in G major. She plained of love, she longed for wings. So, too, Emma would have liked to escape from life and fly away in an embrace ... The heroine's voice seemed simply the echo of her own consciousness, and all this fascinating make-believe a part of her own life ... But, of course, such happiness must be a fiction, invented to be the despair of all desire. She knew now the littleness of those passions that art exaggerates. Accordingly, Emma strove to deflect her thoughts, to see no more in this reproduction of her sorrows than an embodied fantasy, an ornament for the eye.[31]

While the narrator suggests a possible relationship between his protagonist's and Lucia's predicaments, by having Emma remember her experiences of love through watching Lucia, there is no mention of Emma's *feelings* about her own situation. Such an "objective" presentation of the female protagonist's response to the drama, when compared with the presentation of female protagonists in the same situation by women writers of realist fiction, reinforces the notion that they were seeking to portray female characters' subjectivity in the fiction. In Capuana's *Giacinta* (1879), the female protagonist's responses to hearing her lover-to-be play music to her produces the following desciption: "Gerace also had a particular way of gesturing the notes towards Giacinta; and she, who had realized it, felt them linger around her body, rest on her forehead, creep lightly over her cheeks and around her neck, tickling her."[32] The narrator's description of the music affecting parts of the female body from the head towards the heart – "the forehead," "the cheeks," "the neck" – and a tickling sensation as opposed to an account of the protagonist's responses to the music in her thought processes, presents a very different image of female subjectivity, one which is focused on mapping parts of the female body at the risk of objectifying it.

The "Hysteric" in Realist Fiction

The trope of the "hysteric" appeared for the first time in Flaubert's *Madame Bovary* (1856), with which Italian writers and educated readers would undoubtedly have been familiar.[33] Emma Bovary is a devourer of sentimental novels, which are shown to have a devastating effect on her in terms of her marriage and on her body: she hallucinates, experiences melancholia and hysteria, and eventually takes poison. The topos of the devastating repercussions for the institution of the family that reading romances had on young women became firmly established in nineteenth-century Italian fiction. Capuana includes it in his *Giacinta* (1879), whose eponymous protagonist is an unhappy wife and mother who keeps a lover, devours novels, and experiences hysterical attacks. Refusing to live up to her desired role, like Madame Bovary, she, too, commits suicide. Arguably, the first hysteric to appear in the modern novel in Italy is the eponymous heroine and *femme fatale* from Tarchetti's *Fosca* (1869).

In Flaubert's *Madame Bovary*, the catalyst of the female protagonist's hysterical symptoms is a distressing event: Emma Bovary's hysterical attack occurs when she learns of Rodolphe's desertion of her; in Capuana's *Giacinta*, the eponymous protagonist's hysterical symptoms are triggered by the memory of the young man who raped her as an adolescent. By contrast, in Italian domestic fiction, in which "hysteria" gives way to "nervousness," nervousness is triggered by the protagonists' thought processes – such as their feelings of anxiety or disappointment concerning matters of love, or their fears about remaining spinsters – and are therefore self-motivated because of societal expectations. Given the reader understands such fears and anxieties to be constructs of late-nineteenth-century Italian society's expectations of women, she or he naturally feels sympathy towards the protagonist as she experiencess-ymptoms of nervousness, for which she is presented as having no accountability. Since both Emma Bovary and Giacinta are marked in their respective novels as transgressive for having had extra-marital affairs, the reader's feelings towards them during their respective hysterical attacks are most likely to have been ambivalent. Nervousness as a form of protest against such expectations in women writer's realist fiction, read in conjunction with descriptions of the protagonist's state of mind, has a twofold effect on the reader: on the one hand, it appeals to the reader's sympathies in a way in which realist writings by male writers representing the female protagonist performing an hysterical attack does not; and, on the other hand, it allows the female subject to explore her newfound sexuality in a way that had been hitherto unwritten in fictional form from a female perspective.

The narrators of Flaubert's *Madame Bovary* and Capuana's *Giacinta* describe the symptoms of hysteria as they are played out on the female protagonists' bodies. Emma Bovary, having been deserted by her lover Rodolphe, who has written to inform her of his departure, experiences a hysterical attack, the cause of which leaves her husband, a local doctor, baffled: "They thought she must be delirious. By midnight she was. Brain-fever had set in … She didn't speak, and she didn't hear anything. She appeared even to be without pain, as though body and soul were resting together from all the shocks that they had suffered."[34] The symptoms are presented in a detached, scientific and methodical way, as if being recorded by a member of the medical profession. Similarly, the omniscient narrator from Capuana's *Giacinta* records the protagonist's hysterical symptoms, which are brought on when Giacinta is reminded of the person who raped her in her adolescence:

> Giacinta turned pale and went into a cold sweat. As if on the edge of a precipice, her eyes blurred; she felt dizzy … Thrown on the bed, half undressed, her face sunk between the cushions, her hair loose and her hands groping the covers, Giacinta sobbed, convulsive.[35]

The symptoms are described in the same detached way as in Flaubert's novel, and the use of medical terminology has the effect of somewhat pathologizing the victim. In the above examples, the narrator gazes upon the body of the hysteric and impartially observes her symptoms. The way in which Flaubert and Capuana map the hysteric's symptoms on to the body methodically and mechanically so as to produce a "realistic" portrayal of the pathologized patient recalls the way in which a photographic image of the patient taken at the time of her attack would have been interpreted; indeed, it invokes the photographed images of the hysterics recorded by Bourneville and Régnard in their *Iconographie photographique de la Salpêtrière* (1876–7).[36]

In 1870 Jean-Martin Charcot (1825–1893) began delivering his lectures on hysteria at the Salpêtrière Hospital in Paris. Unable to locate organic lesions in his patients that might help him explain the malfunctions they exhibited, he attributed psychic trauma as a significant agent in the production of hysteria, and used hypnosis to get his patients to reproduce their physical symptoms in order that the physicians might study these. In her book *The Knotted Subject* (1998), Elisabeth Bronfen argues:

> The photographic work of the Salpêtrière served to instil a reciprocity of fascination. Doctors, insatiably seeking images of hysteria (be these live performances or photographic representations) and hysteric patients, complying with this spectacle, outmatching each other with the theatricality of their body poses, came together to stage a scene where hysterical

suffering could be invented and fabricated as an art form, both as a spectacle and as an image.[37]

The inclusion of the female hysteric in realist fiction with the publication of Flaubert's *Madame Bovary* marked what was to become her frequent occurrence in literary form among male writers of Italian realist fiction. Interestingly, at no stage is a diagnosis of hysteria presented in the texts; rather, the reader imputes an understanding of behaviour as hysterical from the adjectives used to describe this. The analysis of the hysteric by Flaubert and Capuana in the two examples cited above is revealing of male writers' use of a scientific language to describe the hysteric's symptoms, which bore a close relationship to that used by the physicians at the Salpêtrière, who sought to fathom the interface of her performance of "fallibility, vulnerability, and abandonment."[38] The construct of the hysteric's public display in photography and medical reports from the Tuesday lectures "became the interface between an articulation of [the hysteric's] own psychic foreign body, the foreign body of already existing cultural iconography (woman as Christ, the ecstatic martyr as seductress, the impulsive, irrational creature) and of Charcot's phantasy of a coherent language of hysteria."[39]

Artists and writers preceded the physicians' medicalization of the hysteric, as this was already taking shape through the relationship set up between the voyeuristic audience of late-sixteenth-century operas and their suffering heroines, both in the visual culture of Italian opera and in French and English literature (from which Italian libretti were adapted).[40] Later, in their book *Studies in Hysteria* (1895),[41] Freud and Breuer defined the hysteric's symptoms as representing a mental conflict that could be freed up through an active process of thinking and talking. Perhaps the more famous of their first patients is Anna O who invented the "talking cure," which led to Freud's discovery of psychoanalysis. Anna O, whose real name was Bertha Pappenheim, was an intelligent, self-sacrificing young woman much like the character Teresa in Neera's novel of the same name, who also experiences hysterical symptoms. Breuer's description of Anna O describes

a girl of an overflowing mental vitality [who] led an extremely monotonous life ... She systematically cultivated the art of daydreaming, calling it her "private theatre." ... Her domestic duties, which she carried out irreproachably, were almost incessantly accompanied by this mental activity.[42]

It bears a striking resemblance to the depiction of the protagonists Denza from La Marchesa Colombi's *A Small-Town Marriage* and Teresa from Neera's eponymous novel, whose daily existence is presented as uniform and repetitive. Denza describes how she daydreams while she looks after her stepmother's baby: "During the monotony of those rainy days in our dreary solitude ... I [would rock] the child, who was irritable from teething, completely absorbed in my own thoughts – imagining myself already married, alone somewhere with him."[43] The "private theatre" to which Breuer refers in Anna O's case is also to be found in the protagonist from Neera's *Teresa*, who

> thought of nothing but Orlandi day and night, completely sacrificing all other affections, and feeling no remorse about it ... In truth, her life was enriched by an inexhaustible fountain of joy. When she sat in the window space, busy for hours with mending clothes, who could stop her going over her talk with Orlandi in her imagination a hundred, a thousand times, until she was completely satiated?[44]

The protagonists' representation in domestic fiction as self-sacrificing mothers, wives, and young women, whose states of mind are presented about the feelings for the men they love, reveals the beginnings of a female subjectivity, which included their (predominantly hetero-) sexual desires and pre-dated Freud and Breuer's "discovery" of a female sexuality.

If – as doctors, scientists, and male writers of realist fiction seem to believe – the hysteric has ontological status insofar as she can be said to exist (or to have existed), following Lacan, I perceive the hysteric as the quintessence of the human subject because "she speaks as agent, from the lacks and gaps in knowledge, language and being. In her 'being' she reveals the incapacity of any human subject to satisfy the ideals of Symbolic identification."[45] The nineteenth-century obsession with staging the suffering heroine in Italian tragic opera demonstrates how artists, writers, and audience members, seeking to reconcile their ambivalent feelings of pity and condemnation towards the "hysteric"/diva, were the first to seek the "coherent language of hysteria," preceding the scientists. "Hysteria," as the psychiatric profession chose to label the condition until around 1980, in whatever form it may take – anxiety, depression, nervousness, panic attacks – continues to affect millions of people's lives today, particularly in capitalist societies. Since 1980, the American Psychiatric Association has officially referred to hysteria as "somatization disorder." Though historically regarded as a malady predominantly affecting women, writing in the year 2000 the psycho-analyst Christopher Bollas described the modern hysteric as male.[46] For me, hysteria is a male configuration applied to women as a social, cultural, and historical discourse rather than a medical condition.

Male writers of realist fiction seeking to depict the hysteric, together with Charcot and his fellow physicians, failed to gain access to the hys-teric's state of mind in the same way, and to the same degree, as did women writers of realist fiction in late-nineteenth-century Italy. Their insight into the bourgeois female psyche, as I have already suggested, prefigured Freud's and Breuer's work on interpreting the hysteric's spoken text, and their descriptions of the hysterical attack or nervous-ness as experienced by the female protagonist probe her state of mind and give the reader a privileged access to first-hand knowledge of her mental pain and experience of suffering. In Neera's novel, Teresa shuts herself away in her room when the judge's wife comments to her that she is becoming an "old maid":

> She was overwhelmed by despair; her body rocked with torrents of hate, wretched emotions, and envy such as she had never before felt.
>
> She twisted in bed, biting her blanket with the insane desire to hurt someone, with the monstrous desire to see blood stream with her tears.
>
> They found her unconscious, ashen, teeth clamped together.
>
> Doctor Tavecchia, called in to calm her mother's fright, pronounced it nervous hysterics and prescribed tranquilizers.[47]

The narrator's choice of verb "to feel" and the noun "desire" to describe the protagonist's state of mind represents a significant departure from the language used by male writers of realist fiction to portray the female pro-tagonist's hysterical attack, whose body, as Catherine Ramsey-Portolano points out, "rebels against the anguish and anxiety … against the passing of her youth and youthful beauty."[48] Realist fiction by male writers has more in common with the final sentence from this passage, which draws meaning from the "objective" narrative gaze rather than from mention of the psychological pain experienced by the protagonist.

Doctors and "Hysterics" in the New Italy

The Church and state divide at the beginning of Italian Unification af-fected peoples' perception of the medical profession: the esteem with which physicians were held in other industrializing nations was less evident in Italy, particularly in rural areas.[49] The Church closely monitored new developments in the medical profession and was, in many respects, indebted to positivist discourses of female intellectual inferiority for upholding the feminine ideal of the Virgin Mary, which women in Liberal Italy were expected to emulate.[50] Despite efforts to dispel the myth that hysteria was a female malady on behalf of positivist thinkers such as Mantegazza, this was still widely believed to be the case. Jan Goldstein's research into the admissions registers of the Salpêtrière and the Bicêtre (the public insane asylums for women and men, respectively) reveals that within the two-year period 1841–2, 7 out of 648 women were diagnosed as hysterical while there were no hysterical men recorded; of the 500 women admitted in the two-year period 1882–3, 89 were diagnosed as hysterical, while among the men there were two cases reported.[51] According to Mark Micale's chronology of the history of hysteria in *The Mind of Modernism* (2004), the first medical books on hysteria started to appear in 1843. In 1867, Henry Maudsley published *The Physiology and Pathology of Mind*, which was translated into Italian as *Fisiologia e patologia dello spirito* in 1872.[52] Goldstein's research shows that hysteria was as prevalent among the working classes as it was among bourgeois women: "Nearly all Charcot's celebrated hysterics, and nearly all of the less celebrated ordinary hysterics admitted to the Salpêtrière, were women of the lower-class."[53] Certainly, the end of the nineteenth century saw an increase in the number of psychiatric patients across Europe, particularly women, as well as a surge in publications on psychiatric illnesses. The year 1865 saw the establishment of the first professorship of psychiatry, and Charcot began to deliver his first lectures on hysteria at the Salpêtrière in 1870. Yet Paul Briquet's work of 1859 had already stressed that hysteria was a disease of the nervous system to be found in both genders, and the period 1885–7 saw an interest in the medical profession in male hysteria.[54] However, as Elaine Showalter argues, "by the end of the century, women had decisively taken the lead as psychiatric patients, a lead they have retained ever since, and in ever-increasing numbers."[55]

Flaubert's *Madame Bovary* – whose protagonist, as we have already seen, experiences hysterical symptoms and who is watched by her baffled husband who is a physician – predates and foretells of the ambivalent relationship between doctor and female patient, which became commonplace in the psychiatric profession around 1870. In Italian realist fiction, the female patient and male physician topos recurs in Capuana's *Giacinta* as well as in the relationship between Amati and Bianca Maria in Serao's *Il paese di Cuccagna* (The land of plenty, 1891). As I have already argued, however, the eroticized relationship between doctor and hysterical patient in psychiatric medicine, which was to become the norm in late-nineteenth-century Italy, had already taken root at the beginning of the century with the emergence of Romantic opera: audiences watching Amina sleepwalk in Bellini's *La Sonnambula*, first performed in 1831, and Lucia's mad scene in Donizetti's *Lucia di Lammermoor*, were acting out, and prefiguring, the analytical role of the physicians at the Salpêtrière. Thus, women as psychiatric subjects were being medicalized in literary and visual culture well before the medical profession made official their supposed psychiatric illness.

Carole Smith-Rosenberg's research highlights the ambivalence felt on behalf of physicians towards their female patients. The doctor saw himself as the therapist thwarted, the child untended, the husband denied nurturance and sex in treating a patient whose symptoms had no organic etiology, a fact which baffled doctors. Indeed, Smith-Rosenberg refers to the contempt physicians felt towards their patients when no organic lesions could be found.[56] Mothers were urged to bring up their daughters with a strong sense of self-discipline, devotion to family needs, and a dread of uncontrolled emotionality, and doctors held that hysterics were ill-behaved children who had not been trained to undertake such duties.[57] Many doctors generally held that a woman's physiology and anatomy predisposed her to hysteria, and that emotional regression and instability were rooted in woman's very nature. Indeed, the female protagonist from Capuana's *Giacinta* laments her failure to be a model wife in a consultation with her doctor. She justifies her behaviour by perceiving it as biologically determined: "We women are mad. We create a web of deceit for ourselves. It is perhaps not all our fault; we are weak."[58] By diagnosing the female hysteric, the doctor had created a bond between himself and his female subject. Georges Didi-Huberman has interrogated the way Charcot's rediscovery of hysteria feeds off an extraordinary complicity between doctor and patient, performing a relationship of mutually dependent desires, gazes, and knowledge.[59] Because physicians had defined hysteria as a disease, its victims could expect to be treated as sick: consciously or unconsciously women had opted out of their traditional role. The doctor, in labelling the hysteric as ill, assigned her the right to absent herself from her duties in the home.

Doctors were caught in a power struggle with the hysteric: they were torn between diagnosing her, thereby allowing her to opt out of her role as wife and mother, and not diagnosing her in the absence of an etiology, thereby allowing her to perform the sense of "fallibility, vulnerability, and abandonment," and, following Lacan, speak as agent from the lack and gaps in knowledge, language, and being.[60] Doctors in realist fiction by female and male authors are portrayed as observers of female hysterics by whom they are enthralled, much in the same way as the physicians of Charcot's laboratory, almost ashamed that they are unable to fathom the cause of the hysteric's symptoms. The following passage from Capuana's *Giacinta* illustrates this point:

> Follini ... studied Giacinta with the cold curiosity of a scientist in front of *an excellent case study*. Natural heredity and social circumstances explained her condition to an extent. But for him, a disciple of De Meis at the University of Bologna, for him who, if he didn't believe in the immortal soul he believed in the soul and the spirit, a passion like that could not simply be explained as a product of cells, nerves, blood. And he wanted to discover the whole process, the essence. He was interested in it for his book *Physiology and Pathology of the Passions,* which he had been working on for two years. For this reason, when it happened, he would skillfully question Giacinta, get her to confess, doing his best to locate her symptoms in their spontaneous action.
>
> One evening when the countess appeared to be very lively making her vibrant and bubbly phrases crackle around her, the doctor sat himself in a corner out of sight to observe her more easily.[61]

The dialectics of reason and madness, presented here through the doctor and Giacinta, respectively, reveal Follini's and the narrator's epistemophilic gazes, which are directed at the female subject. The narrator's use of language aspires to impartiality and objectivity, mirroring the doctor's distancing from, yet fascination with, his "excellent case study." This bafflement at the hysteric's reaction occurs in Flaubert's *Madame Bovary* when Emma is deserted by her lover, and is watched by her physician husband as she experiences a hysterical attack. Flaubert uses irony here to gently mock Charles's diagnosis of cancer:

> They thought she must be delirious. By midnight she was. Brain-fever had set in.

For forty-three days Charles never left her side. He forsook his patients, sat up all night with her ... What alarmed him most was Emma's condition of prostration. She didn't speak, and she didn't hear anything. She appeared even to be without pain, as though body and soul were resting together from all the shocks that they had suffered.

... Sometimes she had pains in her heart, sometimes in her chest, then in the head or limbs. She started vomiting – and in that Charles thought he saw the first signs of cancer.[62]

The Doctor-"Hysteric" Dyad

The above citation also illustrates the doctor's paradoxical predicament in relation to the hysteric: while he is the observer of an objectified "excellent case study," who performs her hysterical attack, the doctor is equally intimidated by her unfathomable behaviour. The doctor in Neera's *L'Indomani* expresses the view commonly held at the time, which was that women deliberately behaved hysterically in order to seek revenge for having to conform to the roles of wife and mother:

Women are not always victims ... they rebel, as they can, when they can. They respond to the monstrous injustice of the *matrimonio combinato* with their thousands of hysterical attacks, with their billions of affairs. If hit, they strike back; if deceived, they deceive; nothing more logical.[63]

This presumption is undermined, however, by the narrator's access to the female protagonist's thought processes: the reader is made aware that the female protagonist's anxieties are the result of the pressure she experiences to conform to a role assigned to her by society, and that she is not purposefully inventing her hysteria in order to opt out of her designated role. In being granted insight into the female protagonist's anxious state of mind, and the cause of this in writings by women, the reader is able to judge the doctors' diagnoses of the protagonists, to observe the doctors' responses to the female protagonists' non-organic complaints, and to make a judgment based on what she or he knows from the narrator. In "Checchina's Virtue" (1883) by Serao, the reader is informed about the anxiety the protagonist feels at the thought of visiting the Marquis, which keeps her awake at night and causes her to feel exhausted when she finally awakes with a bitter taste in her mouth. In an attempt to put her mind at rest, her physician husband patronizingly gives his regular diagnosis:

Every morning Toto would invent something for her.

"It must be the pork chop that has you feeling poorly, Checca my dear."

"If you don't feel well, why don't you take effervescent magnesium citrate? It's a pleasant beverage and it sweeps out your stomach like a broom."

"Checca my dear, the more I look at you the more I think that you must have coprostasis. Really, why don't you opt for a bit of almond oil? Freshly squeezed, at Garneri's, it's a delight."[64]

Serao gently mocks the doctor's self-assuredness in his diagnosis, which the reader knows to be false, thereby creating an alignment between author and reader.

Neera also exposes the fallibility of physicians' diagnoses of female protagonists who suffer from psychosomatic symptoms, though she presents a more verist and empathic relationship between younger doctors and female patients. In *Teresa*, the more experienced doctor prefers not to deal with Teresa's nervous illness out of fear of not knowing what it is, unlike the younger doctor who is instructed in modern theories and versed in pathology and psychiatry and has experienced hysterical symptoms. When he is called to diagnose the protagonist, his diagnoses are assertive and reassuring: "Nothing. Nothing wrong with her heart … physically."[65] He advises Teresa to go on long walks and to rest. The same antidote is offered by Il dottor Gigi in Neera's journal *Vita intima*: "Long walks, good nutrition, possibly a little light exercise, in short everything that benefits muscular development."[66] Serao's ideas of a cure are somewhat different, preferring instead to prescribe unconditional love of one's husband, brother, or father.[67]

As well as drawing attention to the doctor's diagnoses of the hysteric, Neera explores the erotic relationship between doctor and patient from the point of view of the female protagonist. When the younger doctor comes to inspect Teresa, her feelings concerning his examination of her are presented. The narrator observes the struggle for power between the doctor and Teresa, the doctor's stare over Teresa, and her reaction to it, how she succumbs to the doctor's gaze, and stares back, as if she has been tamed:

Teresa felt that look penetrate her body and thoughts. She didn't look at him, but even avoiding his gaze, she felt its intensity. In this way she grew even more strongly aware of it until, attracted by an overpowering magnetism, she returned his gaze. In this stillness, she became suddenly calm.[68]

We learn how Teresa feels desire for the doctor, and how the doctor is also seduced by his patient, mystified by her baffling symptoms as he places his ear to Teresa's chest to listen to her heart, and his hair falls almost to Teresa's mouth. Describing Teresa's reaction to the doctor when he returns to check up on her several days following the initial examination, the reader learns of Teresa's discomfort about being put in a maternal role by the doctor, as well as her sense of discovery of intimacy with him:

> A few days later, he returned to check on the results of his suggestions. When he suddenly appeared, Teresina blushed in confusion with a secret feeling of shame.
> That sort of intimacy with a young man without the bond of love disturbed her. She was amazed at not feeling greater aversion to the contact, surprised to find an autonomous life in her senses, independent of her heart and will.[69]

Teresa's perspective on her response to the doctor is characteristic of domestic fiction, and it provides a female take on the doctor–patient relationship. The reader learns of Teresa's awareness of her feelings of sexual desire for the doctor when he talks and, in particular, when he gives his definition of "true" love:

> The doctor was talking with that male voice that made Teresina tremble. Her thoughts were far away, but the usual magnetic current, purely physical, kept her listening to the young man ...
> Without quite knowing how it came about, he began speaking about love:
> "True love is born from a whole set of circumstances, of infinite and continuous affinities. It's a certain way of looking, of feeling, of expressing ideas; it's the contour of the lip, the voice, gestures, the shape of the hands, the odor of the skin. It's the prolonged attraction of their bodies, when the closer they are the closer they want to be. It's the quick and total exchange of thoughts; it's the binding of the same feeling, the merging, the completion of both in a progressive absorption of mind and senses ..."[70]

Neera expresses her view on love through the figure of the doctor, though this is perhaps not surprising given the emphasis on positivist discourses during this period; it is, however, curious that a doctor is seen as an expert on love. We learn of Teresa's emotional response to the doctor's view on love: "She thought she might die in a rapture of sensual pleasure, in the delicate excitement of that man's voice speaking of love."[71] The love of which the doctor speaks is the romantic love Teresa had experienced for Orlandi, and which the town's infamous spinster, Calliope, had felt for her lover; that the doctor's voice breaks off at this point and the tone of his voice changes is illustrative of his ambivalence. While, on the one hand, he feels sympathy for Teresa's feelings of true love, he cannot condone them, for society does not permit women to explore them, given that they take her away from her proper roles as wife and mother. Neera, thus, uses the guise of fiction and a male character to write openly about romantic love.

Topoi of Auto-Eroticism and Narcissism

For young women, information about sexual desire for, and encounters with, the opposite sex was scarce in late-nineteenth-century Italy. In an attempt to address this issue, women writers of domestic fiction configured their female protagonists experiencing anxiety either at the mere thought of having a sexual encounter with a man or, indeed, of actually experiencing sexual desire while in a man's company, for example, during a public event. Through the guise of fiction, female authors consequently imparted knowledge concerning taboos surrounding female sexuality to young girls or newly married women experiencing similar sexual desires and anxieties in their lives. The presentation of female protagonists' states of mind in domestic fiction uncovers a hitherto unexplored depiction of female sexuality in the fiction. In Neera's *Teresa*, there is a scene in which the protagonist, a fifteen-year-old middle-class girl from the provinces, leaves home for the first time and goes to stay with her aunt and uncle. Away from her recently assumed duties in the domestic sphere as young homemaker, Teresa's discovery of her newfound sense of identity when she wakes up to none of her usual domestic responsibilities is presented as a source of great pleasure for her.[72] Referring to the mattress on which she is lying, the narrator describes how Teresa "delightedly sank" into it, thereby presenting a relaxed image of the position of Teresa's body: "She lay on her side with her hands on her chest, knees slightly bent, head abandoned on the thin pillow."[73] The narrator's depiction of the protagonist's contrasting responses is indeed suggestive of a sympathy expressed on behalf of the narrator towards Teresa's usual experiences of everyday life. The narrator's presentation of Teresa's newfound sense of self is further developed through what we are subsequently told about her response to seeing the four simple pictures on the wall representing the adventures of Telemachus: "Teresina did not wonder if that attire corresponded with classical tradition. She saw only a beautiful woman dressed in pink amid so many others dressed in white, with young Telemachus among them."[74] That Teresa focuses her attention on the "beautiful woman dressed in pink" is suggestive of her idealization of female beauty, and further highlights the beginnings of her newfound sexuality. Continuing to focus attention on Teresa in the room on her own, the narrator somewhat erotically describes how Teresa starts to dress slowly, "tasting the pleasure of walking bare-footed on the rug between the bed and wall and whirling in her skirt without a corset, periodically pulling up the blouse that would slip to her arms."[75] The use of the verb "taste" – its association with eating and devouring, as well as its sexual connotations – is indicative of an exploration of the female self that was taking place for the first time in domestic fiction. Teresa relishes the opportunity to run barefooted in her bedroom, which indeed recalls the flight motif in the novel that I discussed in chapter 3, and its association with the protagonist's escape from oppression and her desire for evasion. References to parts of the protagonist's body (feet, arms), which she appears to be discovering for the first time, are similarly indicative of an exploration of the self. Indeed, so intimately aware of the protagonist's feelings, thought processes and bodily movements is the narrator that she uses free indirect speech to mimic the wonderment in the tone and style of Teresa's thought processes:

How white her arms were! She had never had time to look at them before. They looked like someone else's arms, slender, round, white. She couldn't make out why they were white while her face and even her neck were darker. Only under her collar bone, where her breasts began, did the white reappear.[76]

Middle-class women readers of the time were invited to participate in Teresa's marvelling at her discovery of her naked body, and to identify vicariously with the female narrator's presentation of Teresa, whose self-discovery is portrayed as practically narcissistic as she examines her image in the mirror: "She went up to the mirror to examine herself in detail, up so close she could see her breath on it."[77] Exploring her features and facial expressions, Teresa discovers the sound of her own voice as she speaks to herself out loud in the mirror for the first time:

"I'm beginning to get some self-*esteem!*" she said, smiling to herself in the mirror at the funny idea that she could *esteem* herself. She stood stock-still, struck by the sparkle she saw on her full red lips and dazzling white teeth. She smiled again. How odd! Her whole face changed. Was that the effect she made when she laughed?[78]

Teresa's jubilant state of mind as she explores her personhood within the time and space she has available contrasts sharply with her presentation in the home in which she has the burden of domestic chores.

It is also during her visit to Marcaria that Teresa experiences feelings of excitement and fear at the prospect of dancing with a young man for the first time. While she is dancing, the omniscient narrator informs readers of Teresa's state of mind, her physical movements, and her thoughts and feelings: "She was dying, but didn't have the courage to admit it. She was intoxicated by the movement, the leaping music, the warmth of that body next to hers, the strong smell of jasmine emanating from her partner's hair."[79] These first experiences of sexual feelings reveal their profound psychological effect upon Teresa: as she lies in bed that night she cannot sleep, and she imagines herself dancing with Cecchino, hugging the mattress to her body as if it were him:

> She remembered the accordion refrains and hugged the mattress with her left arm held high, her right arm stretched out in the illusion of dancing again. At dawn she slept.
> On awaking her first thought was of him, but instead of being a gay and happy thought it came almost like pain, like a sharp thorn in her skin.
> As the day passed her melancholy grew. She had never felt such sadness. She felt different, as if a great number of years were weighing on her, along with sad thoughts of death, illness, discomfort, emptiness.
> She touched her dress here and there where he had touched it, and was overcome by a great desire to weep.
> At the dinner hour, her heart was so oppressed she couldn't swallow her food.[80]

Teresa's symptoms of nervousness – insomnia, a pain like a sharp thorn in her skin, melancholy, macabre thoughts, a desire to weep, an inability to swallow her food – act as a metaphor for her anxiety about hitherto unknown experiences of love.

A similar experience occurs in the novel *L'Indomani* (1890) by the same author through its protagonist Marta. Feeling isolated and unloved by her husband, Marta loses touch with her sense of reality during a wedding celebration, and instead responds to her negative thoughts triggered by her feelings about her predicament:

> Tragic thoughts entered her mind: the death of her father, a little boy who she had seen falling from a window, the vaults in hospitals and lunatic asylums; and a pain in her heart she had experienced in her youth, and that could have been incurable heart damage. She looked at Alberto with a passion, with a longing of her whole being that made her face thinner, that robbed her of any other sensation.[81]

Despite her husband's neglect and lack of affection, Marta's overriding sensation is the sexual passion she feels for him. Neera may well be inferring here that Marta's predicament has driven her to insanity, for, as Elaine Showalter has remarked, "Darwinian psychiatry generally held that 'asociality,' the avoidance of company and withdrawal from society into morbid introspection and solitary habits, was 'perhaps the most distinguishing feature of the insane.'"[82] The allusion to the beginnings of a female eroticism in *Teresa* through its eponymous protagonist's awakening is further explored in the following passage from *L'Indomani*, in which Marta awaits her husband's return from his regular evening visit to see his friends at the pharmacy. As the time passes, Marta grows increasingly anxious as she awaits her husband's return. Her statuesque rigidity turns into agitation and frenzy:

> The wait, at first calm and resigned, with the passing of time, turned into general apprehension ... Standing still in the middle of the room she seemed a statue; her feelings centered on an immense and uncontrollable desire to see Alberto.
>
> Time passed by, and from her agonizing immobility Marta entered into a state of sensual hallucination. With her hand she unconsciously undid the fasteners of her dress, loosened her ribbons, and surrendered to a mysterious sense of abandonment, her skin shivering, her mouth thirsty and dry, her arms flung open desperately.
>
> Unable to hold herself up she lent her head on a pillow, on the back of an armchair, on anything that would give her the illusion of a caress. Lost in images of love she let down her hair, and winding it around her face she inhaled its youthful aroma, moaning her own name – Marta, Marta! – to which the night responded with echoes in the deserted countryside – Marta, Marta!

> Time passed by, until the excitement became weaker and left her worn
> out, her limbs aching, her eyes swollen and wavering.[83]

Marta's upright posture relaxes entirely as she undoes the fasteners of
her dress and unties her ribbons, surrendering to a mysterious sensation of abandonment. Her mouth becomes dry and opens, her arms are
limp, and her cheeks caress the side of the sofa while she lets down her
hair. Marta's entrance into a state of sensual hallucination, in which
she fantasizes she is the object of her husband's desire and experiences
an orgasm, points towards the beginnings of an overt exploration of
female sexuality and desire in Italian domestic fiction. The narcissistic eroticism of Marta calling out her name recalls that of the young
Teresa looking in the mirror and breathing onto it. That the protagonists explore self-love (and, therefore, self-esteem) through the imaginary while alone is revealing not only of the protagonist's desire for
intimacy with a man and women's unsatisfied erotic drives, but is also
illustrative of the protagonists' sense of powerlessness. The reader is
interpellated to perceive the protagonists as subjects. This is achieved
through the narrators' reference to the protagonists' emotions and state
of mind mentioned alongside their somatic symptoms. Marta's narcissistic eroticism, expressed when she calls out her name, recalls that of
the young Teresa in the novel of the same name where the protagonist
looks in the mirror and breathes onto it.

Similar examples are found in the domestic fiction by La Marchesa
Colombi and Serao. In La Marchesa Colombi's *A Small-Town Marriage*,
Denza's narcissism and eroticism is presented at the beginning of the
novel: she is delighted when, as an adolescent, her stepmother says she
is beautiful. This prompts her to turn on the lamp when she is undress-
ing, to sit in front of the mirror, and to watch herself undo her plaits and
let her hair down:

> After my stepmother's memorable words about beauty, ... it became im-
> possible for me to go to bed in the dark. I would light the candle, and take
> down my hair in front of a tiny mirror a couple of inches square, the only
> concession to vanity among the furniture in our room, which we hadn't
> had much use for until now.[84]

The protagonist from Serao's "Checchina's Virtue" is also presented
experiencing sexual desire through the narrator's description of her
state of mind. As we saw in chapter 3, at night as she lies awake next

to her husband who is snoring, Checchina imagines herself making her way to the Marquis's house:

> Go, yes, she had to go, since she had said yes that evening when he had kissed her ... And with the lucidity of vision typical of the brains that nocturnal wakefulness exalts, she saw herself leaving the house at four o'clock ... She saw herself entering his house, where he awaited her ... all her nerves shook in vibration and she hid her face in the pillow ... She seemed to have a new strength that she had never felt before, and great courage, an audacity that let her cheerfully overcome any obstacle, and a will so firm that nothing could conquer or break it ... Then, after redoing the same plan twenty times, extending it ... she would always arrive at the extremity of her dream, arrive at that house where he awaited her ... and everything sank in an abyss, in a confusion of fantasies that dreamt the sensations of shadowy tenderness, of warm softness, of deep silence, of the voluptuous caress of rich and beautiful things.[85]

Checchina repeatedly goes over her fantasy in her mind, imagining herself making her way to the Marquis's home. Her sexuality is conveyed through her agency (which is nonetheless an oneiric one) and the desire she expresses to enter the Marquis's home. Her boldness is "masculine," and she explores an aspect to herself hitherto undiscovered: we are told how, upon entering the Marquis's, house she has a nervous reaction, and in her hallucinatory state she hides her face in her pillow at the thoughts and feelings she experiences about her transgression.

In the above examples, the female protagonists' psychical and physical reactions, as in the case of realist fiction by men, are the consequence of thoughts and feelings of love brought on by deeply felt emotions concerning the *homme fatal* in her life. (In domestic fiction the *homme fatal* – who shares many of the characteristics of the modern-day hysteric defined by Bollas – is Mazzucchetti in La Marchesa Colombi's *A Small-Town Marriage*, he is the Marquis in Serao's "Checchina's Virtue," in Neera's *Teresa*, he is Orlandi. In La Marchesa Colombi's *A Small-Town Marriage*, the male protagonist, Mazzucchetti, even confesses he is an *homme fatal* to Denza: "Then he confided that he was a man marked by fate, and he offered proof ... that he would be the ruin of the woman whom he fell in love with, and who fell in love with him."[86]) Through the female narrator's description of the female protagonist's desires, the reader learns of her feelings *about* her transgression; for example, Checchina's anxiety about her desire to enter the Marquis's home;

Marta's anxiety as she awaits her husband's return; Teresa's anxiety as she awakes the day after having danced with Cecchino. As previously mentioned, the revelation of female characters' desires in domestic fiction bears a strong resemblance to the feelings and thoughts revealed by Freud's and Breuer's first patients in their book *Studies in Hysteria* (1895).

Elaine Showalter suggests that the hysteric's symptoms were indicative of a passive, distorted protest against patriarchal culture: "Their bodily symptoms were a covert form of protest: 'the "protofeminism" of hysterical protest.'"[87] If we apply this to the protagonists of Italian domestic fiction, it would suggest that they, too, were protofeminists. The presentation of the protagonists' sexual desires in domestic fiction prefigured what Freud's case study of Ida Bauer revealed in his dream analysis: Dora's sexual oppression, repressed desires, and women's homosexuality. Indeed, Hélène Cixous in *Portrait de Dora* (1976) describes Dora as "the core example of the protesting force of women," "a resistant heroine," the symbol of the "silent revolt against male power over women's bodies and women's language."[88] Freud believed that sexuality is the key to the problem of the psychoneuroses. The birth of psychoanalysis was heralded as a method for treating hysteria: once the unconscious desires of the hysteric were made conscious, the hysteric was cured. Certainly the explosion of representations of hysterical women in literary and visual culture at the *fin de siècle* faded away with the birth of psychoanalysis. Indeed, it was not until physicians had proven with their case studies that hysteria occurred in women *and* men, and that hysteria could be cured by dream interpretation and psychoanalysis, that the hysteric's representations in visual and literary culture occurred with less frequency. The sexuality and subjectivity in the presentation of female protagonists by Italian women writers of the late nineteenth century already invited the writers' female readers to undergo a kind of self-analysis, which perhaps played a greater role in the discovery of psychoanalysis than has previously been recognized: ordinary middle-class women readers were reading of, and experiencing vicariously, the anxieties and sexual desires of middle-class women, who were presented as straying from their prescribed roles; indeed, they were being encouraged to question the very desirability of these roles.

Chapter Five

Female Friendships, Sibling
Relationships, Mother–Daughter Bonds

[Women] did not betray their husbands physically; they cultivated friendships and intellectual ties, literary companionships, elective affinities. They engaged actively, if not by supporting the emancipationist movement, through facilitating the construction of a female solidarity.

Antonia Arslan, *Dame, galline e regine* (1998)

This chapter gives evidence that there was a nascent solidarity taking shape between middle-class women writers and readers across the peninsula in late-nineteenth-century Italy. I provide a close reading of excerpts from domestic fiction in which writers represent female relationships that existed outside the texts between adolescent girls, as well as between married young women, mothers and daughters, as narrated from a female perspective. To argue that such relationships were unambiguous sources of joy, positive mental health, and progressive social change, would be to over-idealize relations between women and to not properly account for the negative feelings of anxiety and personal pain (e.g., jealousy, betrayal, rivalry, and resentment) that were often embedded within them. As I argue in this chapter, Italian women writers were not merely celebrating female relationships in the late nineteenth century as a means towards progressive social change; rather, through their predominantly positive depictions of nurturing female relationships, they were undermining (however consciously) the myth of romantic love in the new Italy, thereby debunking it for the benefit of their readers, who were steeped in its cultural representations in romantic opera and realist fiction by male writers, composers, and librettists.

In early post–Unification Italy, women writers of fiction for and about women did not actively belong to a recognizable political female community in the same way that female emancipationists did. However, by depicting positive female relationships among women in domestic fiction, writers were knowingly helping to forge a sense of solidarity among middle-class women readers, whose predicaments were almost identical to those of the female protagonists they were reading about. As such, domestic fiction for and about women played a crucial role both in raising awareness among readers of their predicaments through the texts' verisimilitude and in addressing themes such as the ideology of separate spheres, women's limited access to education and the professions, and the shame surrounding spinsterhood.

Women Readers and Writers Revisited

In her 1977 article, Sally Mitchell argued that reading offered middle-class women from the late nineteenth century the "vicarious participation, emotional expression, and a feeling of community that arises from a recognition of shared dreams."[1] One can only conjecture that women readers of Italian domestic fiction felt the same disillusion that was expressed through the protagonists' experiences of adolescence, romantic love, marriage, and motherhood. In *The Woman Reader, 1837–1914* (1993), Kate Flint draws on a variety of accounts from Edwardian and Victorian England to show how, in that historical context, the activity of reading was often the vehicle through which an individual's sense of identity was achieved and confirmed. Flint further clarifies this nineteenth-century social and educational assumption, pointing out that

> readers identify almost automatically with the most attractive – if not the most conventional – central woman character available ... That identification was believed to happen when one read, and that it was thought that reading could powerfully instil and confirm desirable moral and social qualities, is exemplified particularly clearly in the numbers of brief biographical compilations produced during the period, and in the language of their prefaces and introductions.[2]

Flint goes on to suggest that "the woman reader was expected, according to the terms of the contemporary psychological and physiological tenets which stressed her innate capacity for sympathy, to find it far easier than a man would do to identify with characters and incidents from her reading material," and that "reading, whether in the company of one's biological mother ... or not, is a means of becoming part of a variety of reading communities."[3] The vicarious participation of readers of domestic fiction was further enhanced because readers generally shared similar backgrounds, and they could relate to the situations and feelings depicted in the works, whose authors were – like their readers – middle-class women whose experiences of growing up in late-nineteenth-century Italy were also similar to those of their protagonists. Adolescence for girls in the world beyond the texts was considered to be a time when the young mind was most susceptible. In domestic fiction, adolescent girls read romantic novels illicitly, as in Serao's "Girls' Normal School" (1886), in which the character Alessandrina Fraccacreta reads Ugo Foscolo's *Ultime lettere di Jacopo Ortis* (The last letters of Jacopo Ortis, 1802) inside a copy of the journal *Piccolo fornaciari*, meaning "The little furnace man."[4] In Serao's *Fantasia* (1883), a discussion on the proscription against reading takes place during a sewing lesson, in which some characters admit to having read books in secret:

> "We aren't allowed to read books by Zola ... Or rather, it's not that we aren't allowed," Minichini observed, "but it wouldn't be proper to say you can read them in front of youngsters." "Oh! How many books I've read that no one knows about," exclaimed Avigliana. "I know of a marriage that never took place because the bride let slip that she had read *The Lady of the Camellias* ..." said Minichini.[5]

Married young women are presented as wanting to read books that are emotionally titillating. In La Marchesa Colombi's epistolary novel *Prima morire* (1881), the protagonist Eva, in a letter to a friend, describes Chateaubriand's *L'Atala* (1801) as "a read that exalts and brings on a fever," and refers to the novels she consumes as those "which make me cry uncontrollably, which keep me afflicted sometimes for a whole week for some improbable catastrophe."[6] The novel in which she is a character, like the majority of novels by women writers from this period, is an indictment of girls reading romantic fiction.

Typically, women writers of Italian domestic fiction presented female protagonists who are entirely conventional and who undergo an inner psychological questioning that leads them to challenge, albeit temporarily, the status quo. Even if in the case of Neera's *Teresa* (1886), the eponymous protagonist's questioning takes the form of a passive rebellion against the law of the father in her refusal to follow in the footsteps of her sisters into an arranged marriage; in La Marchesa Colombi's *Prima morire*, Eva's desertion of her husband and child to be with the man she loves ultimately leads to her returning to her family upon receiving news that her child is sick; in Serao's "Checchina's Virtue" (1883), Checchina is tempted by the Marquis's invitation to his lodgings, but then realizes that she ought not to go through with it for fear of feeling shame; and in La Marchesa Colombi's *A Small-Town Marriage* (1885), Denza spends the best part of the novel believing that she will marry a wealthy man whom she loves, only to be married off at the end to a man who is twice her age with a boil on his face. The effect of these novels on late-nineteenth-century Italian women readers was one of ambivalence: while they provided an outlet for a reader's frustrations of being tied to a monotonous domestic existence, they also taught her to accept her limitations by describing the purely conventional and supposedly "natural" emotional reactions of women. Through the act of reading, the woman reader created a space within which she could be entirely on her own with her personal needs, desires, and pleasures; she could escape from her domestic duties into an imaginary realm.[7]

The depictions in the novels of the degrees of separation among the genders (and the differences in their experiences) in adolescence and adulthood, the different parameters within which women and men are expected to live their daily lives, and the focus on moments considered to be significant in the lives of women, and for which girls are shown to be unprepared (such as a young woman's first outing to the theatre, her first experience of sleeping with a man following her wedding day, and her experience of motherhood), create a sense of shared experience between female characters in the novels, and by extension, between women readers and women writers as well. Thus, a feeling of community and solidarity existed, however partially or implicitly, among and between individual groups (readers and writers), which also, on occasion, extended across boundaries of the characters' social class within the novels. For example, the writers' sympathy expressed for female servants and spinsters, the "estranged woman," like Calliope from Neera's *Teresa*, demonstrates the alliances of middle-class women writers and readers with women from the lower classes, and with women who did not fit into the socially prescribed roles of wife and mother. It should be remembered, however, that the "alliance" felt on the part of Serao towards servants and spinsters, as demonstrated through a reading of her domestic fiction and journalism, was decidedly less strong when compared with the sympathy expressed by Neera and La

Marchesa Colombi, who showed sympathy towards such characters in both their fiction and non-fiction. In this regard, La Marchesa Colombi is the most sympathetic.

Female Friendships

Janet Todd, in her book *Women's Friendship in Literature* (1980), suggests that literary female-friendship representations break down into five categories: sentimental, manipulative, political, erotic, and social.[8] From my reading of domestic fiction from Italy, female friendships fall into just two of these: the sentimental and the social. For Todd, sentimental female friendships are close, emotionally expressive, nurturing, and psychologically enriching, and they also exhibit a passion that is reminiscent of heterosexual romantic love. "Social" female friendships are seen as the conservative variant of political female friendships, which involve an alliance that leads to some action against social systems, institutions, or conventions.[9] Drawing on Freud's notion of the pre-Oedipal mother as the first object of childhood affection, Nancy Chodorow argues that children of both sexes take their mother as their first love object in the pre-Oedipal period, but that there is a crucial difference between a mother's attachment to a female child and her attachment to a male child. A heterosexual mother will become narcissistically attached to a daughter and anaclitically attached to a son. As a result of this narcissistic maternal bond, the female ego develops less rigid boundaries, a less insistent self/other distinction, and the female sense of identity is based on a feeling of similarity with her mother, while the male sense of self is predicated on otherness, on a difference from her.[10] Chodorow also posits a fear of the omnipotent mother from whom both females and males seek to escape, but the girl's primary attachment to her mother is never broken; she merely adds a bond with her father. As a result of this double attachment to both father and mother, heterosexuality fails to gain an exclusive grip on the female psyche: adult heterosexual relationships do not meet a woman's emotional needs. Men, argues Chodorow, are always of secondary importance to women emotionally, and represent an intervention into the unconscious mother–daughter unity. Hence, a specifically feminine homosocial and homoerotic desire stems from this close mother–daughter bond. According to Chodorow, women look to children to recreate the exclusive symbiotic mother–child bond and to provide the emotional intensity that they truly desire in their relationships.

Chodorow's writings privilege the pre-Oedipal mother–child relationship as critical to the construction of self – in contrast to the Freudian and Lacanian focus on the primacy of Oedipal phenomena and the role of the phallus. These also identify men's fear of the pre-Oedipal mother and of losing their sense of masculinity as fuelling male dominance in society. Her work has been criticized for being both overly deterministic in its reliance on the explanatory value of women's mothering and insufficiently attentive to differences among women, but her point about distance between women and men is reinforced from a reading of female friendships in Italian domestic fiction. From a reading of this, it would appear that in the early post–Unification period, young middle-class girls and young women looked to other young girls and women to provide the emotional intensity that they truly desired in their relationships and which they were unable to find in their relationships with men. In *Gender Meets Genre* (2002), Ursula Fanning puts forward the view that one possible reason why women writers in general, and Serao in particular, foreground relationships between women is that by depicting female friendships they can create a version of the mother–daughter bond. Drawing on work carried out by Helene Deutsch, who highlights the adolescent girl's need for independence from the mother and her gravitation towards other girls who function as an alter ego for the mother, Fanning argues that

> linked to the desire to replicate the intense mother–daughter relationship is the equally intense, and paradoxical need to break away from the mother … Nineteenth-century women writers, including Serao, were locked in a painful struggle for self-definition. One way in which female self-definition in general is attained seems to be through an intense attachment to a woman or girl other than the mother.[11]

Fanning shows how Italian women writers' practice of foregrounding female friendships in fiction as psychologically significant began as early as 1881, when Serao's *Cuore infermo* was first published.[12] However, even several years prior to that, the publication of La Marchesa Colombi's conduct manual *La gente per bene* (1877) presented – albeit in "non-fictional" form – the existence of close female friendships in post–Unification Italy. In her chapter on "La signorina," La Marchesa Colombi announces: "A young lady can accept invitations to lunch at a female friend's house, and stay there, even alone, under the care of the lady of the house."[13] Michaela De Giorgio draws attention to a

level of difficulty in establishing close female friendships in early post–
Unification Italy due to domestic isolation, a lack of time, and the un-
availability of comfortable public meeting places for women.[14] Yet close
"sentimental" and "social" female friendships – in particular between
adolescent girls – are represented in Italian domestic fiction, such as
in La Marchesa Colombi's *A Small-Town Marriage* and "Girls' Normal
School." In this latter short story, relationships between adolescent girls
in a boarding school are presented as close and intimate, passionate
and homoerotic (even though the sexual enactment is realized only in
"erotic" female friendships): "One could see the passionate look that
Amelia Bozza, a boarder in the upper class, turned on Caterina Borelli,
a day student in the third class ... and Caterina Borelli twirled in her fin-
gers a wilted rose that Amelia Bozza had given her three days before."[15]
Fanning has shown how passionate friendships between adolescent
girls were common within communities of schoolgirls and how they
revealed female solidarity and support among women to the exclusion
of male characters.[16] As if pointing towards her own conviction in the
existence, or, at least, beginnings of a female solidarity among women
belonging to the same social group (a belief which she never states
explicitly, but which is evident through a reading of her domestic fiction), Serao portrays a close-knit female community of adolescent girls
in "Girls' Normal School" through

> the group of "Saints," the mystical group, the two Santaniello sisters,
> Annina Casale, Signorina Pessenda, Signorina Scapolatiello, Signorina
> Borelli, and Maria Valente, looked severe or scandalized; ... they referred
> to each other as "sisters" among themselves.[17]

Depictions of female friendships between adolescent middle-class
girls are less common in the domestic fiction by Neera and La Marchesa
Colombi. In La Marchesa Colombi's "Racconto alla vecchia maniera"
(Story from old times, 1885), the friendship between the young women
Amelia and Carmela sours when Carmela shows a preference for a man
who is not Amelia's brother: "Amelia, resenting the fact that her friend
had deliberately chosen another over her brother, had started to treat
her with coolness, keeping her at a distance, and a little later she had
got married, and had left with her husband for Oleggio."[18]

Though Italian domestic fiction reveals a social critique of women's
confinement within the home, one positive outcome of the domesti-
cation of young middle-class girls in late-nineteenth-century Italy

was that it brought them together, and it enabled them to forge close ties and friendships with one another and to seek asylum and comfort away from the "harsh" outside world. Friendships among young women waiting for suitable marriage partners were normally between sisters and cousins:[19] Teresa from Neera's eponymous novel and Denza from *A Small-Town Marriage* by La Marchesa Colombi both experience close female friendships as adolescents – the former with a married woman who happens to be the judge's wife, and the latter with her cousin Maria – both of whom take on the role of confidante to the respective female protagonists. In Neera's *Teresa*, the judge's wife adopts the role of surrogate mother to the adolescent Teresa, whose biological mother is represented as constantly absent, tired and ill, and, therefore, inattentive of Teresa's needs and unavailable to her. De Giorgio draws upon the work of Sofia Bisi who has shown that, during the 1880s in Italy, one insurmountable prohibition in the code of female relationships was friendship between a single woman and a married woman; if this were indeed the case, the friendship between the judge's wife and Teresa represents yet another sign of female rebellion against the law of the father.[20] The judge's wife takes Teresa to her first opera performance, counsels her on marriage and love, and offers her the opportunity of an arranged marriage to a widower professor. As the judge's wife grows more aware of Teresa's love for Orlandi and the suffering this causes her, the relationship between the two women grows stronger. The judge's wife helps sustain Teresa's relationship with Orlandi by allowing them to correspond through her even when Teresa's father has forbidden his daughter to have any further contact with Orlandi. Such collusion on the part of the two characters, both of whom are portrayed sympathetically by the narrator, is suggestive of an implicit endorsement by Neera – and enacted through the conventional character of the judge's wife – that the writer condoned such subtle, subversive behaviour among women according to the social norms of the day.

In La Marchesa Colombi's *A Small-Town Marriage*, the protagonist and her cousin Maria are adolescents when they become emotionally close following a trip to the opera during which Maria notices Denza has caught the attention of Mazzucchetti, a young, eligible man from the upper-middle classes. Maria and Denza walk arm in arm when Maria tells her of Mazzucchetti's affections. From this point onwards, Denza relies on Maria (who has connections with friends of Mazzucchetti) to see the man who apparently admires her, and to develop a relationship with him. Of the two cousins, Maria is Denza's favourite, and it is

Maria who sets up Mazzucchetti's and Denza's first meeting and gives Denza the possibility to experience romantic love. The friendship between Maria and Denza develops and grows in intensity as a result of the romantic heterosexual relationship, which is also the case between the judge's wife and Teresa in Neera's novel. Fanning has shown in her discussion of female friendships that, in Serao's novels,

> there are two main areas in which Serao locates her female characters when she presents them locked in intense same-sex pairings. In the first place, such pairings can be contemporaneous with and contingent on the romantic heterosexual relationship. In such instances the latter seems on the surface to take precedence but on closer analysis this is not the case.[21]

The same can be said about the friendships between Maria and Denza and between the judge's wife and Teresa. When Maria marries, the cousins' dynamic changes; it becomes less intense and less driven by the possibility of Denza's fulfilment in romantic love. Denza remarks that Maria, "no longer spoke to me of her marriage, and ... rarely came to see us."[22] As a married woman, Maria tells Denza the news that Mazzucchetti is engaged to be married, and subsequently arranges for the man who has proposed marriage to Denza to be alone with her on Maria's balcony, thus being responsible in part for Denza's acceptance to marry not out of love but out of a sense of duty.

The close bond of friendship between Denza and Maria is underpinned by their use of language, which is direct, sincere, and affectionate: Denza speaks freely with her cousin and is at ease in her company, while the language she uses with Mazzucchetti, in contrast, is less spontaneous, and her responses to Mazzucchetti's comments are a filtered version of her true thoughts and feelings. This is brought to light through the first-person narrator, who gives the reader access to the protagonist's thoughts and feelings about events and people. A similar dynamic of relations between female friends, in contrast to relations with a young man whom the protagonist desires, is found in Neera's *Teresa*. Through the omniscient narrator, the reader gauges the ease with which the protagonist converses with the judge's wife. This contrasts sharply with the lack of dialogue during assignations that take place between Orlandi and Teresa, during which feelings and emotions on the part of the protagonist are described. In fact, as we shall see below where I examine relationships between married women, there is an absence of a spontaneous dialogue between women and men, both married and unmarried, in Italian domestic fiction, in particular from the moment when girls' and boys' upbringings diverge in adolescence.

Authors of Italian domestic fiction highlight the significance of female friendships through foregrounding them to the exclusion of depictions of male friendships. In the fiction by women writers, young boys play together outside the home, or they loaf about. Neera's *Teresa* depicts the eponymous protagonist's brother, who

> studied and studied, squeezing his head in his hands as long as his terrible father stood looking at him. Except for those times when he got his retribution in the solitary grass-covered lanes where his companions were waiting for him, loafing in the warm noon hours, and in the woods where the stream narrowed to a thread of water, where abundant blackberry bushes grew under the long shadow of poplars.[23]

Similarly, in La Marchesa Colombi's *A Small-Town Marriage*, the protagonist's admirer confides to her that he and his friends "had rented a room, which happened to be near our house. They went there in the evenings, put on fezzes and smoked their pipes, and they called themeslves Athos, Portos, Aramis, and d'Artagnan."[24] The "public" and "private" spheres girls and boys occupied provided opportunities for an intimacy and closeness to be established and to develop within the separate social groups defined by gender and class. In *A Small-Town Marriage*, the two cousins rearrange the furniture in their living room to create a space for an intimacy to develop and thrive when, accompanied by their stepmother, Denza and her sister pay them a visit:

> They would move a small bench in front of the window and pull up four very low little armchairs; then they would sit down and have us sit down, and the four of us would put up our feet on the same bench "in order to be closer," they said, as though we were very intimate. But whether we were close together or not, we never knew what to say. However, they were so nice and charming, and they knew so many things, that we were happy just to look at them, and to listen to them chatting about the boarding school where they had been, and about the countryside where they were going.[25]

Although Denza's and her sister's lack of formal schooling exposes their discomfort at socializing with new people, the cousins make a concerted effort to put them at their ease which reveals their compassion for, and acknowledgment of, the differences in upbringing between them. In recounting this scene, the first-person narrator/protagonist emphasizes the low height of the small armchairs, which adds to the sense of closeness and intimacy among the four girls.

Sibling Relationships

Despite the Bonelli cousins' efforts to integrate Denza and her sister in *A Small-Town Marriage,* there remains a distance between them due to the differences in their upbringing: while the Bonelli cousins had received their education in a boarding school, Denza and her sister had been educated at home by their father. The relationship between the two sisters, Denza (the first-person narrator, and the younger and more attractive of the two sisters) and Titina, is ambiguous. It is both intimate and at times hostile, and it encapsulates the notion of sisterhood as equivocal sibling rivalry, which Deborah Cartmell and Imelda Whelehan highlight.[26] The same dynamic characterizes the sibling relationship in La Marchesa Colombi's short story "Una Vocazione" (A vocation, 1884), in which the sisters Paola and Bianca argue over the news that their father is to remarry.[27] In *A Small-Town Marriage* , the sisters' lack of education and guidance in their upbringing is highlighted when their stepmother allows them to accept their cousins' invitation of the regular Sunday *passeggiata.* In a momentary loss of their sense of *pudore,* the narrator describes how the sisters embrace one another only to immediately regret having done so, given it was not typical of them to be demonstrative with one another: "After all this hugging and kissing, we felt somewhat awkward, because we weren't used to such demonstrative behaviour. ... So mortified were we by the scene that we had made that we didn't dare look at one another."[28] Notwithstanding the awkwardness Denza and her sister experience in expressing their feelings for one another, when Titina leaves home to get married, Denza misses her, in particular during festivals such as Christmas: "How bored I was that year with preparations for Christmas, which in our house began a week before the holiday! Usually my sister and I would laugh and laugh as we got up on stoves and tables, on the chest, and even on the top of the fireplace, in order to crown the kitchen pots that hung on the walls."[29] As we shall see, the paradoxical closeness and distance that characterizes the siblings' relationship echoes that between mothers and daughters in Italian domestic fiction.

At age fifteen, Neera's Teresa stays at home, where, "in her duties as young homemaker she still felt the uncertainties of inexperience, but she was sure of her mission to help her mother."[30] Indeed, as the eldest child, Teresa has a certain responsibility towards her younger siblings. This is borne out in her relationships with her brother, her twin sisters, and her youngest sister, for each of whom she acts as a surrogate mother on behalf of their biological mother, Signora Soave. Teresa sends her little sisters to school, is loving and affectionate towards her brother Carlo, and cares for her baby sister Ida. Yet the twin sisters are hostile towards their elder sister, perhaps because of the differences in age and responsibility, and because Teresa is in a position of authority: "The twins, growing older (they were now twelve), harboured feelings of jealousy for that sister everyone loved and who enjoyed some small advantages as older sister."[31] Signora Soave's neglect of her parental role, her inattentiveness towards her children, which translates as an unconscious refusal to "parent" her children, can be seen as a subtle form of protest over the different social expectations of women and men, and it is presented by the narrator in an attempt to raise awareness of middle-class women's struggle to live up to the requirements of ordinary women as "good" mothers and wives in late-nineteenth-century Italy.

Regarding Teresa's relationship with her brother Carlo, this is initially close, but it changes over time, becoming gradually more distant. Their relationship is one of emotional closeness and physical affection on Teresa's part: as the siblings await their father's return from the scene of the flood in the opening pages of the book, Teresa is demonstrative towards her brother, who, although he responds with apparent indifference towards her affections, is nevertheless obliging: "All at once she put an arm around her little brother's neck, bending until her cheek touched his short hair, wiry as a brush. He was unconscious of the caress."[32] Yet, when as a young man Carlo returns home from university, it is clear how his different experiences as a student have distanced him from Teresa, whom he rejects in an almost sexualized way when she demonstrates her affection towards him:

> [Teresa] remained beside him, happily breathing the odour of the cigar coming from his mouth until, overcome by a vertigo of tenderness, she suddenly kissed the corner of his mouth. He pushed her away gently, more gently than other times, giving her a little slap on the cheek. And then he asked point-blank: "Do you have a boyfriend?"[33]

The mechanisms pertaining to the ideology of the separate spheres according to gender were at work from the beginning of a child's life in the context of late-nineteenth-century Italy, and that Neera continuously pits Teresa's destiny with her brother's throughout the novel is an explicit denunciation of the double standards. Girls and boys followed different trajectories from childhood onwards: fathers invested financially in their sons' education, while girls were expected to wait for a marriage proposal. The bodily changes that occurred in young women were read as harbingers of their mission as wives and mothers and, in adolescence, the scission that occurred in sisters' and brothers' lives was to differentiate them ideologically, emotionally, materially, and psychologically for their future roles. De Giorgio draws attention to the positive outcome of the brother–sister relationship for middle-class girls, for this was the only relationship that girls and young women could have with a boy and young man who was not a prospective suitable husband.[34] Yet, while it would seem that there is a closeness and intimacy between same-sex siblings and siblings of the opposite sex as represented in the domestic fiction, the protagonists from the novels and short stories in question are represented as being quite distanced emotionally from their siblings despite spending long periods of time with them and sharing common spaces, such as the bedroom. Juliet Mitchell suggests that the condescending attitude boys demonstrate towards their sisters is explained as a defense mechanism for hiding their anxiety at their sisters' bodily changes: "the boy, by being stronger and more valued, hopes to regain his omnipotence so threatened by the sibling that has arrived from 'nowhere' and through which the girl dreads feeling confirmed in her weakness and lack of social value through the same experience."[35]

Married Women

The arranged marriage (*matrimonio combinato*) was an integral part of Italian life until the first decade of the twentieth century: girls left their father's homes to marry and to enter their husband's homes, taking with them their dowry, while sons took home a wife and her dowry.[36] If a family had the financial means to provide for their daughters, the chances of their children marrying were higher. According to one study, women were chosen as marriage partners if they were strong and healthy in order that they could have children, work at home or in the fields, and take men's places in time of war. The same study affirms that wives were not indispensable: there were many women who died young, almost always in childbirth, and were replaced almost immediately. Women in the workforce and as mothers were easily substituted, while men's ownership and rental of the land was fixed and reliable.[37] Once women were married, they occupied different spaces compared with their husbands: men typically spent time outside of the home, such as in the fields outside their villages, and inside villages, towns, or cities where they frequented cafés and loitered in piazzas, while women occupied more confined, limited spaces, such as inside the home, in particular the kitchen, which men entered reluctantly.[38]

Marriage was a rite of passage for young middle-class women in late-nineteenth-century Italy, and the importance surrounding the event was never underestimated. Women gained a certain degree of power in their new social role as wives, and they were considered with greater respect by their peers and their community as future mothers. The clothes married women wore had a certain symbolic value: they had to wear colours that were toned down and symbolized chastity and honour, whereas girls could wear colourful garments.[39] The lifestyles that married women were expected to lead contrasted sharply with society's expectations of the shift in married men's lifestyles. As Lucetta Scaraffia has shown, the passage from adolescence to womanhood marked by marriage was brutally sudden, and it left many young women feeling fearfully unprepared for their new roles.[40] This is shown to be the case in Neera's *L'Indomani* (1890), in which the reader learns that the protagonist Marta, who has married a man she barely knows – which was indeed typical – is taken to her new home, a place with which she is unfamiliar. Similarly, *Fotografie matrimoniali* (Matrimonial photographs, 1898) by the same author includes a scene in which the free indirect speech narration depicts the newly married female protagonist's sense of nostalgia for a time before she was married, revealing her thoughts on the different ways in which women and men experience love:

Sofia remembers certain moments long ago, when as a young adolescent in the almost dark corner of the fireplace, she would listen to the fairy tales, and in that darkness the charitable fairy's gold cloak and the twinkly dress that the hapless Cinderella had found inside a chestnut seemed to her brighter than ever. And then other more recent times, other fantasies imagined fondly in the darkness of her little bedroom as a young girl, daydreaming about rosy mysteries of love. But she dare not say anything to her husband; he would have laughed at her; he didn't understand. Such a pity! Yet he was a young intelligent, good, gentle man. Would it ever be true (as she had heard her mother say once) that men have a completely different way of loving from women? But Romeo was also a man![41]

A yearning for one's husband's love on the part of the newly married woman is also characteristic of Marta's behaviour in Neera's *L'Indomani*. In her *Teresa*, the first-person narrator remarks on the protagonist's love for Orlandi:

> She burned with the female longing that urges them all, believers and lovers alike, to sacrifice themselves on the altar, to make themselves slaves of God or man.
> This profound desire for chains that torment the beautiful souls of women has an extraordinary will of its own. From weakness they derive the same joys men get through strength, and in surrender they find a greater rapture than men find in conquest.[42]

Neera's insights into women's supposed "desire for chains" are strikingly modern; they predate Freud's and Breuer's discovery of psychoanalysis and Jessica Benjamin's more recent study on this subject, *The Bonds of Love* (1988).[43] Women's social disadvantages as compared with men's in late-nineteenth-century Italy are also highlighted in a dialogue between the protagonist's mother and the servant, which reveals the preference for the birth of a boy over a girl:

> "If only it's a boy!" the woman sighed again.
> "Carlino's not enough for you?"
> "Oh, not for myself. But what can girls, poor things, look forward to in this world?"[44]

Signora Soave's lament about women's prescribed roles as wives and mothers is echoed in *L'Indomani* through the character of Signora Merelli, who became pregnant with her first child as soon as she was married, and she had been so ever since. The scenes elicit the readers' pity, and inadvertently express the authors' ambivalence towards women's condition in late-nineteenth-century Italy.

There were marked differences in the ways in which society viewed married and unmarried women: while the former had the privilege of educating their children, the latter were looked upon with sympathy and pity for being apparently deprived of the possibility to have children. De Giorgio refers to novels, conduct books, and the women's press of the period which testify to the insurmountable gaps between the social groups of married and single women whose difference in civil status bestowed distinctly different behaviour.[45] Indeed, it is apparent in La Marchesa Colombi's *A Small-Town Marriage* and Neera's *Teresa* that the idea of spinsterhood and the fact of remaining a spinster was shameful: in the former novel, Denza marries Signor Scalchi in order not to be an "old maid," and in Neera's story, the protagonist's sisters and their friends make fun of Teresa whom they believe will remain a spinster.[46] The importance of marrying out of a sense of duty is expressed in an article by Eduardo De Albertis in the journal *Il Giornale delle donne* in 1902, which stated the following:

> Let's see now why a woman gets married. She gets married primarily because she would regret remaining a spinster; as a matter of fact, if it were up to her she would get married at the age of eighteen or less. She gets married to achieve a certain position in society ... She rarely does so out of love.[47]

According to De Giorgio, the average age for a woman to marry between 1861 and 1920 was around twenty-five and twenty-six years.[48] However, while many women were anxious not to remain spinsters, the editor of the magazine for women *Cordelia* recommends in a letter to a worried reader that women should wait at least until the age of twenty-five before accepting a marriage proposal: "I find that if you are only twenty years old you can wait without worry even for five years. How many women have ruined their lives by making an unhappy marriage out of fear of remaining a spinster!"[49]

Friendships between Married Women

The passage from being a young and single woman to being married is presented as sudden and dramatic in Italian domestic fiction: unmarried women are described as barely knowing their future husbands before marrying them. In Neera's *Fotografie matrimoniali*, the narrator's curt and yet loaded comment, "Just yesterday, a young girl; today, a wife," epitomizes the suddenness of the change in the female protagonist's identity.[50] In La Marchesa Colombi's *A Small-Town Marriage*, Denza's tête-à-tête with Signor Scalchi, which takes place upon first meeting him, lasts only a few moments before she decides to marry him,[51] and in Neera's *L'Indomani*, when the protagonist wakes up for the first time next to her husband, the omniscient narrator informs readers that "it was strange ... to find herself enclosed in the same room as a man whom, two months previously, she didn't even know."[52]

Through an examination of the marital relationships in Serao's "Checchina's Virtue" and in Neera's *Teresa*, an emotional distance between husband and wife becomes apparent. This can be partly attributed to the ideology of the separate spheres women and men were expected to occupy. Maria Minicuci's study of a Calabrian village, in which she shows how the home is largely associated with women's presence whereas men occupy spaces in the fields or the village, is illustrative of the fictional representations of spaces occupied by women and men in domestic fiction: "The home goes back to being the men's space in the evening, when they return home to eat. Yet they don't feel that the home is their own space, and it is considered ridiculous that they spend too much time there: they therefore leave immediately to go to their clubs."[53] Certainly, in late-nineteenth-century Italy, the domestic sphere was commonly perceived as a female-occupied space in comparison with the public sphere of work and education with which men were largely associated. Thus, newly married women, such as Marta from *L'Indomani* and Sofia from *Fotografie matrimoniali*, did not know their husbands very well nor would they have much occasion to get to know them well, since the only time they would see their husbands would be at meal times and in the bedroom. In *Fotografie matrimoniali*, the narrator even presents the newly married female protagonist as feeling afraid of being alone with her husband in whose company she feels awkward: "They get into the stagecoach. Sofia is very nervous, very affected." The narrator then goes on to report: "A couple of minutes of silence ... Endless silence," after which Sofia's husband asks her what she is thinking about, to which she replies, "You," which the reader knows not to be the case.[54] This snapshot of a scene in the daily life of a newly married couple exposes, albeit in realist fictional form, the awkwardness which women and men experienced in their new roles as wife and husband as a result of the separate spheres to which women and men were limited. Given newly married women's unfamiliar predicaments and isolating circumstances, it is unsurprising that friendships among married women differed from friendships among young single women.

Friendships between married women – if they indeed existed – are frequently represented in Italian domestic fiction as either insincere or detached, in stark contrast to the closeness portrayed in female friendships among single and married women and adolescent girls. Signora

Soave from Neera's novel *Teresa* is isolated, and does not appear to have any friends at all, while the friendship between the protagonist of Serao's "Checchina's Virtue" and Isolina is shown to be exploitative and superficial: Isolina tells her husband she is visiting Checchina, when she is, in fact, visiting her lover. Similarly, when Checchina decides to visit the Marquis, she tells her maid that she is going to see Isolina.[55] In Neera's *L'Indomani*, Marta, who has left behind her friends to move to the village where her husband grew up, is expected to make friends with her husband's friends' wives. Through the omniscient narrator, we learn of Marta's anxiety about asking Signora Merelli about her experiences of being a wife and mother: "How many questions Marta had! That woman who had been married for ten years would have been able to answer so many doubts, but she didn't dare ask."[56] The implied, albeit subtle, critique here is the absence of a discourse between married women and, indeed, between mothers and daughters. This is highlighted at a later point in the novel when Marta, feeling estranged from her husband whom she watches enjoying himself with his friends, suddenly feels the urge to throw herself into her mother's arms:

> An abyss separated her from the man she had given herself to, who was a stranger to her, who didn't have the same blood as her, nor the same thoughts, nor the same soul, who had lived for thirty years without her, whom she had never seen cry, who found it pointless to say to her: I love you ... and an irresistible need to throw herself into her mother's arms assailed her.[57]

The frequency with which this issue is addressed in the domestic fiction is suggestive of a critique on behalf of women writers who problematized the incommunicability, or rather, lack of sincere friendships among married women. Fanning observes how male characters in nineteenth- and-twentieth-century European fiction by men "often have, if not true friends, then at least understanding male acquaintances. Charles Bovary is understood by Homais, while Emma is isolated from female companionship," and that in Italian fiction Verga shows groups of men gathered socially to do mutually profitable work more often than such groups of women. This is also true of Verga's *I Malavoglia* (1881) and *Mastro-don Gesualdo* (1890).[58] Similarly, at the opening of Neera's *Teresa*, the men of the town are shown working together to prevent the flood from worsening, while the women huddle in a little group to pray; and in La Marchesa Colombi's *Prima morire* (1881), the separate spheres occupied by women and men, respectively, are illustrated in a letter from Leonardo to his friend, Augusto, who describes how middle-class men of the provinces gather for an evening at the pharmacy to discuss politics. Through the omniscient narrator we have access to the female psyche in Neera's *L'Indomani*, from which we learn how jealous Marta is of her husband's relationships with other men and how isolated she feels in his company: when her husband is on an outing to the pharmacy for an evening, we learn how Marta thought to herself:

> Our house is much more comfortable, more elegant, we want for nothing; I would adore him, I would like my beauty and my intelligence to be for him only; I know how to talk, too, I am not stupid, but it seems that Toniolo, Merelli, and the others are worth more than me. But I left my mother, my friends, everything to be with him; and he would be enough for me![59]

Figuratively speaking, women writers such as Serao, La Marchesa Colombi, and Neera tell the story of the isolated Emma in Flaubert's *Madame Bovary* from her point of view in order to expose and criticize the lack of friendships married women had with one another. By presenting an absence of solidarity among married middle-class women in their domestic fiction, women writers were questioning it as a "fact" of women's everyday lives, one which they were expected to endure.

Italian domestic fiction frequently represented a wife's primary relationship as being with her servant. In Neera's *L'Indomani*, we learn that in order to pass the time and have company Marta enters the kitchen and sits on a stool while her maid Apollonia carries out her chores.[60] Typically, the relationship between signora and servant was rarely intimate, and boundaries of social class and professional status were most often respected. Interestingly, however, in the case of Checchina and her servant Susanna, in Serao's "Checchina's Virtue," they carry out similar activities in the home: both clean the furniture in the *salotto* as part of their daily routine.[61] The servant–signora relationship is one of long standing that emerges in Italian domestic fiction in a new guise: the role of the female confidante in operas such as Bellini's *Norma* (1831) and Donizetti's *Lucia di Lammermoor* (1835) is played out on the nineteenth-century opera stage in the role of the servant, who is sympathetic to and complicit with the suffering heroine's emotional demands in tragic opera. In La Marchesa Colombi's *A Small-Town*

Marriage, when the aunt is ill and cannot accompany Denza and her sister to church, the narrator refers to "the practice of leaving the girls in the care of a servant who was more or less their own age, and less educated," of which the stepmother disapproves. Without much persuasion, Denza and Titina manage to convince the servant to accompany them to the church attended by Mazzucchetti: "We agreed to instruct the servant not to tell anyone, and we set off in a hurry, because the church was quite far away."[62] Similarly, Serao's "The State Telegraph Office (*Women's Section*)" (1895) depicts the character Giulietta talking about her betrothed to Maria, to whom she complains she has no way of getting her letters to him since her mother sacked their servant, who helped Giulietta.[63] The relationships between servant and signora are slightly hostile in "Checchina's Virtue": Checchina's friend Isolina complains about her maid's lack of commitment to her work, while Checchina deceives her maid by telling her she is visiting her friend, when in fact she is visiting the count. Isolina describes her maid as "a thief, and insolent ... she leaves the house for hours at a time," which recalls Serao's attitude towards servants in her article for *La Stampa*.[64] Susanna and Checchina have a different dynamic: Susanna polices Checchina's behaviour, assuming an authority over her as if she were Checchina's mother in telling her that she should not walk the streets alone.[65]

This tension is absent from Serao's "Terno Secco" (Jackpot, 1887), in which the signora, who has a daughter, is a single mother. In this story, a sympathy prevails between the signora and her servant who, we are told, is pregnant: "Then [the servant] stared into her mistress's eyes and the two mothers understood one another tacitly, such was the young woman's pain, such was the affectionate compassion of the older woman."[66] In Serao's "Giovannino, or death" (1888), we learn of a different kind of dynamic between servant and signora – that of complicity, which echoes the relationship between Denza, her sister, and their maid in La Marchesa Colombi's *A Small-Town Marriage*. Though the relationship between servant and signora in Italian domestic fiction was typically one of solidarity, there are some exceptions: in "Checchina's Virtue" and Neera's *L'Indomani* there is a quasi-maternal element to the relationship between servant and signora. Checchina is in an infantile role in fearing she will be found out by her servant, Susanna, for attempting to conduct an affair with the count, and in Neera's *L'Indomani*, Marta sits and listens attentively to Apollonia tell of her husband's past while she carries out her chores.

Motherhood

Realist fiction by male writers typically depicts mothers as either accepting their prescribed roles and as being possessive of their sons or as sexual beings and generally neglectful of their offspring, such as Emma in Flaubert's *Madame Bovary* (1856), and Giacinta in Capuana's novel of the same name (1879). The latter novel is revealing of how mothers were held responsible for their daughters' upbringing, while fathers were typically responsible for the upbringing of their sons. In the context of a discussion of the relationship between the protagonist and her parents, the narrator remarks: "Mothers have to take care of their little girls. If it had been a boy, then yes, he [the father] would have had to take care of him!"[67] In this, the narrator informs us that when Giacinta was born, "she hadn't brought her mother great joy," for whom "maternity was … an unbearable burden, an unwanted annoyance," and the mother is consequently held responsible by the reader (and society) for Giacinta's life of debauchery and subsequent suicide in adulthood.[68]

In contrast, and interestingly (though perhaps not surprisingly), sympathetic representations of motherhood recur frequently in Italian domestic fiction. In Serao's short story "Silvia" from her collection *Dal vero* (1879), at the moment of her death, the protagonist feels close to the mother she never knew, and thinking out loud in the presence of her father, she utters the words "… she knew it. Children can't survive without their mothers."[69] The portrayal is similar in other writer's nonfiction. In Neera's collection of essays *Confessioni letterarie* (1891), she laments the loss of her mother: "When she died, everything got worse: lifestyle, relationships, customs. I had scarcely had a glimpse of society when the house fell silent like a cloister."[70] In both cases, there is an implied negation of the role of the father, who, contrary to the way in which the husband's role is defined in Pisanelli's Civil Code of 1866, is seen as a less significant authority figure. One could even extend this argument to suggest that, in focusing their attention on the mothers' predicaments, women writers were attempting to identify a maternal subject – a matriarchy as opposed to a patriarchy – incorporating the mother's desire much in the same way that French post–Lacanian feminists Cixous, Kristeva, and Irigaray search for a representable femininity that displaces phallocentrism.[71]

De Giorgio observes that around 40 per cent of women born in Italy between 1851 and 1871 had an average of five children; mothers held the authority in the home in practice; and they were expected to be devoted to family life.[72] Typically, as we have seen, women writers represented the mother through the point of view of the female narrator. In Neera's *L'Indomani*, the protagonist Marta, who has had an arranged marriage, is depicted living a monotonous, unhappy, and isolated existence. She is described as "almost monastic," which echoes the description of Serao's protagonist Silvia from her short story of the same name. Silvia, also recently married through a marriage of convenience to a man nearly twice her age, is presented as a kind of automaton, "walking with slight and moderate footsteps, upright in the rigid folds of her black dress, almost like a nun ... speaking very little, smiling much less, hardly thinking."[73] It is only when the protagonists from both stories are pregnant that they are represented by their respective authors as being fulfilled. In "Silvia," we learn of the protagonist's new identity as an expectant mother: "No longer the woman she once was ... a complete, alive, strong and good woman had taken her place: the mother."[74] This chimes with Neera's celebratory response to Marta's pregnancy at the end of *L'Indomani*: "She felt her guts moving under the impulse of a live person, with the strange revelation of another being inside her. It seemed as though a little hand was beating against her breast and saying: let me out, I am Love and Truth."[75] Signora Soave's experiences a sense of fulfilment of her prescribed role as wife and mother as she anticipates giving birth to her fifth child, as she gazes at the ornament in her bedroom, a glass bell which contains the wax image of a baby boy:

> Signora Soave's glance rested on a small wax baby boy under a glass bell. That yellow baby with two small black spots for eyes above a small protuberance simulating the nose; that baby with a sweet and resigned expression, lying for more than twenty years amid the paper flowers and silver stripes decorating his crib. That naked and holy baby drew tender feelings from the woman, making her melt with love and respect, with a desire to weep, to kiss it, to commend herself to its tiny blessed hands. The grandeur of God represented by that little baby boy struck her with pious, devout awe. She got up and, moving with difficulty, went to place a kiss on the glass bell. Then with hands clasped she stood still, absorbed in sorrowful contemplation.[76]

The above examples carry strongly religious dimensions of the Virgin Mary, the *mater dolorosa* or sorrowful mother figure so prominent in Catholic iconography, and which Angela dalle Vacche has recently argued is the stereotype that mostly fits the diva's acting style in early silent Italian films.[77] In Italian domestic fiction there is a distinction between society's expectation of mothers and mothers' actual experiences. This characteristically presents the everyday existence of mothers as a struggle, both physically and emotionally, and mothers are often represented with sympathy and pity: in Serao's short story "Terno Secco," the signora and the mother-to-be, Tommasina, have to work constantly to make a living for their families and are quickly tired out. Similarly, Teresa's mother in Neera's *Teresa* is regularly represented lamenting her lot. In the domestic fiction of La Marchesa Colombi, Serao, and Neera, portrayals of motherhood are implicitly critical and, at the same time, celebratory.[78]

Mother–Daughter Relationships

In collaboration with Mantegazza, Neera published her conduct book *Dizionario d'igiene per le famiglie* ('Dictionary of hygiene for families') in 1881. In her entry on "adolescence," which is addressed to mothers, she offers advice on whether or not they should talk to their daughters about menstruation, which she refers to as an "illness," or, using more religious terminology, as "the Messiah" and "the baptism."[79] Interestingly, Neera recommends that mothers only to speak to their daughters about the "disturbances of the uterus" if they are sure their daughters know something about menstruation. In her short story "Paolina" (1881), Neera highlights the silence and embarrassment with which young girls starting their periods in Liberal Italy were met. In this story, the eponymous protagonist's governess alludes to the changes that will shortly be taking place in Paolina's body without naming them: "You are by now a young lady, and certain things, you can understand … Do you know that great things are about to happen?" The first-person narrator reveals the shame and anxiety she feels upon learning of the bodily changes she will soon experience: "I started like a frisky colt. All changes alarmed me; I was reactionary down to the marrow of my bones."[80] In Neera's *Teresa*, the protagonist's mother, who, about to give birth to her fifth child, tells her daughter, "Tonight you'll have another little baby brother or sister … something you'll understand later … but you're the oldest, you should know about it. Now go to bed,"[81] thus making a strikingly similar allusion to the changes that are about to take place in Teresa's body. Upon hearing this from her mother, Teresa experiences the same sense of *pudore* as Paolina:

> Teresina leaned against the door frame, frozen, her throat constricted by unexpected excitement ... The few words her mother had just spoken at the door had made a profound impression in the general excitement of that night. She felt she had all at once become a woman – with a sudden premonition of future sorrows, with a new responsibility, with a peculiar modesty mixed with extraordinary sweetness.[82]

Luce Irigaray in *Speculum de l'autre femme* (1974) and *Éthique de la différence sexuelle* (1984) suggests that relations between mothers and daughters (whether symbolic or spiritual) are likely to be conflictual, since our culture displays a quasi-total absence of adequate representations of the mother–daughter relationship that would permit women to negotiate new relations with one another.[83] According to Irigaray, patriarchy functions by separating women from one another and by suppressing the possibility of a maternal genealogy. Irigaray believes that the establishment of symbolic mother–daughter relationships is essential to women's autonomy and identity, *as women and not just as mothers*.[84] In modern Italian feminist thought on sexual difference, Carla Lonzi's 1970 *Manifesto di rivolta femminile* (Manifesto for women's revolt) rejected notions of equality between the sexes "because [they] promote male models that women are told they should aspire to rather than criticize and create alternatives to."[85] Following Irigaray's line of thinking, in 1987 Luisa Muraro, co-founder of the Verona-based group Diotima, suggested the notion of entrustment (*affidamento*) between women as a way of establishing a paradigm of women's relations connecting "weaker" and "stronger" women in symbolic mother-daughter relationships; the idea being that the "symbolic mother," usually, but not necessarily an older woman, guides the "daughter" in an exploration of the issues of sexual difference.[86] It is curious, therefore, that mother–daughter relationships are frequently portrayed in different ways in Italian domestic fiction, and that, taken together, the recurring topoi of female friendships and relationships in domestic fiction would appear to be working against gender oppression. In Serao's "Terno Secco," mother and daughter are seen together throughout the narrative as if to suggest that neither has meaning without the presence of the other and that a symbiotic bond justifies their existence. Mother and daughter live their daily lives together – they sleep in the same bed, eat together, and follow one another around the house. The mother is depicted as having to work long hours to earn a living to support her daughter, and she even plays the lottery in order to provide for herself and her daughter. The mother eats only a beaten egg in the morning and remains without food for the whole day, during which she must give lessons in English and French.[87]

The mother–daughter relationship in Neera's novel *Teresa*, in which the narrator conveys an intimacy between the protagonist and her mother through their shared experience, is similarly shot through with ambiguity. While changes in the Caccia family are taking place – Teresa's sisters are engaged to be married and her brother is training to be a lawyer – "Teresina live[s] almost exclusively in the company of her ill mother – both protected from the breezes with their feet on the same stool, smiling sadly."[88] Teresa and her mother are represented feeling affection and love for one another, and Teresa's mother is able to influence her father's decisions regarding Teresa's invitations; it is because of Teresa's affection for and loyalty towards her mother that she chooses not to run away with Orlandi. Yet there is also a distance that separates mother and daughter. Due to a sense of shame and embarrassment, there are certain things mothers and daughters cannot talk about, such as menstruation. Thus, Teresa is unable to tell her mother about the young man she dances with for the first time when she visits her aunt:

> Teresina had the crazy impulse to reveal her secret, but she didn't dare right at that moment ...
>
> It was a good opportunity. Cecchino's name burned on the girl's lips. She had only mentioned the dance in order to talk about him; she wanted to tell her mother everything. But that name wouldn't come out. Two or three attempts were aborted. An inexplicable knot squeezed her throat, and her heart beat crazily.[89]

Despite this common tension in the relation between mother and daughter, there exists an implicit, almost visceral, understanding between them:

> Teresa felt a tenderness, a veneration for her mother, and her mother returned it with a sad affection, full of implied sorrow. They had never exchanged confidences. They didn't have the temperament for it, perhaps

even lacked the opportunity to begin. However, in times of rest during Ida's naps or absences, when the two women sat next to the eternal window, their silence had a voice.[90]

Teresa is unable to bring herself to tell her mother about Orlandi, yet thanks to the spiritual and emotional bond between Signora Soave and Teresa, the former has already instinctively sensed her daughter's love. When Teresa receives a marriage proposal, the mother knows instinctively that it is from Orlandi:

> She knew nothing of her daughter's love from her actions or from confidences shared, but she had seen it fluttering in the air, had guessed it from her daughter's distracted ways – perhaps she had deluded herself in a mother's blind affection, in a woman's tender faithfulness to the idea of love despite disappointment. She certainly didn't need to ask the name of Teresina's lover.[91]

Neera concludes the chapter with a poignant depiction of mother and daughter reading a letter Teresa had received from Orlandi that evening in which he swears eternal love: "Mother and daughter wept as they read it."[92] Such female closeness goes against Sandra Gilbert and Susan Gubar's assertion that the theme of the separation from the mother is caused by the precedence of the female love relationship, that "women writers … have described female sexual initiation in terms of the myth of Persephone, with its themes … of sorrowful separation from female companions."[93] Rather, Neera's domestic fiction along with Serao's and La Marchesa Colombi's, illustrates what Marianne Hirsch in referring to the "feminist family romance" of the 1970s has described as "the concentration on mother–daughter bonding and struggle, and the celebration of female relationships of mutual nurturance [which] leave only a secondary role to men."[94]

The unspoken understanding in matters of romantic love between mother and daughter through the characters of Teresa and her mother reappears in Neera's *L'Indomani*, which charts the protagonist's slow realization of the myth of romantic love as she lives out her first few months as a wife. Her question, "Why had they not told her 'You will enter, a stranger, into the bed of a stranger; your contact will be without delirium and your hearts will come close together without merging'?"[95] reveals Marta's sense of disappointment at the lack of communication between women (mothers, daughters, and friends) about the realities of life as a woman in late-nineteenth-century Italy. This contradicts Neera's aforementioned view in her entry on "Adolesence," put forward in her *Dizionario d'igiene*, that mothers ought not to feel under pressure to communicate with their daughters about the changes in puberty. At the end of the novel when Marta's mother visits her daughter, the same distance and yet intimacy, borne of "*pudore* and a woman's pride,"[96] is shown to bind them:

> They fell silent, both distracted by their thoughts, divided in such a way that after a while they looked at one another, disorientated. They both had a lot to say to one another; the desire to ask, to confide was immense ... To get her to speak, Signora Oldofredi took an interest in her daughter's new relationships.[97]

The ensuing conversation centres on a discussion of practical matters as opposed to matters of the heart: Marta's mother provides her daughter with news about friends in her hometown, and weddings that have taken place and that are due to take place. The narrator refers to mother's and daughter's likeness in temperament and appearance, commenting on "the same melancholic smile" that both have, which recalls the similar dispositions of Signora Soave and her daughter in Neera's *Teresa*. Marta's mother holds a more resigned and accepting approach to women's prescribed role, and adopts the view that women, like men, cannot "live with the continuous illusion of love; for this reason we have religion and maternity."[98] Marta, on the other hand, refuses to believe that love does not exist, and chooses not to listen to her mother – "Marta only heard the murmuring of her mother's words."[99] Instead, she channels her romantic love for her husband into love for the unborn child inside her. Such a transference of love onto Marta's unborn child, while rejecting her mother's view that romantic love does not exist, is also symbolic of Marta's endorsement that love exists, but not in the way she had been brought up to believe. Marta reinforces her mother's view in her realization of her "proper" role, and substitutes her romantic love for a maternal love, confirming the ideological view expressed time and again in the novels that the two cannot exist simultaneously.

The protagonists in *Teresa* and *L'Indomani* both implicitly reject their mothers as examples of womanhood: Marta rejects her mother's view that true love does not exist, and Teresa rejects the prescribed path as wife and mother. Italian domestic fiction's concentration on recurring depictions of close female friendships *to the exclusion of* representations of male friendships points towards the writers' endorsement of women's confinement to the home insofar as this brought young girls, signore, mothers, and maids together, enabling them to forge close ties and friendships with one another in the majority of cases. Equally, it points towards the writers' (unconscious?) attempt to forge a female solidarity among middle-class women readers and writers in late-nineteenth-century Italy and to promote positive relations between women that, in the everyday, outside the texts, may not have been quite so prevalent.

Conclusion

My central argument in this book has been that the depiction of girlhood and womanhood in Italian domestic fiction and journalism as written by women functioned as a type of conduct manual that taught women how to deal with their predicaments and limitations in everyday life. In contrast to the themes their male contemporaries addressed in their writings, Italian women writers illustrated a predominantly female world, one in which men formed the backdrop, and whose setting was typically the home, in order to present slices of "believable" female characters' lives in a seemingly impartial way. I hope to have demonstrated that we need a broader definition of women's writing, one that will allow us to better assess experiences of womanhood in the everyday and the role of women writing in the Italian nineteenth century. While Neera, Serao, and La Marchesa Colombi expressed conservative views on women's roles as mothers and wives in their non-fiction writings, their unprecedented focus on female relationships in their fiction (between young girls, mothers and daughters, siblings, and married women and servants), and the way in which this was represented as contradictory – intimate while at the same time being hostile – suggests a refusal of distant and acrimonious female relationships, and appeals to women readers to rethink their relationships with one another in the new Italy in terms of them being less equivocal and conflictual.

To return to the notion of "solidarity," this suggests a feeling of shared interests and concerns among a group of people of both genders. "Sisterhood," on the other hand, connotes an exclusively female body of people who share a feeling of closeness to one another, and who are linked by their gender as well as by a common political interest. Salvatore Battaglia's entry on sisterhood ("sorellanza") in his *Grande dizionario della lingua italiana* (1998) provides the following definitions: "a natural and affective bond which unites sisters; female complicity; solidarity among women,"[1] while the historical use of the term has links to the Church (the term "vergine sorella" [virgin sister], according to Tommaseo's and Bellini's dictionary [1861–79], refers to a nun of Saint Chiara).[2] Arguably, the first official sisterhood to establish itself in the newly unified Italy – if it can, indeed, be argued that there existed a sisterhood at all – comprised the group of emancipationists from the late 1880s and 1890s who were active principally in the cities of the North. As Michela De Giorgio has shown, the correspondence between the founder of the journal *La Donna*, Gualberta Alaide Beccari, the Piedmontese actress Giacinta Pezzana (1841–1919), and the emancipationist Giorgina Crawford Saffi, is revealing of their intense and passionate friendship, as well as a shared commitment towards the ideals put forward by the emancipationist movement to which they belonged.[3]

It is highly questionable whether women writers such as Serao, La Marchesa Colombi, and Neera were perceived as belonging to a sisterhood of writers given their apparent endorsement of the status quo concerning the "woman question," and, in the case of Neera and Serao, their disagreements with emancipationists. Though they started to become known to the public at around the same time as the protofeminists began their campaigns, there is little evidence to suggest that they shared a set of political beliefs, and their choice of profession was not overtly inspired by any particular political manifesto. Indeed, most women writers from this period harboured a conservative stance vis-à-vis women's roles. Fazia Amoia has written that "the majority of women writers at the turn of the century – Liala, Invernizio, Neera, Colombi, Vivanti – were, like most of their contemporaries, anti-feminist and anti-divorcist," and Antonia Arslan has commented that an open commitment to feminism might have led to the loss of their women readers' approval.[4] Suggestive of what could be regarded as a "sisterhood in-the-making" among some circles of women writers is the emphasis on the common themes in their domestic fiction and journalism, which offered first-hand "social documentary" of predominantly middle-class female experience to their female readers, told from a woman's perspective. This is also apparent through a reading of journals and conduct manuals for women from this period. Female-authored reviews of writings by women were, more often than not, very positive: an anonymous review, written by a woman, of La Marchesa Colombi's conduct manual *La gente per bene* appeared in the journal *Museo di famiglia* on

15 January 1877, describing the book as "modern, elegantly written and a pleasure to read."[5] Even when disagreeing with them on political or ideological grounds, women readers still demonstrated admiration for women writers: Emilia Mariani, in her "Lettera Aperta a Matilde Serao" (Open letter to Matilde Serao), which appeared in *La Donna* on 10 October 1883, tells Serao, "I am an admirer of your intelligence," and Adele Maiani Nulli's open letter to Neera, which was published in *L'Italia femminile* on 16 April 1899, describes Neera as an "intellectual."[6] It is quite likely that such displays of deference on behalf of female critics towards women writers contributed in no small measure to women writers' growing sense of self-confidence and self-esteem in the public eye.

Lucienne Kroha makes two points concerning the position of women writers in late-nineteenth-century Italy. First, that Italian women writers from the late nineteenth century were without literary mothers ("there were no George Eliots, George Sands, Jane Austens, Madame de Staël or Brontë sisters to stand behind the fledgling female novelist"), and second, that "women writers of this period, independently of their feminist or anti-feminist stances on other issues, unanimously rejected the traditional literary depiction of women and of women's experiences." She states that

> writing novels in [such a] prescriptive climate was difficult enough and a source of conflict in and of itself; going so far as to challenge canonical representations was an anxiety-provoking experience which called women writers into question as both women and writers.[7]

Indeed, Serao in her *Parla una donna* (1916), speaks of female writers and poets, whom she clearly believes were different from other women. Serao's awareness of herself as a writer, and the link between her and other writers, illustrates a point made by Showalter in her discussion on English writers that "women novelists' awareness of each other and of their female audience showed a kind of covert solidarity that sometimes amounted to a genteel conspiracy," and that although "few English women writers openly advocated the use of fiction as revenge against a patriarchal society, ... many confessed to sentiments of maternal feeling, sisterly affection, *esprit de corps* for their readers,"[8] which could well be applied to the Italian context. In *The Proper Lady and the Woman Writer* (1984), Mary Poovey shows how Mary Wollstonecraft, Mary Shelley, and Jane Austen not only explicitly discuss propriety in their works; implicitly, in both their works and their life choices, they also replicate tensions, paradoxes, and contradictions that we see in their conduct material.[9] A similar phenomenon was taking place in the Italian late nineteenth century: along with other women writers, La Marchesa Colombi, Neera, and Serao embodied the tensions and contradictions that are to be found in their writings, yet which were also embedded in the fabric of the culture and society of the time. The paradoxes and contradictions of this period in Italian history were being played out in the themes, subject matter, and narrative style of women writers' works focusing on domestic issues.

While it would be practically impossible to measure the extent to which domestic fiction tapped into discourses on the role of women and shaped changes in women's social and legal situation during the period 1870 to 1910, to suggest that the popularity and circulation of domestic fiction had no influence whatsoever on perceptions of and discussions about "the woman question" in the collective consciousness, and on changes made in law in favour of women's rights, would be tantamount to stating that literary texts exist in a vacuum, and simply describe the world they depict rather than shape people's perceptions of the world. That domestic fiction was so popular during the first half of this period, and particularly during the 1880s compared with the second half of the period when improvements in access to education and the professions were being made, provides at least some evidence of its role in raising awareness among its middle-class women readers of what they endured in their everyday lives. Italian domestic fiction articulated and drew attention to the various forms of exploitation and oppression of women, and to some extent, men, in a subtly and socially acceptable way; indeed, so subtle was its presentation that it almost went unnoticed.

Appendix

Maria Antonietta Torriani (1840–1920)

La Marchesa Colombi was born in Novara in Piedmont on 1 January 1840. Her father was a watchmaker who died a year after her birth, aged thirty-two. Her mother, who was a teacher, remarried an elderly widower in 1847, a landowner and pharmacist with whom she had a child.[1] La Marchesa Colombi attended her mother's primary school and spent four years at the Bellini d'Arti e Mestieri institute, where she received good grades and a prize in Italian literature. She studied in a convent in the Lake Orta region from where she gained a teaching diploma. La Marchesa Colombi would read the journal *L'Illustrazione italiana* in private while she was in the convent, and she had struck up a correspondence with the journalist Eugenio Torelli-Viollier, whom she married in 1875, and who founded and ran the *Corriere della sera* a year later. In 1865, La Marchesa Colombi's stepfather died leaving her a large sum of money. It is most likely that she moved to Milan at the end of 1866; indeed, her application for a mortgage to buy a property from 1 January 1870 lists her as a journalist living in Milan.

In 1870, La Marchesa Colombi met the Milanese female emancipationist and campaigner for women's rights Anna Maria Mozzoni. La Marchesa Colombi befriended her, and for a while together they were active in spreading the ideals of the female emancipationist movement. They delivered lectures at the Liceo-Scuola Superiore femminile Agnese in Milan, and in the spring of 1871 they organized a series of conferences in Genoa, Florence, and Bologna; Mozzoni spoke on politics and philosophy; Torriani spoke on the importance of education for women through lectures on "Victor Hugo e la povera gente" (Victor Hugo and the poor), "La storia delle rose" (Story of the roses), and "Giulia Modena." In Bologna, La Marchesa Colombi met Enrico Panzacchi and Giosuè Carducci. From the year of her marriage to Torrelli-Viollier, La Marchesa Colombi was at the heart of the cultural life of Milan, and would frequent *salotti* where she became friends with authors such as Salvatore Farina, Giovanni Verga and Iginio Ugo Tarchetti. Among the journals on which she collaborated as literary critic, storyteller, and fashion and lifestyle expert are the following titles: *Il Passatempo*, which became *Il Giornale delle donne* in 1872; *Corriere della sera*; *L'Illustrazione italiana*; *Museo di famiglia*; *Il Fanfulla*; *Nuova Antologia*; *Cronaca Bizantina*; and *Vita Intima*. La Marchesa Colombi also wrote a conduct book, *La gente per bene* (Respectable society, 1877), of which, by 1893, twenty-two editions had been published. She also wrote two opera libretti – the first melodrama was entitled *La Creola*, which she co-wrote with Torelli-Viollier with music by Gaetano Coronaro, and which was first performed in the autumn of 1878 at the Teatro Comunale in Bologna; and the second was entitled *Il violino di Cremona*, which had its first night performance at La Scala in Milan in the spring of 1882, with music by Giulio Litta.[2] In addition, she published many novels and short stories for women readers and children, and translated works from French and English. Her fiction is generally realist, and many of her works focus their attention on the poor working conditions for women.

Her marriage to Torelli-Viollier lasted for around ten years, and following the suicide of her niece, La Marchesa Colombi separated from her husband and moved to Turin. There she withdrew from writing, although she established a *salotto*, which was frequented by musicians, intellectuals, and performers such as Arrigo Boito, Giuseppe Giacosa, Eduardo De Amicis, and Giovanni Camerana. During the last part of her life, La Marchesa Colombi travelled in Europe with her friend Giovanna Macchi. She died in Turin on 24 March 1920. After her death, La Marchesa Colombi was forgotten until her revival, thanks to Natalia Ginzburg, in the 1970s.

La Marchesa Colombi collaborated with Neera, with whom she managed the journal *Vita Intima*, and her archive contains a card from Serao and Edoardo Scarfoglio, which was sent to Torelli-Viollier on their wedding day. On 25 February 1905, Serao published an article in *La Stampa* that attacked female servants for being envious and disloyal. In response to this, La Marchesa Colombi, who had not collaborated on a newspaper for some time, published an open letter to Serao in *La Stampa* on 1 March 1905 in which she defended servant girls. Curiously, however, in *La gente per bene*, La Marchesa Colombi makes a point of stressing in her entry on "Le signorine" that when writing correspondance they should never sign their letters with the word "serva": "The letter should begin with what one has to say, and should finish when there is nothing more to say. This is the only rule that I accept. They should never sign with 'servant,' because ladies are never anyone's servant."[3]

Anna Radius Zuccari (1846–1918)

Neera was born in Milan on 7 May 1846 and died there on 19 July 1918. Her father was an architect. She lost her mother when she was young, and her father lived only ten years after her mother's death. Having no mother, sisters, or close friends, and growing up with her two brothers, two aunts, and father in Caravaggio in the Po valley, she spent hours sewing and doing embroidery. As a young girl, Neera disliked school but loved reading, especially *The Thousand and One Nights* (1706), poetry by Byron and Ossian, prose by Foscolo, and Sterne's *Sentimental Journey* (1768). She began to write when she was ten years old in order to counter the tedium of her daily life. In *Una giovinezza del secolo XIX* (A nineteenth-century childhood, 1919), she comments: "I would write not thinking about writing. If books and a pen were a comfort to me in the tedious monotony of my existence, I nevertheless did not consider them to be my future."[4] Neera married Adolfo Radius, a lawyer, in 1871, with whom she had two children. In 1875, she published her first short story in the periodical *Il Pungolo* with the help of its director Leone Fortis. Henceforth, she began her literary career, frequently travelling while contemporaneously managing the marital home in Via Borgospesso in Milan. She collaborated on various magazines and journals such as *Fanfulla*, *Corriere del mattino*, *Fanfulla della domenica*, *Il Giorno*, *Corriere della sera*, *Corriere di Napoli*, *Nuova Antologia*, *Marzocco*, and *L'Illustrazione italiana*. She founded the journal *Vita Intima* in 1890, and wrote moralistic essays, many of which first appeared in print in the periodical *L'Idea liberale*, and were subsequently collected in volumes such as *Il libro di mio figlio* (1891), *Battaglie per un'idea* (1898), and *L'amor platonico* (1897).[5] Neera's ideological beliefs with regard to the moral consciousness of the individual reinforced her conservative views on gender roles. In her *Le idee di una donna* (The ideas of a woman, 1903) she puts forward the view – somewhat paradoxically considering her own professional status as publicly renowned writer – that women's "proper place" is in the home as wife and mother, which she defines as "real feminism":

> Woman no longer recognizes herself in the integrity of her own worth, and it is this very worth that I defend with sheer ardor, dedicating my efforts to the women who accept with simplicity and nobleness their great mission, promoting real feminism.[6]

Neera's fiction concentrates intensely on the sacrifice and self-denial of its female characters for whom she conveys a deep sympathy – such as for Lydia in her novel of the same name – through her portrayal of the characters, which adopts the naturalist style of fiction by Luigi Capuana. As Antonia Arslan has observed, Luigi Baldacci draws attention to the ambiguities of meaning deriving from Neera's fiction and non-fiction. Highlighting the sympathetic portrayal of the eponymous protagonist from the novel *Teresa*, which he classifies a feminist novel, he comments upon the seemingly antifeminist position that Neera assumes in her non-fictional writing.[7] Neera collaborated on the first manual on women's hygiene with physiologist and anthropologist Paolo Mantegazza, which was published in 1881 as the *Dizionario d'igiene per le famiglie* (Dictionary of hygiene for families), and she corresponded with and caught the interest of several other prominent intellectuals of the day. These included Capuana (for whom she wrote *Autobiografia a Luigi Capuana*, which appeared as a preface to the second edition of *Il castigo* in 1891), Roberto Bracco, Marinetti, De Roberto, Antonio Fogazzaro, and Benedetto Croce.

Matilde Serao (1856–1927)

Serao was born in 1856 in Patrasso, Greece, and died in Naples at her writing desk in her home on 25 July 1927. She was a Nobel Prize candidate in 1926, but this went instead to Grazia Deledda due to Serao's antiwar stance, which was not well received politically in the context of Mussolini's Italy. Her mother was from an aristocratic background and was a teacher. The family moved back to Naples after 1860 where Serao attended the Scuola Normale (a teachers' training college for elementary school teachers). Serao obtained her qualification and then began work as a telegraph operator. Her realist short stories "Scuola normale femminile" (Girls' teacher training school, 1886) and "Telegrafi dello Stato" (State telegraph operators [*women's section*], 1895) draw on her own experiences to investigate the options open to women of the middle classes who had to find some means of supporting themselves. The stories present a damning critique of the working conditions of young women teachers and telegraph operators, and were first published in Milan's official literary journal for the *veristi* and *scapigliatura* movement, *La Farfalla*.[8] Meanwhile, Serao's father, who was a freelance journalist, had introduced her to the world of journalism, to which Serao was drawn. She published her first book *Opale* in 1878. In 1881, her first novel – *Cuore infermo* (Frozen heart) – appeared, and she began working as a journalist, having secured a post as editor of *Capitan Fracassa* in Rome. The director of the journal Luigi Vassallo singled her out for her talent and ambition, and for being the first woman to secure a post as editor of a journal in Italy:

> Before her, other women of real value had written for newspapers, but theirs had been a simple collaboration: the director published those articles which he believed were publishable without any obligation on either side for further collaboration. Not Serao: she had become a permanent editor, ready to carry out on a daily basis the work she was required to do. And she was the first to assume such a role.[9]

Serao married journalist and writer Edoardo Scarfoglio in 1884, with whom she had four children. Together they founded the *Corriere di Roma* in 1885, and Serao began her column, "Api, mosconi e vespe" (Bees, flies, and wasps), which she wrote under the pseudonym Gibus, and which was to last for forty-one years.[10] The *Corriere di Roma* went bankrupt in 1887, and subsequently the couple moved to Naples where, with the help of the rich banker Matteo Schilizzi, in 1888 they founded the *Corriere di Napoli*. In 1892, they merged the *Corriere di Napoli* and the *Corriere del Mattino* and set up *Il Mattino*. Serao worked as a journalist and novelist while raising her four children. In 1902, Serao and Scarfoglio founded and directed *La Settimana. Rassegna di Lettere, arti e scienze*. Serao separated from her husband, and in 1905 she had a daughter, Eleonora, with Giuseppe Natale, a lawyer. She founded her own newspaper, *Il Giorno*, in 1904, which she directed until her death in 1927. Serao wrote around forty works of fiction ranging from sentimental novels to realist novels and, later, melodramatic and gothic novels. Like Neera, Serao positioned herself politically as upholding the status quo in her works of non-fiction regarding the "woman question": she spoke and wrote against campaigns for female suffrage and defended the indissolubility of marriage.

Notes

Preface

1 Sibilla Aleramo, *Una donna* (1906; reprint, Milan: Feltrinelli, 1998), 121.
2 Tania Modleski, "Introduction to the Second Edition," in *Loving with a Vengeance: Mass Produced Fantasies for Women*, 2nd ed. (New York: Routledge, 2008), xxv.
3 Elizabeth Merrick, *This Is Not Chick Lit: Original Stories by America's Best Women Writers* (New York: Random House, 2006), ix. See also Janice A. Radway, "Women Read the Romance: The Interaction of Text and Context," *Feminist Studies* 9, no. 1 (1983): 53–78.

Introduction

1 Elaine Showalter, *A Literature of Their Own: From Charlotte Brontë to Doris Lessing* (Princeton: Princeton University Press, 1977; London: Virago, 1999). Antonia Arslan's *Dame, droga e galline: romanzo popolare e romanzo di consumo fra '800 e '900* (Padova: CLEUP, 1977), published in the same year as Showalter's book, and Ellen Moers's *Literary Women* (London: W.H. Allen, 1977), brought to readers' attention a selection of the popular serialized fiction by renowned women writers from the end of the nineteenth century, including Carolina Invernizio and Annie Vivanti. This was followed by studies such as Giuliana Morandini's anthology of Italian women's writings from the 1800s and the 1900s, *La voce che è in lei: antologia della narrativa femminile italiana tra '800 e '900* (Milan: Bompiani, 1980), which looked still further back in the past to examine women's writing from the 1800s, and Anna Santoro's *Narratrici italiane dell'Ottocento* (Naples: Federico and Ardia, 1987) discussed eleven authors from the second half of the nineteenth century in response to Moers's omission of names of Italian women

writers. More recently, the University of Chicago Library has established an "Italian Women Writers" project, http://www.lib.uchicago.edu/efts/ IWW/ (last accessed on 16 June 2013).

2 Maria Antonietta Torriani adopted her pseudonym in 1875. It is the feminine form of the protagonist il Marchese Colombi, a bizarre and original character, from Paolo Ferrari's play *La satira e Parini* (Milan: Sanvito, 1856).

3 "La Serao è mirabile quando si muove nella luce del giorno, quando guarda e vede. Ha bisogno di concretezza, ha bisogno di aggirarsi tra luoghi e oggetti solidi e tangibili e tra gente legata a problemi semplici, chiari e reali; il suo sguardo è così vivo che può dar vita ai sentimenti e ai temperamenti di alcuni tra i suoi personaggi e renderli memorabili, eppure a volte conserviamo di alcuni suoi racconti o romanzi il ricordo intenso e profondo non già di un'indole umana ma di uno stato d'animo o di un colore." Cited in Gianni Infusino, "Aristocrazia e popolo (Le donne negli scritti di Matilde Serao)," in *Matilde Serao tra giornalismo e letteratura*, ed. Gianni Infusino (Naples: Guida Editori, 1981), 66. Ginzburg had republished Serao's short story "Checchina's Virtue" (La virtù di Checchina, 1883) two years previously: see *La virtù di Checchina*, ed. Natalia Ginzburg (Milan: Emme Edizioni, 1974). Unless otherwise stated, all translations of primary and secondary sources are mine.

4 Luigi Baldacci, "Nota introduttiva," in Neera, *Teresa*, Centopagine 42 (Turin: Einaudi, 1976), v. Benedetto Croce had published a collection of Neera's most popular works in 1943. See *Neera*, ed. Benedetto Croce, 2nd ed. (Milan: Garzanti, 1943). Neera borrows her pseudonym from the Roman satirist and poet Horace (65 BC–8 BC), whose poem, "Odes" (book 3, poem 14), refers to the nymph, Neaera. The name also calls to mind its male equivalent "Nero," and invokes the Roman emperor Claudius Caesar Nero (AD 37–AD 68), who purportedly was licentious and engaged in petty amusements while neglecting the problems of the Roman city and empire. It is significant that Zuccari chooses a pseudonym whose connotations invoke a period in classical history, and a prominent person who put personal desires before duty. Neera explicitly calls upon a time during which the foundations of a new civilization were being laid and cities were being built, as if to draw a parallel with the period in which she is writing, which was one of political, economic, and social ferment. The emperor whose name she invokes neglected his duty to his people in the same way that Neera perceived herself as neglecting her duties as housewife and mother by choosing to write.

5 For recent work on women writers and the "questione della lingua," see Helena Sanson, "Women Writers and the Questione della Lingua in

Ottocento Italy: The Cases of Caterina Percoto, La Marchesa Colombi, and Matilde Serao," *Modern Language Review* 105, no. 4 (2010): 1028–52.

6 Ugo Ojetti, *Alla scoperta dei letterati* (Milan: Dumolard, 1895), 236–7: "Se la mia lingua è scorretta, se io non so scrivere, se io ammiro chi scrive bene, vi confesso che, se per un caso imparassi a farlo, non lo farei. Io credo con la vivacità di quel linguaggio incerto e di quello stile rotto di infondere nelle opere mie il *calore*, e il calore non solo vivifica i corpi ma li preserva da ogni corruzione del tempo." Serao's italics.

7 See Catherine Ramsey-Portolano, "Neera the Verist Woman Writer," *Italica* 81, no. 3 (2004): 351–66, for a re-evaluation of Neera's contribution to verismo and naturalism in the Italian context.

8 For recent work on female solidarity in late-nineteenth-century Italy, see Katharine Mitchell, "'Sorelle in arte (e politica)': The 'Woman Question' and Female Solidarity at the Fin de Siècle," in *Women and Gender in Post–Unification Italy: Between Public and Private Spheres*, ed. Katharine Mitchell and Helena Sanson (Oxford: Peter Lang, 2013), 197–224.

9 For recent work arguing for a consideration of women writers alongside their male counterparts, see Ann Hallamore Caesar, "Writing by Women in Post–Unification Literary Culture: The Case for De-segregation," in *Women and Gender in Post–Unification Italy: Between Public and Private Spheres*, ed. Katharine Mitchell and Helena Sanson (Oxford: Peter Lang, 2013), 225–45.

10 Ann Hallamore Caesar and Michael Caesar, *Modern Italian Literature* (Cambridge: Polity, 2007), 130–1.

11 Gayle Rubin, "The Traffic in Women: Notes on the 'Political Economy' of Sex," in *Feminism and History*, ed. Joan Wallach Scott (Oxford: Oxford University Press, 1996), 111. First published in *Monthly Review Foundation* (1975).

12 Judith Butler, *Gender Trouble: Feminism and the Subversion of Identity* (1990; reprint, New York: Routledge, 1999), 187.

13 Henri Lefebvre, *Everyday Life in the Modern World* (London: Penguin, 1971), 14.

14 Lefebvre, "The Everyday and Everydayness," *Yale French Studies* 73 (1987): 10.

15 See Michel De Certeau, *The Practice of Everyday Life*, trans. Steven Rendall (Berkeley: University of California Press, 1984).

16 My take on the everyday is in sync with the view put forward by S. Rowbotham who, in *Hidden from History* (London: Pluto, 1973), 53, argues that "in referring to the everyday rather than the field of studies known as 'popular culture' the intention is to separate the project from the critique of populism. Cultural populism assumes a critical stance against the dangers of

passive consumption of mass-produced poor quality goods which permeates the literature of critical theory and tends to stop at a generalised crude interpretation before reaching the evidence of lived experience."

17 For a recent collective volume on late-nineteenth-century Italy focusing specifically on print culture, see *The Printed Media in Fin-de-Siècle Italy: Publishers, Writers, and Readers*, ed. Ann Hallamore Caesar, Gabriella Romani, and Jennifer Burns (London: MHRA and Maney, 2011).

18 Ester De Fort, "Storia della scuola elementare," in *Italia*, vol. 1, *Dall'Unità all'età giolittiana* (Milan: Feltrinelli, 1979), 49.

19 Giuseppe Farinelli, *Storia del giornalismo italiano: dalle origini ai nostri giorni* (Turin: UTET, 1997), 212.

20 Denis Mack Smith, *Modern Italy: A Political History* (New Haven: Yale University Press, 1997), 221.

21 See Beatrice Pisa, *Venticinque anni di emancipazionismo femminile in Italia: Gualberta Alaide Beccari e la rivista "La Donna" (1868–1890)* (Rome: Elengraf, 1982), 68.

22 Lucienne Kroha has made this point in relation to Neera's work in her book *The Woman Writer in Late-Nineteenth-Century Italy: Gender and the Formation of Literary Identity* (Lewiston, NY: E. Mellen Press, 1992), 68–9: "Recent criticism, aware of the 'two faces' of Neera, has tended ... to polarize her work into fiction and non-fiction, depicting the latter as representative of a theoretical conservatism, the former of an 'intuitive' feminism ... Neera's contradictions are to be found not only in the incompatibility of fiction and non-fiction, but within the fabric itself of both these components of her work."

23 Franca Pieroni Bortolotti, *Sul movimento politico della donna. Scritti inediti*, ed. Annarita Buttafuoco (Rome: Utopia, 1987), 22–34.

24 For a study of divorce laws in the new Italy, see Mark Seymour, *Debating Divorce in Italy: Marriage and the Making of Modern Italians, 1860–1974* (New York: Palgrave Macmillan, 2006).

25 Lesley Caldwell, *Italian Family Matters: Women, Politics and Legal Reform* (London: Macmillan, 1991), 105.

26 Simonetta Ortaggi Cammarosano, "Labouring Women in Northern and Central Italy in the Nineteenth Century," in *Society and Politics in the Age of the Risorgimento*, ed. John A. Davis and Paul Ginsborg (Cambridge: Cambridge University Press, 1991), 171.

27 See Carmela Covato, "Educate ad educare: ruolo materno ed itinerari formativi," in *L'educazione delle donne: scuole e modelli di vita femminile nell'Italia dell'Ottocento*, ed. Simonetta Soldani, 2nd ed. (Milan: Franco Angeli, 1991), 138.

28 See Marino Raicich, "Liceo, università, professioni: un percorso difficile," in *L'educazione delle donne: scuole e modelli di vita femminile nell'Italia
dell'Ottocento*, ed. Simonetta Soldani, 2nd ed. (Milan: Franco Angeli,
1991), 157. According to Raicich, the press reacted with indifference to
Paper's success. During the previous century, however, in 1777 when
Maria Pellegrina Amoretti received a degree in law from the University
of Pavia, she was given attention in the press, and was presented with
celebratory poems, songs, and sonnets (151–2). The second woman to
graduate in Liberal Italy was Velleda Maria Farné, who received a degree
in medicine from the University of Turin in 1878. It was not by coinci-
dence that both women graduated in medicine: "Ultimately, teaching and
practicing medicine on children were considered almost as a projection
of the maternal function." Furthermore, in Tuscany, twenty-two years
went by before another woman graduated in medicine following Paper's
success.

29 Soldani, "Premessa," in *L'educazione delle donne: scuole e modelli di vita
femminile nell'Italia dell'Ottocento*, ed. Simonetta Soldani, 2nd ed. (Milan:
Franco Angeli, 1991), xii–xiii.

30 Sharon Wood and Joseph Farrell, "Other Voices: Contesting the Status
Quo," in *The Cambridge Companion to Modern Italian Culture*, ed. Zygmunt
G. Barański and Rebecca J. West (Cambridge: Cambridge University Press,
2001), 145.

31 Such an ideological stance is by no means limited to women writers from
late-nineteenth-century Italy. Natalia Ginzburg, writing in 1973, also
positioned herself as anti-feminist. See Natalia Ginzburg, "La condizione
femminile" in *Vita Immaginaria* (Milan: Mondadori, 1974), 182–90.

1. Italian Domestic Fiction, Its Readers, and Its Writers

1 See Nina Baym, *Woman's Fiction: A Guide to Novels by and about Women in
America, 1820–1870* (Ithaca, NY: Cornell University Press, 1978), 47.

2 See Letizia Panizza and Sharon Wood, eds., *A History of Women's Writing in
Italy* (Cambridge: Cambridge University Press, 2000), 3. Prior to the 1850s
in Italy, women writers were typically from aristocratic backgrounds and
wrote letters and poetry.

3 Cited in Giovanni Ragone, "La letteratura e il consumo: un profile dei generi e dei modelli nell'editoria italiana (1845–1925)," in *Letteratura italiana
II: produzione e consumo* (Turin: Einaudi, 1983), 695n18.

4 Lucienne Kroha, *The Woman Writer in Late-Nineteenth Century Italy: Gender
and the Formation of Literary Identity* (Lewiston, NY: E. Mellen Press, 1992), 17.

5 Anna Santoro, *Narratrici italiane dell'Ottocento* (Naples: Federico and Ardia, 1987), 54. In 1858, Percoto published *Racconti* in Florence. She collaborated on various journals and was esteemed by famous literary men, including Tommaseo, Lambruschini, Tenca, Correnti, Manzoni, and Carducci (25). Saredo's work was also lauded by literary men during her career. In the 1850s she published *Pia de' Monteroni* (Turin, 1852) and *Le farfalle di provincia* (Milan, 1857).

6 Niccolò Tommaseo suggested that women could also read history books, emphasizing that women should learn only enough to "say with propriety and clarity a part of what they feel in their hearts." See Niccolò Tommaseo, *Degli studi che più si convengono alle donne* (Milan: G. Agnelli, 1868), 410–15.

7 See *Donne e giornalismo: percorsi e presenze di una storia di genere*, ed. Silvia Franchini and Simonetta Soldani, Studi e Ricerche di Storia dell'Editoria, 23 (Milan: Franco Angeli, 2004), 7. In her article "Passion and Sexual Difference," Lucia Re refers to the "innumerable examples of tranquil domestic scenes in the realist work of the Italian macchiaioli ... depicting bourgeois women holding books or with books on their laps or at their sides ... where the book is an icon of respectable female leisure," and in particular highlights that "while portraits abound of men at their desks writing, the equivalent for women is extremely rare." See Re, "Passion and Sexual Difference: The Risorgimento and the Gendering of Writing in Nineteenth-Century Italian Culture," in *Making and Remaking Italy: The Cultivation of National Identity around the Risorgimento*, ed. Albert Russell Ascoli and Krystyna von Henneberg (Oxford: Berg, 2001), 156–8.

8 See Ian Watt, *The Rise of the Novel: Studies in Defoe, Richardson and Fielding* (London: Hogarth Press, 1987).

9 See Sergio Pacifici, *The Modern Italian Novel from Manzoni to Svevo* (London: Feffer and Simons, 1967; Carbondale: Southern Illinois University Press, 1967), 5.

10 Il dottor Gigi, "L'arte di vivere," *Vita Intima*, 17 June 1890, 21: "... sanno di non dover leggere e che leggono appunto per questo ... romanzi naturalistici, veristi, come li vuol chiamare, ma quasi sempre o pornografici, o pessimisti, che vengono letti a scatti, con la repugnanza di fare una cosa proibita." Arslan conjectures that Neera, who was the director of *Vita Intima*, was probably the author of the column and used "Il dottor Gigi" as a pseudonym. See Antonia Arslan, "Un progetto culturale temerario e il suo fallimento: Vita Intima (1890–91)," in *Donne e giornalismo*, ed. Franchini and Soldani, 222.

11 Il dottor Gigi, "L'arte di vivere," *Vita Intima*, 17 June 1890, 21; author's italics: "Molto spesso, è questo stato di agitazione continua dello spirito

costituito dal rimorso di far male, il desiderio di farlo, e la paura che lo si sappia, insieme a quel genere di letteratura che creano la nervosità di tante fanciulle." On the figure of the late-nineteenth-century Italian female reader, see Olivia Santovetti, "The Cliché of the Romantic Female Reader and the Paradox of Novelistic Illusion: Federico De Roberto's L'Illusione, 1891," in *The Printed Media in Fin-de-siècle Italy:* Publishers, Writers, and Readers, ed. Ann Hallamore Caesar, Gabriella Romani, and Jennifer Burns (London: MHRA and Maney, 2011), 49–63.

12 Carlo Cattaneo, "Sul romanzo delle donne contemporanee in Italia," in *Opere edite e inedite*, ed. Agostino Bertani (Florence: Le Monnier, 1863), 380: "... una squisita analisi del sentimento, una delicata e finissima conoscenza del cuore umano, un amore della verità che vince e sorpassa ogni illusione."

13 Niccolò Tommaseo and Bernardo Bellini, *Dizionario della lingua italiana* (Turin: UTET, 1861–79), 442: "Componimento narrativo in prosa, di ampio respiro imperniato sui casi di uno o più personaggi – rispondente al gusto del grosso pubblico ma di scarso valore letterario."

14 Angelica Palli, "Una parola sul giornale La Donna," in *La Donna*, 12 April 1868, 2: "... scrivere di letteratura e di educazione, cose che può fare anche accanto alla culla dei suoi bambini."

15 Angelo De Gubernatis, *Dizionario biografico degli scrittori italiani* (Florence: Le Monnier, 1879), cited in Michela De Giorgio, *Le italiane dall'Unità a oggi: modelli culturali e comportamenti sociali* (Rome: Laterza, 1992), 377. This figure is compared with 4,525 male writers.

16 Antonia Arslan, *Dame, droga e galline: romanzo popolare e romanzo di consumo fra '800 e '900* (Padova: CLEUP, 1977), 23–4.

17 Cited in Americo Vespucci, "Pubblicazione raccomandata," in *Il Giornale delle donne*, 5 March 1878, 45.

18 Kroha, *The Woman Writer*, 10.

19 Neera, *Il libro di mio figlio*, in *Neera*, ed. Benedetto Croce, 2nd ed. (Milan: Garzanti, 1943), 739. Somewhat paradoxically, in the same passage, Neera expresses her view that women should not receive an education: "I know that some chuckling modern reformer will say to me: 'Oh you sentimental naïve woman! Do you really think you will help the poor person better by giving him a consecrated wafer of the eucharist rather than a grammar book?' Well actually I do, because while people can live without grammar books they cannot live without ideals; and for the vast majority of people religion is the only possible ideal" (Lo so che qualche moderno riformatore sogghignando mi può dire: "Oh ingenuità sentimentale! Crede di giovare meglio al povero lasciandogli l'ostia che dandogli una grammatica?"

Veramente lo credo, perchè senza grammatica si può vivere, e senza
ideale, no; e per una classe infinita di persone la religione è il solo ideale
possibile).

20 Neera, *Una giovinezza del secolo XIX* (Milan: Feltrinelli, 1975), 93: "Quando
qualcuno vuol sapere gli studi preparatori che feci per scrivere la trentina
di volumi da me pubblicati, rispondo: calze, camicie, camicie e calze."

21 Neera, "Le donne del secolo XVIII," *Il Giornale delle donne*, 16 March 1877,
123: "Angeli smarriti e battaglieri che tuffano nell'inchiostro la punta delle
loro ali." Neera makes her remark in the context of a discussion on Madame de Staël, whom she describes as "an exceptional woman, a woman
who must be judged by men's standards, or better, by standards all of her
own" (Una donna a parte, una donna che va giudicata alla stregua degli
uomini o meglio con una misura tutta propria).

22 Sibilla Aleramo, *Una donna* (1906; reprint, Milan: Feltrinelli, 1998), 121:
"Tutta l'opera letteraria muliebre del paese mi pareva deficiente: grandi
frasi vuote, senza nesso e senza convinzione."

23 Cited in Alessandra Briganti, "Matilde Serao: un profilo," in *Svelamento,
Sibilla Aleramo: una biografia intellettuale*, ed. Annarita Buttafuoco and Maria
Zancan (Milan: Feltrinelli, 1988), 188: "Scrivo dappertutto e di tutto con
audacia unica, conquisto il mio posto a furia di gomitate, di urti, con fitto
e ardente desiderio di arrivare, ... non do ascolto alle debolezze del mio
sesso e tiro avanti per la via come fossi un giovanotto." I have not been
able to find evidence of La Marchesa Colombi's attitude towards herself as
a writer.

24 Maria Teresa Cometto alludes to "that feeling of 'sisterhood' that linked
many intellectual women at the time, and that helped them to feel less
alone and less defenseless." See her "Marchesa Colombi e Neera," in
Ritratto di signora: Neera (Anna Radius Zuccari) e il suo tempo, ed. Antonia
Arslan and Marina Pasqui (Milan: Comune di Milano, 1999), 76.

25 See Hélène Cixous, "The Laugh of the Medusa," in *The Signs Reader:
Women, Gender, and Scholarship*, ed. Elizabeth Abel and Emily K. Abel
(Chicago: University of Chicago Press, 1983), 283: "Writing is precisely the
very possibility of change, the space that can serve as a springboard for
subversive thought, the precursory movement of a transformation of social
and cultural structures." The emphasis is the author's. See also Luce Irigaray, *This Sex Which Is Not One*, trans. Catherine Porter with Carolyn Burke
(Ithaca, NY: Cornell University Press, 1985).

26 Neera, *Una giovinezza*, 19: "Esiste ancora un dagherrotipo dove sono ri-
tratte tre giovani signore, mia madre e le sue due sorelle, sedute in
fila ..."

27 Letizia Panizza and Sharon Wood, introduction to *A History of Women's Writing,* ed. Letizia Panizza and Sharon Wood (Cambridge: Cambridge University Press, 2000) 1. The authors do not subscribe to the notion of *écriture féminine* (as, indeed, nor do I) that the very act of writing is gender-determined, as if there were an essentialist distinction between the way women and men use language. See Cixous, "The Laugh of the Medusa," 279–97.

28 Ugo Ojetti, *Alla scoperta dei letterati* (Milan: Dumolard, 1895), 236.

29 Serao, cited in ibid., 236–7: "Noi quattro (intendo Verga, De Roberto, me e un po' Capuana) accusati di scorrettezza abbiamo un pubblico che ci segue e ci legge: perchè nella posterità dovremmo morire? Il romanzo è recente forma d'arte, e non ci sono argomenti storici in contrario. Staremo a vedere." Interestingly, in the same passage, Serao reveals that in her view the reason she cannot write in "good" Italian is due to gaps in her education: "I don't know how to write well because of ... a poor and incomplete education (I studied at a teacher training college)" (non so scriver bene per ... gli studii cattivi e incompiuti [ho fatto tutta la Scuola normale]).

30 Neera, *Le idee di una donna e confessioni letterarie* (Florence: Vallecchi, 1977), 29: "Non credo che questo amore del minuto, dell'intimo, del femminile mi venga dall'essere donna, perché altre scrittrici non lo hanno e predomina invece in tutti gli scrittori psicologici, come ho già detto, dimostrando che è una conseguenza di temperamento e non di sesso."

31 Friedrich Nietzsche, *The Will to Power,* trans. Walter Kaufmann and R.J. Hollingdale (New York: Vintage, 1968), section 481.

32 An exception to this might be autobiography. Literally meaning "a biography of the self," the autobiographical narrative is based upon the writer's memories, which are in any case selective and change over time. Thus, autobiography is also, arguably, a kind of fiction.

33 Catherine Belsey, *Critical Practice* (London: Routledge, 1980), 73: "Classic realism tends to offer as the 'obvious' basis of its intelligibility the assumption that character, unified and coherent, is the source of action. Subjectivity is a major – perhaps the major – theme of classic realism."

34 Louis Althusser, *Lenin and Philosophy, and Other Essays,* trans. B. Brewster (London: New Left Books, and New York: Monthly Review Press, 1971), 168.

35 La Marchesa Colombi, *Prima morire* (Rome: Lucarini Editore, 1988).

36 Serao, "La virtù di Checchina," in *La virtù delle donne* (Rome: Avagliano Editore, 1999).

37 In her discussion of La Marchesa Colombi's *Prima morire,* whose protagonist Eva is a devourer of novels, Ann Hallamore Caesar argues that

the novel "draws on the literature it condemns – a brew of Werther and Ortis, Tarchetti's musicians, and Fogazzaro's Malombra. La Marchesa Colombi's intentions in writing this book were no doubt honorable, but it is a dishonest novel because it pretends not to be doing what it is in effect doing. Although punishment is duly meted out and the unhappy endings distributed, it nonetheless affords its women readers the very kind of pleasurable identification that it then condemns as threatening the very foundations of woman's moral standing and family life. What it so elegantly demonstrated is that, once the whole vexatious question of women and novel reading escaped the hands of priests, parents, and politicians and fell into the hands of writers and artists, those very same arguments about the dangers of allowing women free access to novels could themselves be enacted within the art under the guise of moral rectitude while communicating that very same frisson of pleasure to the reader." See Ann Hallamore Caesar, "Women Readers and the Novel in Nineteenth-Century Italy," *Italian Studies* 56 (2001): 97. Caesar's argument can well be applied to the novels and short stories of domestic fiction, which afforded women readers the same pleasurable identification with their female protagonists' fantasies of experiencing romantic love with an albeit unattainable marriage partner.

38 See Gino Tellini, *Il romanzo italiano dell'Ottocento e Novecento* (Milan: Bruno Mondadori, 1998), 184.

39 Wanda De Nunzio Schilardi, *L'invenzione del reale: studi su Matilde Serao* (Bari: Palomar, 2004), 14. The relationship that Serao establishes with her readers through adopting a personalized, subjective voice that gives the reader the sensation of listening to a confession is discussed by Serao in her article "Romanzi d'amore," which appeared in *Fanfulla della domenica* 38 (1884): 151–2.

40 See Catherine Ramsey-Portolano, "Neera the Verist Woman Writer," *Italica* 81, no. 3 (2004): 351–66, for a discussion of how Neera actively participates in and contributes to the literary movement of *verismo*.

41 See Neera's "Falena," [1893] in *Monastero e altri racconti: Neera*, ed. Antonia Arslan and Anna Folli (Milan: Scheiwiller, 1987), 114–18. For a recent English translation, see Martha King's version in "Rethinking Neera," ed. Katharine Mitchell and Catherine Ramsey-Portolano, special supplement, *The Italianist 30* (2010): 154–6.

42 Verga, "Nedda," in *Cavalleria Rusticana and Other Stories*, trans. with an introduction by G.H. McWilliam (London: Penguin, 1999), 4: "Era una ragazza bruna, vestita miseramente, dall'attitudine timida e ruvida che danno la miseria e l'isolamento."

43 Neera, *Teresa*, trans. Martha King (Evanston: Northwestern University Press, 1998), 50: "Il primo pensiero, svegliandosi, fu per lui; ma invece di essere un pensiero gaio e sorridente, le si affacciò quasi come un dolore, come una spina acutissima passata nella pelle."

44 Ann Hallamore Caesar, "Writing by Women in Post-Unification Literary Culture: The Case for De-segregation," in *Women and Gender in Post-Unification Italy: Between Public and Private Spheres*, ed. Katharine Mitchell and Helena Sanson (Oxford: Peter Lang, 2013), 231–2.

45 Franchini and Soldani, *Donne e giornalismo*, 24–5.

46 Kroha, *The Woman Writer*, 18; author's italics.

47 La Marchesa Colombi, "Impara l'arte e mettila da parte," in *Serate d'inverno* (Ferrara: Luciana Tufani Editrice, 1997), 19: "Odda aveva finito un quadro di genere; e l'aveva mandato all'esposizione di Brera. Non quest'anno però; le prego signore lettrici, non cerchino sul catalogo, non voglio fare personalità."

48 Sandra M. Gilbert and Susan Gubar, *The Madwoman in the Attic*, 2nd ed. (New Haven: Yale University Press, 2000), 80.

49 Anna Santoro, *Narratrici dell'Ottocento* (Naples: Federico and Ardia, 1987), 20.

50 La Marchesa Colombi, *Un matrimonio in provincia* (1885; reprint, Novara: Interlinea, 1999), 18–19: "C'insegnava lui di quando in quando a leggere, scrivere e far di conto. E durante le nostre passeggiate faceva la nostra educazione letteraria. Almeno lui lo credeva, perché ci raccontava l'Iliade, l'Eneide, la Gerusalemme … il povero babbo era tutto ansimante ed in sudore, come se quelle gesta le avesse fatte lui."

51 Neera, *Una giovinezza*, 119: "Dei classici trovati nella libreria di mio padre non ne lessi neppure uno; li giudicavo noiosi e freddi."

2. Journalism, Essays, Conduct Books

1 Sections of this chapter draw substantially upon my article "La Marchesa Colombi, Neera, Matilde Serao: Forging a Female Solidarity in Late Nineteenth-Century Journals for Women," *Italian Studies* 63, no. 1 (2008): 63–84, and "'Sorelle in arte (e politica)': The 'Woman Question' and Female Solidarity at the *Fin de Siècle*," in *Women and Gender in Post-Unification Italy: Between Private and Public Spheres*, ed. Katharine Mitchell and Helena Sanson (Oxford: Peter Lang, 2013), 197–224.

2 The women's journals *Il Giornale delle donne* and *L'Italia femminile* were on sale in Europe. Serao, Neera, and La Marchesa Colombi were known beyond Italy, in particular thanks to their contributions to the literary and

cultural journal *Nuova Antologia* (founded in Florence in 1866). Neera's contribution lasted from April 1882 to October 1913; La Marchesa Colombi published in the journal from July 1881 to March 1884; Serao, who published 20 short stories, 4 novels, and 5 articles in the journal, contributed pieces from October 1882 to July 1927.

3 I adopt the term "emancipationist" rather than "feminist" to avoid anachronism. Salvatore Battaglia's *Grande dizionario della lingua italiana*, vol. 5 (Turin: Unione Tipografico-Editrice, 1998), 808, highlights that the word "femminismo" was borrowed from the French "féminisme," and was first used in Italy to refer to the movement for female emancipation during the first decade of the twentieth century.

4 Claudia Gori, "Oltre domani: futuro, progresso e divino nell'emancipazionismo italiano tra Otto e Novecento," *Storia delle donne* 1 (2005): 240.

5 Beatrice Pisa, *Venticinque anni di emancipazionismo femminile in Italia: Gualberta Alaide Beccari e la rivista "La Donna" (1868–1890)* (Rome: Elengraf, 1982), 63.

6 My italics. Neera, *Lydia* (Lecco: Periplo, 1997), 161: "Passò due giornate intere presso la poltrona dello zio, a legger*gli* la *Revue*."

7 Luigi Capuana, *Giacinta* (Rome: Riuniti, 1980), 172.

8 Neera, *L'Indomani* (Palermo: Sellerio, 1981), 74: "... [d]ava qualche punto, leggicchiava il giornale, sbadigliava."

9 La Marchesa Colombi, "Impara l'arte e mettila da parte," in *Serate d'inverno* (Ferrara: Luciana Tufani Editrice, 1997), 33: "[Odda] ebbe appena il tempo di sedere in una poltroncina e di far mostra di leggere un giornale ..."

10 Matilde Serao, "The State Telegraph Office (*Women's Section*)," in *Unmarried Women: Stories*, trans. Paula Spurlin Paige (Evanston, IL: Northwestern University Press, 2007), 144: "La Borrelli piegò un giornaletto letterario che stava leggendo di nascosto, la *Farfalla*, se lo cacciò in tasca ...", in *Il romanzo della fanciulla* (Naples: Liguori, 1985), xx.

11 La Marchesa Colombi, "Cronaca," *Museo di famiglia*, 1 June 1876: "le vede spesso scorrere con uno sguardo curioso le pagine del giornale in cerca della novità, – della vita."

12 The first issue of the journal came out on 3 June 1890 and contains the following reference to her comment and analysis of culture and society. In this case, the discussion concentrates on spring festivals: "[M]any newspapers mentioned that these May festivals ..." (Parecchi giornali dissero che queste feste di maggio ...), and in her entry of the issue from 17 June 1890, she comments on titles of recent newspapers to have emerged.

13 Neera, *Fotografie matrimoniali* (Catania: Niccolò Giannotta Edit, 1898), 54:
    "dopo aver acceso il sigaro prende un giornale sul tavolino e legge."
14 Silvia Franchini draws attention to the connection between women reading
    newspapers and journals and their probable emancipationist sympathies
    in "Donne e Stampa Periodica: Un Nuovo Repertorio Regionale," in *Gior-
    nali di donne in Toscana: Un catalogo, molte storie (1770–1945)* (Florence: Leo
    S. Olschki, 2007), 11: "For the women of the middle classes, a subscription
    to a journal included with a daily newspaper or a travel magazine, a maga-
    zine about current affairs or light reading for entertainment, would not
    have come without suspicions of dangerous emancipationist tendencies."
15 Verina Jones, "Journalism, 1750–1850," in *A History of Women's Writing in
    Italy*, ed. Letizia Panizza and Sharon Wood (Cambridge: Cambridge Uni-
    versity Press, 2000), 120.
16 Ibid., 124.
17 Ibid., 127.
18 Emilio Treves's *Museo di famiglia* (1869–79) from Milan, Americo Ves-
    pucci's Turin based *Il Passatempo*, which became *Il Giornale delle donne* in
    1872, were financed and directed by men, while *Vita Intima* (1890–1) was
    founded and directed by Neera but financed by Guido Marcati, and *La
    Cornelia*, founded in Florence on 1 December 1872, was directed by Aurelia
    Cimino Folliero de Luna. Still in the 1950s it was very rare for women
    to be directors of journals or magazines; there is the example of Alba de
    Céspedes with her own cultural journal immediately after the war (aimed
    at women and men), and *Noi donne*, which had always been directed by
    women.
19 La Marchesa Colombi's first article appeared in the issue 28–9 March 1876.
20 In her article "Le vie dolorose" (The via dolorosa) for *Corriere di Roma*, pub-
    lished on 25 July 1886, Serao speaks in defence of Italia Donati, a teacher
    who committed suicide on being slandered by her community for having
    purportedly become the mayor's lover.
21 "E io, antica, ostinata combattendo l'emancipazione femminile, nemica di
    tutta la rettorica di voti politici, di avvocatesse, di deputate e altre miserie
    consimili, dal mio umile posto di lavoratrice saluto questo forte campione
    del lavoro muliebre." Titles of her other articles included: "Il lavoro dei
    fanciulli: dove la legge non arriva" (Children's work: What the law does
    not cover), 2 February 1886 and 10 February 1886; "Esame di coscienza"
    (Test of conscience), 31 December 1885; "La donna reclame" (The woman
    advertiser), 1 December 1886.
22 "Esso vuol essere un libro di letture gradevoli ed insieme istruttive, morali
    senz'essere puerili, che si possa mettere nelle mani dei giovani come degli

adulti, che si leggono con diletto nelle sere invernali e negli ozii estivi. Saremo felici di poter presentare alle famiglie italiane una pubblicazione che possa stare a pari di quelle d'ugual genere che escono all'estero con tanta fortuna."

23 "Non posso entrare in relazione colle mie gentili lettrici, senza una formale presentazione. – E quando avrò detto che mi chiamo *la marchesa colombi*, sapranno che fui contemporanea di Parini … e tanto basta." La Marchesa Colombi, "Cronaca," *Museo di famiglia*, 1 June 1876; author's italics.

24 "Il MUSEO DI FAMIGLIA, serio, istruttivo, s'era tenuto estraneo fino a ieri al chiasso della vita cittadina, per evitare gli urti della folla, la leggerezza del mondo elegante, le liti da piazza ed i pettegolezzi da salotto … Ed in omaggio ai loro vent'anni, il MUSEO, o chi per lui, ha fatto una transazione colla sua gravità, e mi ha detto: 'Lei, Marchesa, che ha avuto in casa l'afflizione di tanti pettegolezzi … [s]ente di poter parlare di novità, d'arte, di teatri, di mode, di quella parte infine degli umani eventi che può interessare le signore, evitando il pettegolezzo, e la frollaggine de' suoi tempi … e dei nostri, e le pedanterie della sua età?' – Consultai la mia mente. Mi parve di potermi ancora assumere quell'impegno, e l'ho assunto." (*Museo di famiglia*, 1 June 1876)

25 Antonella Gramone, "La Marchesa Colombi tra mode e modelli," *La Marchesa Colombi: una scrittrice e il suo tempo* (Novara: Interlinea Edizioni, 2001), 40.

26 La Marchesa Colombi, *La gente per bene* (1877; reprint, Novara: Interlinea Edizioni, 2000), 1–2 (the italics are the author's): "Lei, Marchesa, che vive da tanti e tanti anni nella società elegante, che ha potuto osservarne i costumi durante tre o quattro generazioni, dovrebbe scrivere un libro, che trattasse appunto *dei doveri e delle convenienze sociali*. … Ora, il genere di libro che mi disponevo a scrivere doveva avere per critici naturali le signore."

27 "Ma temo assai che non paia lunga questa mia cronaca."

28 "Io, che di latino non so che il *Pater noster*."

29 La Marchesa Colombi, "Cronaca," *Museo di famiglia*, 22 October 1876: "The elections, then the elections, and still the elections! … In the electoral struggle all men are athletes. In the battle to vote, the most pacifist citizens become heroes. Their interest in their home, their emotional attachments, their projects, their habits, everything is neglected, forgotten, in the orgasm of elections" (Le elezioni, e poi ancora le elezioni, e sempre le elezioni! … Nelle lotte elettorali tutti gli uomini sono atleti. Nelle battaglie dell'urna i più pacifici cittadini diventano eroi. Gli interessi della loro casa, le loro affezioni, i loro progetti, le loro abitudini, tutto è trascurato, dimenticato, nell'orgasmo delle elezioni).

30 La Marchesa Colombi, "Cronaca," *Museo di famiglia*, 31 May 1876. She concludes her article in an almost slapstick yet nevertheless very "true" fashion for the social context of the time, with: "Better late than never" (Meglio tardi che mai).

31 Gualberta Alaide Beccari, "Giannina Milli," *La Donna*, 30 October 1876: "[e]lla ha rinunziato al suo posto di professore di Storia e Geografia e di Direttrice nella Scuola magistrale di Roma."

32 Neera, "Conversazioni con mia figlia," *Museo di famiglia*, 22 July 1875: "l'individuo che lavora acquista un diritto maggiore alla vita."

33 Kristeva's notion of the *chora* is based on what Plato, in *Timaeus*, calls the *chora*. The *chora* is a "receptacle, unnameable, improbable, hybrid, anterior to naming, to the one, to the father and consequently maternally connoted." See Julia Kristeva, *Desire in Language*, trans. Leon S. Roudiez (Oxford: Basil Blackwell, 1980), 133.

34 *Il Passatempo*, 10 October 1869; my italics.

35 "The old spinster – age thirty-seven, with a hard and opaque face, pale eyes, thin lips … she has already embroidered twenty-four metal fastenings on sleeves for blouses … a stupendous trousseau, a wealth of work and material to enchant someone. It's true, the husband is missing. He should have arrived earlier, he got married elsewhere, he has already produced a big grown-up son … A yellowish paleness ruins the old spinster's face the most." (La vecchia zitella – trentasette anni, volto opaco e duro, occhi smorti, labbra sottili ... ha già ricamato ventiquattro speroni di camicie con le relative maniche ... un corredo stupendo, una ricchezza di lavoro e di materia da incantare. È vero, manca ancora lo sposo. Avrebbe dovuto giungere prima, si è ammogliato altrove, ha già fatto un figlio grande e grosso ... Un pallore giallognolo guasta maggiormente il volto della vecchia zitella.) Serao, "Poesia Casareccia," *Il Giornale delle donne*, 17 February 1880. The article had appeared previously in *Il Piccolo*, and was re-published in *Il Giornale delle donne*.

36 Matilde Serao, *Saper vivere: norme di buona creanza* (1900; reprint, Florence: Passigli Editori, 1989), 240–1: "Dai quarant'anni in poi … si può uscire sola; viaggiare sola; vivere sola; con qualche fedele persona familiare; ricevere sola: tutto ciò, senza che nessuno vi trovi a ridere … Si può andare, venire, discorrere, scrivere, partire, ritornare, senza dare troppi conti a nessuno."

37 See Neera, "Importanza della bellezza," in *Il Giornale delle donne*, 5 June 1879.

38 Neera, "Lui: pensieri di una mamma," in *Il Giornale delle donne*, 17 January 1879: "E il latino? Signora maestra, sa tradurre lei Marco Tullio Cicerone?

E le matematiche? Saprebbe dirmi cosa sono i logaritmi, il calcolo integrale e il calcolo differenziale? ... Ah! no, pur troppo, non conosco i logaritmi, nè il calcolo e nemmeno Marco Tullio Cicerone. Vedo che bisogna rassegnarsi."

39 Neera, "Le donne del secolo XVIII," *Il Giornale delle donne*, 16 March 1877: "Un raro e delicato ingegno femminile," "donna di gran spirito," who possessed "una certa grazia ingenua."

40 Neera, "Le donne milanesi: cherchez la femme," in *Il Giornale delle donne*, 5 May 1881.

41 "Le donne milanesi": "Nelle altre provincie d'Italia, anche in molte città principali, le donne fanno una vita così casalinga, solitaria e monotona, tra il marito e la calza, che ben a ragione stupiscono di questo correre vertiginoso della milanese da un negozio a un teatro, da una casa a un'altra, da un libro a un cappellino, da un concerto a una conferenza, sempre lesta, vivace, guizzante."

42 "I suoi teneri anni sono generalmente assai duri, poverina! ... Più tardi comincia a emanciparsi ... Fra i tredici e i quattordici anni sparisce. ... È un po' malata; è troppo alta per gironzolare tutto il giorno; molte volte il vestito le è diventato corto, e in attesa di poterne fare un nuovo sta in casa a sbucciare le patate alla mamma. ... Molte di esse sono brave ragazze, in fondo; si maritano presto, hanno i loro figliuoli che spesso allattano, diventano grasse e non portano più i vestiti a cuore." (Neera, "Le donne milanesi")

43 Eduardo De Albertis, "Fra una pagina e l'altra di un libro nuovo," in *Il Giornale delle donne*, 19 July 1881.

44 Neera, "Al Signor De Albertis"; my italics. The letter's emancipationist ideology is very apparent:

> Dunque a lei non piace il mio *Castigo*? ... Se mi permetto di dirigerle questa lettera è perchè lei uscendo dal merito intrinseco del libro (dico merito per modo di dire, sa?) ha voluto accusare il genere ... Lei, signor De-Albertis, è padronissimo di volere *i libri che si leggono ad alta voce in famiglia*, ma se tutta la letteratura da Omero a Virgilio, da Ariosto a Shakespeare, da Foscolo a Musset, da Balzac a Dumas, si fosse limitata a scrivere su questo tema, il repertorio non sarebbe troppo variato – lei si troverebbe bene, lo capisco, ma i gusti sono tanti ... Laura è una dei tipi i più umani che si possano immaginare. [...] Sicuro non è simpatica, ma ha ella pensato la triste vita che le toccò fino ai trent'anni? ... Sa lei comprendere cosa vuol dire, essere ingannata sempre, sempre delusa, vivere senza amare in mezzo all'amore ... *Ah! loro uomini sono sempre a posto, e soddisfatti, contenti, giustamente equilibrati di spirito e di corpo, trovano nobile, coraggioso e onesto di deridere o di insultare le misere donne, cui l'amore fu vietato per tutta la vita; le chiamano zitellone isteriche, e si meravigliano che un autore raccolga le loro lagrime e ne comprenda i segreti martiri. E io capisco,*

sa, come lei non trovi un solo moto di simpatia per questa donna inasprita e malata – lei la giudica troppo dalla sua posizione fortunata di uomo.

45 "Non è letterario, né artistico, nel solito significato. Si rivolge alle donne, a tutte, *anche alle illetterate* e che pure leggono." My italics. The extract from the letter is cited in Patrizia Zambon, "Riviste fiorentine e milanesi dell'ultimo Ottocento nel carteggio Angiolo Orvieto-Neera," in *Il sogno aristocratico. Angiolo Orvieto e Neera: corrispondenza 1889–1917*, ed. Antonia Arslan and Patrizia Zambon (Milan: Guerini Studio, 1990), 31n5.

46 Zambon, ibid., 30. The second italics are my own and draw attention to Neera's attempt in her letter to Orvieto to play down her role as a woman writer in the public eye, as if to suggest this were somehow shameful.

47 Neera's "Farfalle nere" columns were published along with her narrative, *Fotografie matrioniali* (Catania: Niccolo Giannotta Edit, 1898), 152–94.

48 Neera, "Manine Bianche," *Vita Intima*, 3 June 1890: "Cara donna ideale ... così tu devi essere: bella e pudica, religiosa e mesta, devota alla tua casa e ai dolci affetti!"

49 See Antonia Arslan, "Un progetto culturale temerario e il suo fallimento: 'Vita Intima' (1890–91)," in *Donne e giornalismo*, ed. Silvia Franchini and Simonetta Soldani (Milan: Franco Angeli, 2004), 222.

50 Il dottor Gigi, "L'arte di vivere," *Vita Intima*, 3 June 1890:

> Quando poi si pensi all'enorme distacco fra ogni periodo della vita femminile, per cui l'adolescente ha bisogni e sensazioni profondamente diversi della fanciulla, la pubere ha funzioni così opposte a quelle dell'adolescente, la sposa vita così nuova in confronto di quella della pubere, la madre così diversa da tutte, un igiene speciale per la donna apparirà indispensabile ... Io prenderò il tipo femminino, la madre; la inizierò man mano nei segreti della educazione fisica della sua bambina. La prenderemo appena nata, e la accompagneremo insieme attraverso a tutte le età della vita: infanzia, fanciullezza, adolescenza, paternità, maternità, età critica, vecchiezza, la studieremo nei suoi rapporti con la casa, con l'uomo, con l'ambiente, col mondo in cui viviamo.

51 Arslan has been unable to trace any letters from La Marchesa Colombi in Neera's archive, which, given their close collaboration leading up to the launch of the journal, she finds curious, conjecturing that the folding of the journal had something to do with a fallout between them. Further, La Marchesa Colombi suddenly stops writing her column on 20 January 1891. See Arslan, "Un progetto culturale temerario e il suo fallimento," 223.

52 "Per Te, che leggi," *Vita Intima*, 3 June 1890: "Per Te, che leggi. *Vita Intima* ti saluta, graziosa lettrice. – Essa è nata e vuol vivere soprattutto per te; vuol diventare la tua più fida amica, chiedendoti solo in ricambio un po'

d'affetto. Gli uomini hanno i loro giornali che leggono per le vie, nei caffè, nei clubs, nei teatri, un po' dappertutto e in ogni tempo; giornali gravi, fitti di politica noiosa, alla quale tu volgi l'occhio e il viso con un'amabile smorfietta."

53 "Mi si disse ingiusta, pessimista, partigiana del mio sesso, quando in lavori scritti col più ardente amore del prossimo osai difendere la donna, la donna pura, la donna caduta ... vale a dire oppressa." Cited in Antonia Arslan, *Dame, galline e regine: la scrittura femminile italiana fra '800 e '900*, ed. by Marina Pasqui, with a preface by Siobhan Nash-Marshall (Milan: Guerini Studio, 1998), 59.

54 Pisa, *Venticinque anni*, 30–1.

55 *La Donna*, 25 December 1873: "Di mantenere rapporti vivaci con le nostre sorelle di altri paesi ... di unire tutte le donne pensanti e ragionanti del mondo."

56 Sibilla Aleramo, *Una donna* (Rome: Feltrinelli, 1998), 155: "La solidarietà femminile laica non esisteva ancora."

57 Pisa, *Venticinque anni*, 24.

58 Giannina Milli's poem "Ad Alessandro Manzoni" was published in the issue of 26 July 1868, and La Marchesa Colombi's poem "La povera gente" appeared in the issue of 27 March 1873.

59 "I nostri lettori sanno che nell'università di Michigan, come in tutte le università degli Stati Occidentali d'America, le donne sono ammesse a studiarvi leggi e medicina come gli uomini e sovra un piede di perfetta eguaglianza con essi."

60 Serao, "Domenica," *La Donna*, 20 November 1879: "Nel cuore inaridito delle zitelle mature rientra un po' di speranza, esse pongono una veletta rosea sul volto che s'ingiallisce, cercano di dimenticare il passato, ahi troppo lungo! e sorridono all'avvenire."

61 "Medaglioni: Neera," *L'Italia femminile*, 22 January 1899: "È una gentildonna, nel significato migliore della parola. Parla poco, e mai di se stessa, ma pensa assai; ciò vedete negli occhi nerissimi, molto belli ... È una vera fortuna per noi averla a collaboratrice."

62 Emilia Mariani, "Lettera Aperta a Matilde Serao," *La Donna*, 10 October 1883. In a footnote written by Beccari, the editor comments: "I believe that our *Civil Code* would be reformed where our sex is concerned, and reformed according to justice. It is a pity that Serao sets about debating on what she knows nothing about!" ([I]o credo che il nostro *Codice Civile* verrebbe in breve riformato in quella parte che riguarda il nostro sesso, e riformato secondo giustizia. Peccato che la Serao si metta a discutere su ciò che non conosce affatto!)

63 Adele Maiani Nulli, "Lettera aperta a Neera," *L'Italia femminile*, 16 April 1899: "E se il marito non si trova? E se trovatolo, in nome di quel tal articolo del nostro codice che dice: 'esser la donna in certi casi obbligata a concorrere al mantenimento della famiglia' come potrà farlo se, non essendo operaja, ella non avrà quella coltura necessaria in oggi, per accostarsi a una professione, o per procacciarsi un impiego?"

64 Bruno Warroij, *Storia del pudore: la questione sessuale in Italia 1860–1940* (Venice: Marsilio, 1990), 9.

65 Matilde Serao, *Saper vivere: norme di buona creanza* (Florence: Passigli, 1989), v.

66 La Marchesa Colombi, *La gente per bene: leggi di convenienza sociale* (Novara: Interlinea, 2000), 221: "Following a woman or a young lady in the street, walking under her windows, sending her messages via the domestic staff, are impertinences unworthy of an educated man." (Seguire una signora o una signorina in istrada, passeggiare sotto le sue finestre, mandarle ambasciate dalle persone di servizio, sono impertinenze indegne di un uomo educato.)

67 "Farfalle nere e farfalle bianche" in Neera, *Fotografie matrimoniali* (Catania: N. Giannotta, 1900), 153: "Il rispetto è senza alcun dubbio la maggior prova d'amore per parte di un uomo"; 159: "Alcuni uomini, ignari delle alte fonti della compassione, sciupano quel poco di cui possono disporre per le donne perdute. Mi fanno l'effetto di uno che avendo solo tozzo di pane lo desse un cane."

68 Niccolò Tommaseo and Bernardo Bellini, *Dizionario della lingua italiana* (Turin: UTET, 1861–79), 1316: "Sentimento che avverte lo spirito di cosa moralm. sconveniente; è segno esteriore di tal sentimento. Il pudore nell'uomo è istinto; e pare certi animali ne abbiano uno assai somigliante; e i più gentili e amabili tra loro più ne dan segni, e quelli che non paiono averlo, più ci fanno schifo e ribrezzo. Nell'uomo ha una radice morale; è il buon senso della decenza."

69 See La Marchesa Colombi, *La gente per bene*; Serao, *Saper vivere*; Paolo Mantegazza and Neera, *Dizionario d'igiene per le famiglie* (1881; reprint, Florence: R. Bemporad and Figlio, 1901). Both La Marchesa Colombi's *La gente per bene* and Serao's *Saper vivere* have recently been republished.

70 Paolo Mantegazza and Neera, *Dizionario d'igiene per le famiglie*, 2nd ed. (1881; reprint, Florence: R. Bemporad and Figlio, 1901). Arslan and Ganazzoli conjecture that the idea to write a conduct manual with Mantegazza was Neera's. See Antonia Arslan and Margherita Ganazzoli, "Neera e Paolo Mantegazza: storia di una collaborazione (con 32 lettere inedite)," in *La rassegna della letteratura italiana*, 1–2 (January-August 1983), 106.

71 See Arslan and Ganazzoli, "Neera e Paolo Mantegazza," 110 n1.
72 La Marchesa Colombi, *La gente per bene*, 119.
73 Ibid., 85.
74 Ibid., 87: "I know some adorable ones, in whose company I have spent
    delightful days" (Io ne conosco di adorabili, la cui compagnia mi ha fatti
    passare giorni deliziosi).
75 La Marchesa Colombi, *La gente per bene*, 211.
76 Neera, *L'amor platonico* (1897) in *Neera*, ed. Benedetto Croce, 2nd ed.
    (Milan: Garzanti, 1943), 765: "Se poi ci facciamo a considerare le vecchie
    zitelle, queste evanescenti figure di zie, di cugine e di maestre, di cameriere
    fedeli e devote che hanno cucito intorno a noi tanti e tanti metri di stoffa,
    che hanno fatto tante tante calze per i figli degli altri, e che arrossiscono
    ancora se qualcuno le prende per donne maritate, quante donne timide e
    ardenti, tutte meste, tutte segnate dalle stigmate crudeli e talvolta ironiche
    del destino!" For recent work on the figure of the spinster in Neera and
    Serao's writings, see Lucy Hosker, "The Spinster in the Works of Neera
    and Matilde Serao: Other or Mother?" in *Women and Gender in Post-
    Unification Italy: Between Public and Private Spheres*, ed. Katharine Mitchell
    and Helena Sanson (Oxford: Peter Lang, 2013), 67–92.
77 Neera, *Dizionario d'igiene*, 144: "Per la maggior parte di essi lo studio è
    una catena che devono trascinare tutta la vita al tavolino convenzionale
    dell'impiego ... La donna padrona della casa, padrona del suo tempo, fra
    occupazioni tranquille, nei dolci lavori della famiglia – col suo ricamo,
    co'suoi libri, nell'angolo lieto del focolare, nel vano verdeggiante della
    finestra – la donna co' suoi privilegi, la donna co' suoi diritti, non ti sembra
    più libera e più felice dell'uomo?"
78 La Marchesa Colombi, *La gente per bene*, 58: "If girls don't speak about poli-
    tics, it is because they know it is a tiresome subject; they have learned it by
    men ... If [girls] wanted to, with those little intelligent and erudite minds,
    they would hold their own in politics. They do well not to try, though."
    (Se le ragazze non parlano di politica, è perchè sanno che è cosa uggiosa;
    l'hanno imparato studiando gli uomini ... Se [le ragazze] volessero, con
    quelle piccole menti intelligenti ed erudite, terrebbero testa agli uomini
    anche in politica. Fanno bene a non tentarlo, del resto.)
79 Ibid., 97: "There are three alternatives. She can like the man, not like him,
    and be indifferent to him. The *signorina* has to say frankly in which of these
    three cases she finds herself. And if she likes him, she has to say without
    undue emphasis. And if she doesn't like him, she has to say so without
    scorn, and above all without ever caricaturing a fault of his or of his pro-
    fession." (Le alternative sono tre. Il signore può piacere, può dispiacere, e

può essere indifferente. La signorina deve esprimere francamente in quale di questi tre casi si trova. E se le piace, deve dirlo senza enfasi. E, se le dispiace, senza disprezzo, e sopra tutto senza fare mai la caricatura d'un suo difetto e della sua professione.)

80 Serao, *Saper vivere*, 238. Serao's italics: "… badare moltissimo al [loro] contegno, in pubblico: contegno riservato, ma grazioso: contegno gentile, ma non famigliare: conversazione vivace, – se è vivace – ma non eccessiva: allegra moderata, non musoneria: giusta serietà e non *posa* di tristezza."

81 Anna Maria Mozzoni, *La donna e i suoi rapporti sociali* (Milan: Tipografia Sociale, 1864), ix.

82 Neera, *Battaglie per un'idea* (Milan: Baldini and Castoldi, 1898), 90–91: "Non è vero che la donna sia un grazioso animaletto messo al mondo per il piacere del sesso forte … Non si apprezza abbastanza la virtù femminile; non si apprezza, strano a dirsi, dai più interessati ad averla, che sono gli uomini."

83 Neera, *Battaglie per un'idea*, 70: "Senza la donna non avremmo i nostri capolavori, Shakespeare e Goëthe non avrebbero scritto, nè Raffaello dipinto. Come? In fondo ad ogni gloria d'uomo si legge il nome di una donna, in ogni casa fiorente si trova l'opera della donna, in ogni infanzia felice la donna, in ogni ardore di carità la donna, in ogni azione generosa od eroica la donna, la donna sempre, ispiratrice, consolatrice, amica, custode, arca sacra di popoli che verranno, e si osa dire che ella non ha nulla da fare, che non ha mai fatto nulla e che farà solo qualche cosa quando studierà il latino."

84 Virginia Woolf, *A Room of One's Own* (1919; reprint, London: Penguin Books, 1945), 29.

85 Mozzoni, *La donna e i suoi rapporti sociali*, xv.

86 Ibid., xv.

87 Ibid., 163.

88 Neera, *Battaglie per un'idea*, 120–21: "Si dice che il cervello della donna pesa meno, ma poi si dice anche che tutta la donna pesa meno, per cui si esclude la particolarità del peso del cervello e resta solo un minor peso generale … Ma forse che gli uomini che pesano sessanta o settanta chilogrammi sono ritenuti inferiori a quello che raggiunge il quintale? … Infine il cervello di molte bestie non pesa più di quello dell'uomo?"

89 Ibid., 132: "Più difficile ancora che per l'uomo la scelta giudiziosa è per la fanciulla, poichè grandi e belle cose avrà imparate a scuola e in famiglia, ma non certamente la conoscenza degli uomini, conoscenza che io nego possa venir mai concessa alla donna se non dopo il matrimonio."

90 Mozzoni, *La donna e i suoi rapporti sociali*, 182–3.

91 Neera, *Battaglie per un'idea*, 124: "la sensibilità al dolore è eguale nei due sessi e che solo ne varia la manifestazione per cause esterne ed accidentali."

92 Ibid., 122: "Non si è pensato che le signore, nel gabinetto del dentista, sotto le mani di quell'operatore quasi sempre giovane, in un contatto così immediato che i respiri si confondono, col salotto vicino dove aspettano le amiche, le rivali, forse un adoratore, hanno mille ragioni per frenare un grido inestetico ed irritante? … Per civetteria o per timidezza la donna tace; e poi la donna, colta o no, sa che l'uomo è propenso a trovarle il lato debole, a deriderla, e tra le forme del suo pudore c'è anche questa, di nascondere le sofferenze fisiche."

93 Mozzoni, *La donna e i suoi rapporti sociali*, 180–1.

94 Serao to Olga Ossani, 26 January 1882, in Anna Garofalo, "Lettere di Matilde Serao a Olga Ossani Lodi (Febea)," *Nuova Antologia* 85 (1950): 119: "Scusa se non ti ho mandato ancora il capitolo. Penso che in questa settimana potrò mandarlo. È sempre la stessa storia. Con la casa in disordine, il *Fracassa* senza collaboratori, le visite di arrivo e un ostinato raffreddore che mi ingomma il cervello, arrivo alla sera, senza aver potuto concentrare la mia presenza su questo benedetto capitolo che desidero sia potente."

95 See Ida Baccini, *La mia vita* (Rome and Milan: Società Editrice Dante Alighieri, 1904); Bruna Conti and Alba Morina, eds., *Sibilla Aleramo e il suo tempo* (Milan: Feltrinelli, 1981); and Antonia Arslan, "Un'amicizia tra letterate: Vittoria Aganoor e Neera (Con appendice di lettere)," *Quaderni veneti* 4, no. 8 (1988): 35–74.

96 Matilde Serao, *Ricordando Neera* (Milan: Fratelli Treves Editori, 1920), 24–5.

97 Neera, *Una giovinezza del secolo XIX* (Milan: Feltrinelli, 1975), 117–18.

98 La Marchesa Colombi to Giovanni Marano, 2 March 1882, in Maria Teresa Cometto, *La Marchesa Colombi: la prima giornalista del Corriere della Sera* (Turin: Blu, 1996),162: "Mi trovai guarita e potei sopportare le fatiche della fine di carnevale, gli ultimi balli, ed ora le serate della Sara Bernart [*sic*]. Non potete farvi un'idea della bellezza affascinante e del talento artistico di questa donna. Appena la Patti m'inspirò un'ammirazione simile; ma questa è assai più bella ed elegante, e m'entusiasma di più." Interestingly, Serao is more sparing in her praise towards Sarah Bernhardt. In her letter to Hérelle dated 26 January 1898, Serao confesses: "Je n'ai aucune foi en Sarah Bernhardt!" See Raffaele Giglio, *Per la storia di un'amicizia: D'Annunzio, Hérelle, Scarfoglio, Serao: documenti inediti* (Naples: Loffredo, 1977), 150.

99 See *Lettere: Matilde Serao a Eleonora Duse*, ed. Matilde Tortora (Naples: Graus, 2004).

100 Wanda De Nunzio Schilardi, *L'invenzione del reale: studi su Matilde Serao* (Bari: Palomar, 2004), 10.
101 De Nunzio Schilardi, *L'invenzione del reale*, 13.
102 My italics. Gardenia, review of "La virtù di Checchina," by Matilde Serao, *La Donna*, 15 July 1884:

> E con quanta maestria l'Autrice ci dipinge quella disparità di educazione, di gusti, di abitudini, che nonostante i principj di eguaglianza da noi professati, separano e separeranno sempre le varie classi della società! E come è ben delineato il ritratto della donna timida e ignorante, racchiusa fra le pareti domestiche, sotto il tirannico giogo del maritale dispotismo e della superstizione, che condannando all'inerzia le più nobili sue facoltà, l'abbandonano senza sostegno alle lotte snervanti fra la taccagneria di un marito grossolano ed egoista e l'amore innato del bello e del benessere, che naturalmente datasi l'occasione propizia, scuote, alletta e conquide l'anima agghiacciata da una vita passiva e unicamente dedita a quelle materiali occupazioni casalinghe: le quali, mentre richiedono quotidianamente gran tempo, lasciano lieve traccia, anzi somigliano la tela di Penelope, nè potendosene mostrare l'equivalente a contanti agli occhi di alcuni, non hanno valore ... Ma quello che ci sorprende è che da lei parta l'avvertimento; da lei, che in parecchi scritti notissimi, si è dichiarata pubblicamente avversa alle donne che chiedono si apra più vasto campo all'intelligenza, all'attività loro; alle donne che aspirano ad essere non umili ancelle o schiave spregiate e vilipese dall'arbitrio dispotico di un padrone; ma coadjutrici e compagne dell'uomo nella via della vita. Quello che ci sorprende è che mentre la signora Serao vuol riguardare questa elevazione morale e intellettuale, come un privilegio estensibile solo a poche elette, grandi intelligenze, scelga poi a soggetto de' suoi lavori letterarj la misera sorte della donna ch'è umile, semplice, timida, sottomessa e povera di spirito. *Non pensa ella forse che così facendo serve alle avversarie più che se scrivesse un trattato in appoggio delle loro teoriche?*

103 Virginia Olper Monis, review of *Teresa*, by Neera, *La Donna*, 20 February 1887, 237–8.
104 Mozzoni, *La donna e i suoi rapporti sociali*, v–vi.
105 Emmanuelle Genevois, "Da Maria Antonietta Torriani a 'La Marchesa Colombi': gli esordi di una scrittrice tra giornalismo e letteratura," in *La Marchesa Colombi: una scrittrice e il suo tempo: Atti del Convegno Internazionale, Novara 26 maggio 2000*, ed. Silvia Benatti and Roberto Cicala with an introductory essay by Antonia Arslan (Novara: Interlinea Edizioni, 2001), 30.
106 Genevois, "Da Maria Antonietta Torriani," 23.
107 Luigi Baldacci, "Nota introduttiva," in Neera, *Teresa*, Centopagine 42 (Turin: Einaudi, 1976), vii.

108 Giuliano Manacorda, "L'opera di Matilde Serao entro l'ipotesi gramsciana di una lettura nazional-popolare," in *Matilde Serao tra giornalismo e letteratura*, ed. Gianni Infusino (Naples: Guida Editori, 1981), 21–2.

109 Anna Banti, *Serao* (Turin: UTET, 1965), 185.

110 Nancy Harrowitz, *Antisemitism, Misogyny, and the Logic of Cultural Difference: Cesare Lombroso and Matilde Serao* (Lincoln: University of Nebraska Press, 1994), 99.

111 Francesco De Nicola, in Francesco De Nicola and Pier Antonio Zannoni, *Scrittrici, giornaliste: da Matilde Serao a Susanna Tamaro* (Venice: Marsilio, 2001), 16. De Nicola argues that both La Marchesa Colombi and Matilde Serao shared in common a commitment in favour of the emancipation of women.

112 Silvia Franchini, "Cultura nazionale e prodotti d'importazione: alle origini di un archetipo italiano di 'stampa femminile,'" in *Donne e giornalismo*, ed. by Franchini and Soldani (Milan: Franco Angeli, 2004), 101.

3. Gendering Private and Public Spheres

1 Sibilla Aleramo, *A Woman*, trans. Rosalind Delmar (Berkeley: University of California Press: 1980), 6: "[Mia madre] non rievocava quasi mai davanti a me la sua fanciullezza, la sua gioventù; dal poco che avevo sentito, però, avevo potuto formarne una vision e assai meno interessante di quella suscitata dai ricordi di mio padre."

2 Ann Hallamore Caesar, "Women Readers and the Novel in Nineteenth-Century Italy," *Italian Studies* 56 (2001): 94.

3 Neera, *L'Indomani* (Palermo: Sellerio editore, 1981), 72: "Ella lo seguiva, attraverso il cortile, fino alla porta di strada; quando egli era in fondo alla via, si voltava indietro. Marta rientrava in casa momentaneamente lieta, sentendo la sua dignità di moglie e di padrona, decisa ad occuparsi dei suoi doveri di massaia."

4 Cesare Balbo, *Delle speranze d'Italia* (Florence: Le Monnier, 1844), 181: "... la cui cura è assegnata per 'ordine naturale' alle donne."

5 For recent work on women in the public sphere in nineteenth-century Italy, see Katharine Mitchell and Helena Sanson, eds., *Women and Gender in Post–Unification Italy: Between Public and Private Spheres* (Oxford: Peter Lang, 2013).

6 See Judy Attfield, *Wild Things: The Material Culture of Everyday Life* (Oxford: Berg, 2000); Leonore Davidoff, "Regarding Some 'Old Husbands' Tales": Public and Private in Feminist History," in *Worlds Between: Historical Perspectives on Gender and Class* (Cambridge: Polity, 1995), 227–76; Amanda

Vickery, "Golden Age to Separate Spheres: A Review of the Categories and Chronology of Women's History," *Historical Journal* 36, no. 2 (1993): 383–414. For theoretical analyses, see Michel de Certeau, *The Practice of Everyday Life* (Berkeley: University of California Press, 1988); Henri Lefebvre, *The Production of Space*, trans. Donald Nicholson-Smith (Oxford: Blackwell, 1996).

7 See Perry Wilson, "Introduction: Gender and the Private Sphere in Liberal and Fascist Italy," in *Gender, Family and Sexuality: The Private Sphere in Italy, 1860–1945*, ed. Perry Wilson (Basingstoke: Palgrave Macmillan, 2004), 2–4; Elizabeth Eger, Charlotte Grant, Cliona Ó Gallchoir, and Penny Warburton, eds., *Women, Writing and the Public Sphere 1700–1830* (Cambridge: Cambridge University Press, 2001); Jane Rendall, "Women and the Public Sphere," *Gender & History* 11, no. 3 (1999): 475–88.

8 Patrizia Gabrielli, "Protagonists and Politics in the Italian Women's Movement: A Reflection on the Work of Annarita Buttafuoco," *Journal of Modern Italian Studies* 7, no. 1 (2002): 84. See also Annarita Buttafuoco, *Questioni di cittadinanza: donne e diritti sociali nell'Italia liberale* (Siena: Protagon Editori Toscani, 1997), 59.

9 Jürgen Habermas, *The Structural Transformation of the Public Sphere: An Enquiry into a Category of Bourgeois Society*, trans. Thomas Burger, with the assistance of Frederick Lawrence, 9th ed. (Cambridge: Polity, 2006).

10 On Habermas's notion of the "public sphere" and feminist criticisms of his social theory as gender blind and in many respects androcentric, see J. Meehan, ed., *Feminists Read Habermas: Gendering the Subject of Discourse* (New York: Routledge, 1995), esp. chps. 1, 2, and 3.

11 See Linda Colley, *Britons: Forging the Nation 1707–1837* (London: Vintage, 1996), 237–83.

12 See Nancy Armstrong, *Desire and Domestic Fiction: A Political History of the Novel* (New York: Oxford University Press, 1987), 3.

13 Cecilia Dau Novelli, "Modelli di comportamento e ruoli familiari," in *Borghesi e imprenditori a Milano: Dall'unità alla prima guerra mondiale*, ed. Giorgio Fiocco (Bari: Laterza, 1984), 217.

14 Brooks adds that "realism more than almost any other mode of literature makes sight paramount – makes it the dominant sense in our understanding of and relation to the world." Peter Brooks, *Realist Vision* (New Haven: Yale University Press, 2005), 3.

15 In her discussion of Neera's *Fotografie matrimoniali* (1898), in which photographs are represented in the text in short prose chapters made up of dialogue (similar in format to a play), Silvia Valisa shows how the text "frames" its female subjects and "thematizes technology as masculine." See Silvia Valisa, "Still Figures: Photography, Modernity and Gender in

Neera's *Fotografie matrimoniali,*" in "Rethinking Neera," ed. Katharine Mitchell and Catherine Ramsey-Portolano, special supplement, *The Italianist* 30 (2010): 45.

16 Colley, *Britons: Forging the Nation*, 254.

17 See "Terno Secco [1887]," in *La virtù delle donne* (Rome: Avagliano Editore, 1999), 82: "La ragazza pensava alla casa senza un soldo, senza una serva, alla casa donde avrebbero dovuto andar via, forse fra poco" (The girl thought about the house with no money, with no maid, about the house which they would have to leave, perhaps soon).

18 Neera, *Una giovinezza del secolo XIX* (Milan: Feltrinelli, 1975), 57: "A quattordici anni avendo terminato i corsi lasciai la scuola … Incominciò allora la mia esistenza casalinga, metodica come una regola di convento; alzata alle otto, rifatta la camera e la sala di ricevimento (dove non entrava mai nessuno) preso posto verso le dieci al tavolino da lavoro, dal quale non mi muovevo più sino alle quattro, con una zia da una parte e una zia dall'altra."

19 While the original was published in 1885, I will be referring to the 2001 English translation of her novel in this chapter. La Marchesa Colombi, *A Small-Town Marriage*, trans. Paula Spurlin Paige (Evanston, IL: Northwestern University Press, 2001), 13–14: "Le ragazze non debbono diventar dottoresse. Ora è tempo che [le ragazze] imparino a tenere la casa in ordine, a cucire, a stirare, a cucinare, ad essere buone massaie."

20 Serao, "Terno Secco," in *La virtù delle donne*, 105.

21 Neera, *Teresa*, trans. Martha King (Evanston, IL: Northwestern University Press, 1998), 41: "Tanto felice, tanto felice che se le avessero detto di volare, ne avrebbe fatto subito la prova." Ellen Moers was the first feminist critic to identify the significance of birds and flight in women's writings. For a discussion on flight imagery in the work of Grazia Deledda (1871–1936), see Ursula Fanning, "Enclosure, Escape and the Erotic: Shadows of the Self in the Writings of Grazia Deledda," in *Grazia Deledda: The Challenge of Modernity*, ed. Sharon Wood (Leicester: Troubador, 2007), 215–36.

22 La Marchesa Colombi, *La gente per bene: leggi di convenienza sociale* (Novara: Interlinea, 2000), 54.

23 Emilia Nevers, *Il galateo della borghesia: norme per trattar bene* (Turin: Biblioteca per le signore, 1877), 4: "Dimmi come alloggi e ti dirò chi sei."

24 Neera, *L'Indomani*, 124: "La casa non doveva essere il suo regno, il suo orizzonte, il suo tutto?"

25 La Marchesa Colombi, *Prima morire* (Rome: Lucarini Editore, 1988), 163: "Tu mi rappresenti ora; porti il mio nome, sei la mia famiglia, e toccherà a te fare gli onori della nostra casa."

26 Neera, *Teresa*, trans. King, 19: "Stramba nemica degli uomini, a cui faceva gli sberleffi come un monello, dietro le ferriate del piano terreno."

27 La Marchesa Colombi, *A Small-Town Marriage*, trans. Spurlin Paige, 3: "Una zitellona piccola, secca come un'aringa, che dormiva in cucina dove aveva messo un paravento per nascondere il letto, e passava la vita al buio dietro quel paravento."

28 Describing the change in Teresa's brother's physical appearance when he returns from being away at university for the first time, the narrator recalls "the naughty little boy who played in the middle of the street." Neera, *Teresa*, trans. King, 72: "Il monello che giuoca in mezzo alla strada."

29 La Marchesa Colombi, *A Small-Town Marriage*, trans. Spurlin Paige, 51: "For a number of years they had rented a room, which happened to be near our house. They went there in the evenings, put on fezzes and smoked their pipes, and they called themselves Athos, Porthos, Aramis, and d'Artagnan. He was Porthos" (Avevano affittata una camera, appunto vicino a casa nostra, già da vari anni. E la sera andavano là, si mettevano un fez, e fumavano nella pipa, e si chiamavano Athos, Portos, Aramis e d'Artaganan. Lui era Portos).

30 La Marchesa Colombi, *La gente per bene*, 74: "Ed ora, signorine mie, le conduco in un luogo dove non sono mai state." Although the passage is addressed exclusively to "signorine," indubitably all women readers would have been curious to read it.

31 Neera, *Teresa*, trans. King, 27–8: "Few people entered the study, and never without a specific reason. In the mornings, Signora Soave would come in timidly to straighten it up a little, taking infinite precautions ... Precisely at four, opening the door only halfway, Teresina would say from the other side: 'It's time to eat.'" (Poche persone, e mai inutilmente, entravano nello studio. La signora Soave, al mattino, per mettere un po' di ordine, timidamente, usando precauzioni infinite ... Teresina, alle quattro precise, schiudendo l'uscio solamente per metà, coi piedi fuori, dicendo: – È in tavola.) Similarly, Checchina in Serao's "Checchina's Virtue" enters her husband's office rarely, and only when absolutely necessary.

32 Neera, *Teresa*, trans. King, 30: "Difficilmente il signor Caccia entrava nel gineceo, e se per caso appariva, sembrava sospendersi subito quella dolce intimità di madre e figlia."

33 See Ann Hallamore Caesar, "Crossing the Public/Private Divide: The *Salotto* and the Theatre in Late-Nineteenth-Century Italy," in *Theatre, Opera, and Performance in Italy from the Fifteenth Century to the Present: Essays in Honour of Richard Andrews*, ed. Brian Richardson, Simon Gilson, and Catherine Keen (Leeds: Maney, 2004), 216.

34 See Philippe Hamon, *Expositions: Literature and Architecture in Nineteenth-Century France*, trans. Katia Sainson-Frank and Lisa Maguire (Berkeley: University of California Press, 1992), 4.

35 La Marchesa Colombi, *A Small-Town Marriage*, trans. by Spurlin Paige, 12–13: "Noi ce ne facevamo una festa. Correvamo in sala, e stavamo là sedute colla bocca aperta a sentire cosa dicevano. Persino la zia, sedotta da quella novità, si messe un abito più liscio, più nero, più aderente che mai, una cuffia d'una bianchezza abbagliante con una bella gala insaldata che le incorniciava il viso, e venne a sedere in sala, sorridente e muta, colle mani incrociate in grembo." The *salotto* in La Marchesa Colombi's *Prima morire* is similarly presented as a space that comes to life in the home when a young woman marries and is permitted to receive guests. Accompanied into her *salotto* for the first time, Mercede is told by her husband: "Questo è il tuo salotto … Riceverai le tue visite" (This is your *salotto* … You will receive your guests here) (163).

36 Mariuccia Salvati, "A proposito di salotti," in *Donne e spazio*, ed. Dianella Gagliani and Mariuccia Salvati (Bologna: CLUEB, 1995), 50.

37 La Marchesa Colombi, "Winter Evenings," trans. Lina Insana, in *Writing to Delight: Italian Short Stories by Nineteenth-Century Women Writers*, ed. Antonia Arslan and Gabriella Romani (Toronto: University of Toronto Press, 2006), 85–92: "Sono l'incubo di mezzo mondo quelle lunghe, lunghe sere d'inverno, che durano dalle sette alle dieci; tre ore per lo meno; … Di gente che passa la sera come la passavamo noi, ce n'è un numero sterminato … Queste persone solitarie ed annoiate, in quelle ore di solitudine e di noia, sono disposte all'indulgenza, come eravamo io ed i miei fratelli nelle nostre serate di famiglia."

38 Neera, *Teresa*, trans. King, 84: "Many times when he entered the parlour where his mother and sister were sewing, buried under a mountain of material, he would grab them both around the neck, and taking Teresina by the waist, would drag her to the porch, whistling a waltz." (Molte volte entrando nel salotto, dove la madre e la sorella cucivano, sepolte sotto una montagna di cenci, saltava al collo di entrambe, e prendendo Teresina per la vita, la trascinava sotto il portico, suffolando un valzer.)

39 Serao, "Checchina's Virtue," trans. Tom Kelso in *Writing to Delight: Italian Short Stories by Nineteenth-Century Women Writers*, ed. Antonia Arslan and Gabriella Romani (Toronto: University of Toronto Press, 2006), 27: "Ella sedeva sul divano, ritta sul busto … Toto Primicerio si lasciava vincere dall'irresistibile sonno degli uomini adiposi, che hanno molto mangiato e molto bevuto."

40 La Marchesa Colombi, "Winter Evenings," 86: "Il capo di casa ottuagenario, che sonnecchiava in una poltrona accanto al camino."

41 Neera, *Le idee di una donna*, 10: "Terminato [il pranzo], mio padre si abbandonava sul divano in un dormiveglia melanconico e le mie zie sedute accanto al muro, immobili, colla testa ritta a guisa di cariatidi, recitavano mentalmente le loro orazioni."
42 Salvati, "A proposito di salotti," 53.
43 Neera, *L'Indomani*, 29: "Tre finestroni la illuminavano facendo penetrare i raggi del sole attraverso un ricco cortinaggio di stoffa a fiori sopra un fondo cilestrino. Della medesima stoffa era il parato del letto, altissimo, ampio, per metà ricoperto di un piumino di seta celeste, sull'orlo del quale ricadeva, accuratamente stirata, la trina del lenzuolo. Sulla pettiniera un'altra trina, nel festone della quale serpeggiava un nastro celeste, faceva da sopporto a un servizio di cristallo lucentissimo. Sugli specchi, sulle cornici non si scorgeva un atomo di polvere."
44 Neera, *Teresa*, trans. King, 13–14: "... nell'inginocchiatoio, tutto pieno di libri, col predellino incavato dalle lunghe genuflessioni; nello specchio piccolo, verdognolo, appeso troppo in alto, dove non si vedeva che la faccia; nelle tende della finestra, lavorate da lei, a rombi, con un uccellino e una palma alternate per ogni rombo; nei due unici quadri, in cornice di legno nero, rappresentanti il matrimonio di Maria Vergine."
45 Serao, "Terno Secco," 83: "... la stanzetta da letto era presa dal grande letto di ferro, proprio di quelli napoletani ...; vi era un cassettone, dal piano di legno, una *toilette* piccola piccola, meschina meschina, di noce dipinta, un attaccapanni e un paio di sedie."
46 *L'Indomani*, 32: "Tre giorni interi coi dolori e poi un male, un male ... è una brutta parte che il Signore ha dato a noi donne. Gli uomini hanno tutto di buono, essi!"
47 *L'Indomani*, 76: "Veniva sovente, ora, a trovare l'Apollonia; seduta su quella seggiolina, seguiva per ore intere i movimenti della buona donna."
48 Serao, "Checchina's Virtue," 33: "[Checchina] ebbe una mezz'ora di annullamento nella desolazione, mentre in cucina Susanna grattava la tavola con un grosso coltello."
49 Neera, *L'Indomani*, 65: "... più volte, senza una ragione apparente [Marta] era corsa a nascondersi nella sua camera per piangere."
50 La Marchesa Colombi, *A Small-Town Marriage*, trans. Spurlin Paige, 50.
51 La Marchesa Colombi, "Racconto alla vecchia maniera," in *Cara Speranza*, ed. by Silvia Benatti and Emmanuelle Genevois (Novara: Interlinea, 2003), 122.
52 Neera, *Teresa*, trans. King, 46.
53 Ibid., 161.
54 La Marchesa Colombi, "Learn a Trade for a Rainy Day," trans. Lina Insana in *Writing to Delight: Italian Short Stories by Nineteenth-Century Women*

Writers, ed. Antonia Arslan and Gabriella Romani (Toronto: University of Toronto Press, 2006), 113: "Si alzò con un singhiozzo strozzato in gola, salì frettolosa nella sua stanza, e si abbandonò ad un pianto disperato."

55 Serao, "Checchina's Virtue,"39: "Fra quelle glaciali lenzuola di tela Checchina sentiva crescere in sé, di nuovo, il desiderio, vivo, forte, di andare, quel venerdì, dalle quattro alle sei, in quell'appartamento di via Santi Apostoli ... Nella notte, nella solitudine, fissando gli occhi ardenti che l'insonnia spalancava, nelle tenebre, ella si sentiva piena di coraggio. Questo grosso uomo ... non le faceva più paura."

56 Serao, "O Giovannino o la morte," in *La virtù delle donne*, 169: "Non trovò più sonno ... La notte riaccendeva il lume, passeggiava per la stanza, scriveva, poi lacerava le lettere piene di strazio che le uscivano dalla penna, dirette a Giovannino."

57 Neera, *Teresa*, 111: "Ogni sera baciava quel monogramma come avrebbe baciata un'immagine benedetta."

58 Ibid, 50: "E poi le venivano in mente i ritornelli dell'organetto, e si stringeva al materasso, col braccio sinistro arrotondato in alto, il braccio destro teso, nell'illusione di ballare ancora."

59 Ibid., 72: "Nella camera di Carlino le finestre erano spalancate, tutte e due; e dalle ampie aperture entrava una luce allegra, sfacciatella, che frugava per ogni angolo, dal pavimento al soffitto. Le pareti, quasi nude e bianche, rifrangevano i raggi del sole nella crudezza di un mattino splendido."

60 Neera, *Teresa*, 81.

61 Ibid., 83.

62 See Ugo Ojetti, *Alla scoperta dei letterati* (Milan: Dumolard, 1895), 233–4, which includes the transcript of an interview with Serao held in the author's house in Naples in December 1894: "E libri vedo tutt'attorno in bell'ordine e belle rilegature, su tavole lunghe, dentro armadi chiusi, su scaffali girevoli. Dalla camera vicina viene un suono lieto di voci infantile."

63 La Marchesa Colombi, *Prima morire*, 80: "È una camera vasta, ariosa, disadorna, con una grande tavola quadrata nel centro, una scrivania per me, poche sedie altissime perchè s'adattino alla statura dei bambini."

64 Neera, *Teresa*, 27: "... faceva riscontro una piccola libreria, un po' tarlata, con qualche vetro rotto, e mobigliata a metà di libri vecchi, disposti in bell'ordine."

65 La Marchesa Colombi, "Winter Evenings," 90.

66 La Marchesa Colombi, *A Small-Town Marriage*, 6, trans. Spurlin Paige: "Il suo studio non era preso d'assalto dai clienti. [Il babbo] [t]eneva un giovane praticante, e lui solo con quell'aiuto bastava a tutto."

67 Serao, "Checchina's Virtue," 36: "... dormiva, russava sopra un grosso libro, con la bocca socchiusa e storta."
68 See John. E. Crowley, "Inventing Comfort: The Piazza," in *American Material Culture: The Shape of the Field*, ed. Ann Smart Martin and J. Ritchie Garrison (Winterhur, DE: Henry Francis du Pont Winterhur Museum, 1997), 277–315.
69 Neera, *L'Indomani*, 53: "... prendeva il fresco sulla soglia della sua farmacia, coi pollici nei taschini del panciotto, seguendo con occhiate lunghe e profonde tutte le donne che passavano."
70 Serao, "Checchina's Virtue," 56: "Ma sulla soglia, sbarrando la metà dell'entrata, appoggiato al muro, vi era il portinaio, un uomo alto e grosso, dalla faccia volgare e irsuta di peli bigi, con un fazzoletto di lana rossa al collo e un berretto con la visiera, messo un po' di traverso. Fumava la pipa, guardando in aria."
71 La Marchesa Colombi, *A Small-Town Marriage*, trans. Spurlin Paige, 43.
72 Serao, "Checchina's Virtue," 23: "Un mercoledì, nel pomeriggio, ella cuciva dietro i vetri del suo balcone, rimettendo i polsini a una camicia vecchia di suo marito, e il marchese d'Aragona, passando nella via, salutò."
73 La Marchesa Colombi, "Dear Hope," trans. Lina Insana, in *Writing to Delight Italian Short Stories by Nineteenth-Century Women Writers*, ed. Antonia Arslan and Gabriella Romani (Toronto: University of Toronto Press, 2006), 117: "Intutta la persona dell'Amalia si vedevano le traccie della vita e dei lavori delle risaie."
74 Serao, "Terno Secco," 89: "... uno dei suoi grandi divertimenti, mentre era una signora che poteva mandare ogni mattina la cuoca al mercato, era di chiamare su i venditori, sul pianerottolo, e discutere il prezzo di un chilo di pesche, per un'ora."
75 Ibid., 91: "... [s]otto il portone Mariangela discorreva con Gelsomina. Mariangela era la cameriera della marchesa Casamarte ... Gelsomina era la figliuola del portinaio del palazzo Ricciardi."
76 Ibid., 79–80: "... lentamente, lentamente, saliva i tre piani, vacillando, ansando, socchiudendo gli occhi per la pena"
77 Neera, *Teresa*, 106: "... salì adagino, cauta, ma non più timorosa, meravigliata ella stessa di sentirsi così forte."
78 Ibid., 14–15: "Questa notte avrai un altro fratellino ... sono cose che capirai piú tardi ... Teresina rimase immobile, appoggiata allo stipite dell'uscio, con una oppressione in gola e un turbamento improvviso." This recalls a scene in La Marchesa Colombi's *A Small-Town Marriage* where the protagonist, upon fetching some water from the kitchen, overhears her father and

stepmother through the doors discussing a marriage proposal someone has offered her for the first time.

79 Ibid., 93.
80 Ibid., 200: "Nel momento che Teresa varcava la soglia, avendo già consegnato il biglietto, l'amica le si slanciò contro, abbracciandola. Voleva dirle qualche cosa ancora, ma ammutolí nell'amplesso."
81 See Silvia Valisa, "Gendered Quests: Analysis, Revelation, and the Epistemology of Gender in Neera's *Teresa, Lydia* and *L'Indomani*," *The Italianist* 28 (2008): 110, and Lucienne Kroha, *The Woman Writer in Late-Nineteenth-Century Italy: Gender and the Formation of Literary Identity* (Lewiston. NY: E. Mellen Press, 1992), 92.
82 La Marchesa Colombi, *La gente per bene*, 64: "È affatto provinciale l'usanza di certe signorine, di offrire alle figlie delle visitatrici di passare in un'altra stanza, o di andare con loro al balcone ... L'uscire sul balcone poi, perchè sono signorine, mentre le signore rimangono in sala, vuol dire: 'Dacchè non abbiamo ancora trovato un compratore, andiamo a metterci in mostra; chi sa?'"
83 La Marchesa Colombi, *A Small-Town Marriage*, trans. Spurlin Paige, 43: "One day, when I was on the Bonellis' balcony, Mazzucchetti turned around three times to look up as he crossed the street, and he stopped for several minutes before he turned the corner." Later on in the story, the first person narrator-protagonist reveals, "The four of us were on the balcony, watching the crowd of peasants dressed in their holiday best" (46).
84 Neera, *Teresa*, 139: "Due belle ragazze, civettine emerite, che dal loro balcone li tentavano continuamente."
85 Ibid., 89: "Non la si vede mai in paese ... Ma nemmeno alla finestra ..."
86 Ibid., 20: "Teresina, alla finestra, seguiva coll'occhio la carriola, e quando non la vide più, rimase ancora a guardare la strada lunga, colle sue case allineate."
87 Ibid., 33: "Egli era partito, un mattino, vestito elegantemente, con una valigetta di pelle di Russia."
88 Neera, *L'Indomani*, 55: "I due amici si erano affacciati alla finestra; le loro teste, nella luce crepuscolare, apparivano giovani, quasi somiglianti ... Ridevano."
89 La Marchesa Colombi, *Prima morire*, 178: "... più d'una volta immobile dietro le vetrate del balcone in salotto, guardando la finestra [dell'ex-amante]."
90 Neera, *Teresa*, 94: "Stasera, dalle dieci alle undici, passeggerò finché ella abbia la bontà di aprire la finestra terrena."
91 Ibid., 33: "La primavera non portava nessun cambiamento alle abitudini monotone della famiglia; ma si aprivano le finestre, e dalla via entrava

un raggio di luce nuova, il rumore dei passi, il bisbiglio delle voci … Le finestre delle altre case si aprivano, scoprendo i tendoni di mussolino, insaldati di fresco: sui davanzali sporgevano i vasi di fiori tenuti chiusi per il freddo."

92 La Marchesa Colombi, "Una Vocazione," in *Cara Speranza*, ed. by Silvia Benatti and Emmanuelle Genevois (Novara: Interlinea, 2003), 105: "Io ho ventidue anni, mi so custodire da me, e tu pure; ed usciamo così poco che non può dar [al babbo] fastidio l'accompagnarci; in casa non vien mai nessuno …"

93 La Marchesa Colombi, *A Small-Town Marriage*, trans. Spurlin Paige, 17: "Tutti mi guardavano e sorridevano, e bisbigliavano fra loro … Molte volte avevo colte al volo certe parole di quei signori che mi guardavano in istrada … 'Bel pezzo di giovane … Bella faccia … Begli occhioni … Fresca come una rosa.'"

94 Neera, *Teresa*, 37: "Attraversando il paese, fu un trionfo. Luzzi, che stava sul caffè fumando un sigaro, la scappellò così profondamente ch'ella si sentí diventare tutta rossa; don Giovanni Boccabadati, che gli era accanto, indolente e distratto con gli occhi per aria, la guardò anche lui, chiudendo un poco le palpebre. Il farmacista si fece sulla soglia della sua bottega, allungando il collo. Presso la chiesa due signore, la moglie del sindaco e alla sorella del dottor Tavecchia, le sorrisero benevolmente."

95 La Marchesa Colombi, *A Small-Town Marriage*, trans. Spurlin Paige, 42. The third walk of the day takes place after supper, and involves running to the other end of Novara and circling around a palazzo.

96 Ibid., 13: "La sola volta che si vedesse qualche persona civile e ben vestita, era appunto quando si traversava la città, dopo cena, per andare sotto i portici del mercato. Addio! Non ci si andò più."

97 Ibid., 14: "Per conseguenza anche le lunghe strade maestre, bianche di neve e di polvere, furono abbandonate, e si cominciò tutt'altra vita."

98 Matilde Serao, "Domenica," *La Donna*, 20 November 1879. The italics are the author's.

99 La Marchesa Colombi, *A Small-Town Marriage*, trans. Spurlin Paige, 50.

100 See Neera, *Teresa*, 86, and La Marchesa Colombi, *A Small-Town Marriage*, 22, where Spurlin Paige translates the expression "fare la signora/ina" as "to live the life of a very elegant young lady."

101 La Marchesa Colombi, *A Small-Town Marriage*, trans. Spurlin Paige, 27: "In istrada guardavo con attenzione tutti gli uomini un po' grassi, e mi pareva d'aver sempre abborrito i magri. Però guardavo i grassi giovani e svelte."

102 Ibid., 34: "Io camminavo tutto impacciata, co' piedi fuori della gonnella, ed i polsi rossi pel freddo che si vedevano tra la manica ed il guanto, senza mantello di nessuna specie, senza manicotto, colle mani in mano."

Per un pezzo non osai parlare, e pensavo che Maria forse si vergognava di farsi vedere in giro con me, perché non mi diceva nulla, ed aveva un fare superbiosetto che non le avevo mai veduto."

103 Neera, *Teresa*, trans. King, 120: "Tutti avevano veduto Orlandi nella via di San Francesco, e ne indovinavano il perché."

104 Serao, "Checchina's Virtue," trans. Kelso in *Writing to Delight*, 23: "... le belle frascatane."

105 La Marchesa Colombi, *A Small-Town Marriage*, trans. Spurlin Paige, 41: "Non c'era chi potesse accompagnar noi alla messa. E, per quanto ne dispiacesse alla matrigna ed al babbo, che disapprovavano molto – 'l'abitudine di affidare le ragazze ad una serva, press'a poco della loro età, e meno educate di loro' –, per quella volta dovettero rassegnarsi, e mandarci a messa colla serva."

106 Ibid., 41: "Lei non fece opposizioni. Ci mettemmo d'accordo per dire alla serva che non ne parlasse con nessuno e via di corsa, perché era assai lontana quella chiesa." The role of the maid complying with her mistress's wishes in matters of romantic love is also a feature of Serao's "O Giovannino o la morte," in which the maid makes every effort to keep Chiarina away from the home when Giovannino and Chiarina's stepmother are conducting an illicit affair. It is also a feature in opera plots dating back to the time of the *opera seria* of Metastasio.

107 Serao, "Checchina's Virtue," trans. Kelso in *Writing to Delight*, 52.

108 Ibid., 53.

109 Serao, "Terno Secco," 117: "L'avranno trattenuta in istrada a parlare del terno."

110 Serao, "Checchina's Virtue," 48: "Non conviene proprio a una donna onesta camminare sola, a quest'ora. Girano tanti malintenzionati. E poi, è proprio l'ora per essere presa per una di quelle."

111 La Marchesa Colombi, *La gente per bene*, 221: "Seguire una signora o una signorina in istrada, passeggiare sotto le sue finestre ... sono impertinenze indegne di un uomo educato."

112 Neera, *Teresa*, 7.

113 Ibid., 39: "Si incontra [Orlandi] dappertutto: oggi qui, domani a Mantova; la mattina in sediolo per le campagne, la sera a Parma o a Cremona."

114 La Marchesa Colombi, "Learn a Trade for a Rainy Day," 105: "È ... sempre in giro per mondo. Fra un mese ... a Londra o a Parigi o a Paraguay ..."

115 Serao, "Checchina's Virtue," 25: "Alla mattina non si era potuto andare alla messa in sant'Andrea delle Fratte, e Susanna era implacabile, quando non aveva potuto ascoltar la messa."

116 La Marchesa Colombi, *A Small-Town Marriage*, trans. Spurlin Paige, 71: "Sebbene di solito non fossi divota, quell'anno, uscii ogni mattina alle sette colla zia che faceva la novena di Natale a San Marco ... M'inginocchiavo in atto compunto nella chiesa buia, e fissando con occhio supplichevole la luce lontana delle candele sull'altare, sussurravo fervidamente: 'Oh Gesù, fatelo tornare!'"

117 Ibid., 58–9:

> Fin dalla prima sera, dopo pochi minuti che ero in chiesa, ... alzai gli occhi con un gran batticuore, ... / Mi fissò negli occhi, e finché durò la funzione, stette a guardarmi, insistente, instancabile. / ... La sera seguente, e tutte le altre, tornò alla stess'ora ...; si mise allo stesso posto, mi dette le stesse occhiate intense e lunghe. Però la seconda sera ci fu un avvenimento. Al momento della benedizione, quando ... tutti chinano il capo divotamente, io lo rialzai pian piano, e guardai Onorato. / Lui aveva avuto lo stesso pensiero e guardava me. In quel silenzio profondo e solenne, come isolati e soli al disopra di quelle teste chine, in quel profumo eccitante dell'incenso, in quella luce misteriosa, in quell'ambiente di preghiera, i nostri occhi si unirono in un solo sguardo arditamente amoroso, si confusero, si strinsero, si baciarono lungamente.

118 La Marchesa Colombi, "Racconto alla vecchia maniera," 120

119 Neera, *Teresa*, 90: "... le donne tiravano adagio adagio la sedia per appoggiare i piedi sulla sedia davanti; ... [t]utti si mettevano comodi, allargando i gomiti per non essere troppo pigiati ... / [il curato] capiva forse di non essere ascoltato; e vedendo quelle teste abbassarsi via via sui petti, ciondolanti, vinte dal sonno; vedendo quella interminabile fila di sbadigli, quella immobilità rigida dei corpi intorpiditi, egli, il buon curato, precipitava le parole affogandole in gola, troncando le finali; finché la predica si riduceva ad un mormorio indistinto, dolce come una ninna nanna, più dolce, più cullante che mai in quella brutta giornataccia di novembre, propizia al sonno."

120 La Marchesa Colombi, *A Small-Town Marriage*, trans. Spurlin Paige, 41: "... come fanno i giovinotti, forse per dimostrare che sono là contro la volontà ed impazienti d'andarsene."

121 La Marchesa Colombi, "Una Vocazione," in *Cara Speranza*, 108: "Sicuro della sanità delle sue idee, si mise ad adocchiare le donne che incontrava, specialmente all'uscire dalla chiesa, per esser certo d'imbattersi in una sposa timorata di Dio."

122 Neera, *Il libro di mio figlio*, in *Neera*, ed. by Benedetto Croce, 2nd ed. (Milan: Garzanti, 1943), 739.

123 Lucetta Scaraffia, '"Christianity Has Liberated Her and Placed Her alongside Men in the Family': From 1850 to 1988 (Mulieris Dignitatem)," in *Women and Faith: Catholic Religious Life in Italy from Late Antiquity to the Present*, ed. Lucetta Scaraffia and Gabriella Zarri (Cambridge, MA: Harvard University Press, 1999), 250.

124 Serao, "Checchina's Virtue," 35: "Il padrone non ci crede, perché sa come è fatto dentro l'uomo e perché vede morire di mala morte tanti cristiani. ... Ma già questi uomini sono tutti a un modo: stanno bene e si ridono della religione e peccano come tante anime dannate; poi, quando sono ammalati, chiamano Dio e la Madonna."

125 Serao, *Saper vivere: norme di buona creanza* (1900; reprint, Florence: Passigli, 1989), 11.

126 La Marchesa Colombi, "In provincia," in *Serate d'inverno* (Ferrara: Luciana Tufani Editrice, 1997), 109–10: "Di quando in quando c'è uno spettacolo teatrale: e dappertutto sono sempre le stesse persone che si trovano, si ritrovano, si guardano, si conoscono, si studiano, si sanno a memoria a vicenda, e vedono nell'interno delle famiglie e dei cuori come in un guanto rovesciato."

127 Neera, *Teresa*, 57: "Teresina era ormai una giovane fatta e, se volevano maritarla, bisognava pure che si facesse vedere."

128 Ibid., 58: "Affacciatasi al palchetto, vide ... giú abbasso tutte quelle teste, e su in alto tante altre teste ancora. Le sembrava che tutti la guardassero."

129 La Marchesa Colombi, "Racconto alla vecchia maniera," 121: "[Mario] s'era messo a passare parecchie volte al giorno sotto le finestre della Carmela, a seguirla in istrada, da lontano, perché, naturalmente, lei non usciva sola, a fissarla col cannocchiale tutta la sera, quando gli accadeva di vederla in teatro."

130 Serao, *Saper vivere*, 148: "... prima di presentare un signore ad una signora – giacchè *mai, mai* si presenta una signora a un signore – ... o nel suo palco ... o in un pubblico ritrovo, bisogna assolutamente chiederne il permesso." The emphasis is Serao's.

131 La Marchesa Colombi, *La gente per bene*, 161: "... sono le provinciali che si credono in obbligo di alternarsi ad ogni atto, per mutar prospettiva, come se facessero parte dello spettacolo."

132 La Marchesa Colombi, *A Small-Town Marriage*, trans. Spurlin Paige, 22: "Cambiavamo posto ad ogni atto per avere tutte il piacere di stare un tratto al parapetto, ai due lati del palco, dove si vedeva e si era vedute meglio."

133 Neera, *Teresa*, 60: "La tragica fine di Gilda, intanto che lo scettico passa nel fondo canterellando la sua canzone, quella fine la colpì profondamente. Dovette ritirarsi, nell'ombra, a nascondervi le sue lagrime."

134 La Marchesa Colombi, *A Small-Town Marriage*, trans. Spurlin Paige, 26: "Da quella sera vissi sempre colla mente lontanissima dalla mia casa e dalle mie occupazioni. E l'avere un pensiero nuovo, e di tutt'altra natura di quelli che avevo avuti fin allora, mi alleviava di molto l'uggia della casa ed il peso delle occupazioni."

135 Neera, *Teresa*, trans. King, 48: "Non vide nessuno, non guardò niente; a passi da sonnambula raggiunse l'angolo più buio; c'era una seggiolina umile, dimenticata nel vano della finestra, dove aveva servito per appendere una coperta bianca a guisa di cortinaggio. Teresina sedette là, e vi rimase come inchiodata."

136 Ibid., 49–50: "Teresina ripiombò nel buio. Non aveva più coscienza di se stessa, girava, girava ... / Moriva; ma non ebbe il corraggio di confessarlo, inebbriata dal moto, dalla musica saltellante, dal calore di quel corpo stretto al suo, e dall'odore di gelsomini, acutissimo, che emanavano i capelli dal suo ballerino / La seconda, la terza volta che ballò con Checchino, non aveva più tanta suggezione; ma il turbamento cresceva."

137 La Marchesa Colombi, *A Small-Town Marriage*, trans. Spurlin Paige, 63.

138 Neera, *L'Indomani*, 116: "Marta vedeva tutto ciò nella impassibilità letargica di un sogno, trovandosi sempre più isolata e più triste. Le venivano in mente cose tragiche: la morte di suo padre, un fanciullo ch'ella aveva visto cadere da una finestra, le crociere degli ospedali, i manicomi; e poi un dolore al cuore ch'ella aveva provato, da giovinetta, e che avrebbe potuto essere vizio cardiaco incurabile."

139 Neera, *Teresa*, 161: "Era la prima volta che si trovava in istrada a quell'ora; e nella condizione di esaltamento in cui l'aveva posta l'improvviso incontro di Orlandi, avrebbe voluto camminare sola nel buio, nel fresco, nel silenzio. / [Se]nza accorgersene riprincipiò a correre, illudendosi di essere padrona di se stessa, provando, in questo inganno, una delle gioie più inebbrianti della sua vita. / Ma la voce dell'esattore chiamò in falsetto: – Teresina! – e l'incantesimo cadde. Il padre, la madre, la famiglia, il decoro, le consuetudini, tutte le catene della sua esistenza ripresero il loro posto." This scene recalls one in *L'Indomani* in which, walking along the streets after an evening spent with Marta's husband's friends at the pharmacy, Marta and her husband nearly run into her husband's former lover, who, given she is running in the streets alone at night, is presumably a prostitute.

140 Serao, *Saper vivere*, 241: "... andare, venire, discorrere, scrivere, partire, ritornare, senza dare troppi conti, a nessuno."

141 Neera, *Teresa*, 180: "Passava oramai trent'anni e nessuno si occupava più di lei ... Usciva dal paese ... era stretta da una tale folla di emozioni dolci

e melanconiche, così vive, così intense, che quella passeggiata vespertina segnava l'ora più bella delle sue giornate."

142 La Marchesa Colombi, "Winter Evenings," 85: "I giovinotti hanno riportate le novità raccolte al caffè o al club; chi s'è sposato, o è in procinto di farlo, chi è morto, chi è innamorato; che nuovissime promette il manifesto del Manzoni: chi era la signora più brillante la sera innanzi alla Scala; che cosa combinano di fare gli ammiratori per la benediciata della prima donna o della prima ballerina."

143 Neera, *Teresa*, 101–2.

144 Neera, *L'Indomani*, 71: "Insieme non stavano molto: a colazione e a desinare, raramente nelle ore intermedie'''; and 57: "Un abisso la separava dall'uomo a cui s'era data, che le era straniero, che non aveva lo stesso sangue, né gli stessi pensieri."

145 La Marchesa Colombi, "Winter Evenings," 91: "… numero sterminato di famiglie, in cui il babbo è fuori da un lato, i fratelli dall'altro, e le signore passano la sera in casa tra loro. Poi vi sono le altre in cui la mamma è ancora giovine o crede di esserlo, e va a teatro, va in società; e le signorine che non debbono assistere alla commedia, non debbono vedere le ballerine, non debbono udire una quantità di cose in conversazione, rimangono sole a casa."

146 Neera, *L'Indomani*, 62. There had been an Italian trading presence in East Africa since 1869. Italy proclaimed Eritrea as its first colony in 1890 and seized Libya in 1911.

147 La Marchesa Colombi, *Prima morire*, 181: "Una sera ero entrato per abitudine al caffè …"

148 La Marchesa Colombi, *A Small-Town Marriage*, trans. Spurlin Paige, 63: "… le poche volte che si prendeva un gelato, s'andava ad un caffè modesto e meno frequentato e si entrava per una porticina di dietro, in una sala deserta."

149 La Marchesa Colombi, "In provincia," 111–13: "… tutte le fanciulle ordinate hanno … la loro giornata regolata ad ore fisse … [I ragazzi hanno] teatri … pranzi, lezioni d'equitazione, velocipede, pattinaggio, nuoto…"

150 Armstrong, *Desire and Domestic Fiction*, 29.

151 La Marchesa Colombi, *A Small-Town Marriage*, trans. Spurlin Paige, 54: "… calmata l'inquietudine dei dubbi e l'ansietà di conoscerlo, beata nella sicurezza fiduciosa di quell'amore, ero troppo assorta nella mia nuova gioia, per avvertire le noie della casa, che m'avevano fatto desiderare di maritarmi altre volte."

152 Neera, *Teresa*, 34: "Le sembrò che dovesse essere una bella cosa il volare, volare, volare, come don Giovanni, in un bel mattino d'aprile, con una

valigetta in mano, via per il mondo, incontro all'ignoto; per campagne verdi e fiorite, per laghi azzurri, per monti fantastici ..."

153 Serao, "O Giovannino o la morte," 159: "Oh venisse presto questo giorno in cui ella sarebbe uscita dalla casa dove aveva tanto sofferto."

154 La Marchesa Colombi, *Prima morire*, 96: "Se un giorno amerai, freddo puritano, vedrai il tuo edificio di massime e di doveri, virtuosamente architettato, rovinare, sfasciarsi, pel semplice accelerarsi dei battiti del tuo cuore, come le case di Pompei alle scosse del terremoto."

155 Neera, *Teresa*, 138: "Il suo amore per la fanciulla non era una passione da paladino o da eroe; non si sarebbe gettato incontro alla morte, forse, ma le voleva bene sinceramente. Le avrebbe voluto bene anche se fosse stata un uomo, anche se fosse vecchia, perché in lei amava soprattutto la bontà affettuosa del cuore ..."

156 Peter Brooks, *Realist Vision* (New Haven: Yale University Press, 2005), 3.

157 Bill Nichols, *Representing Reality: Issues and Concepts in Documentary* (Bloomington: Indiana University Press, 1991), 165.

4. Freeing Negative Emotions

1 William James, "What Is an Emotion," *Mind* 9 (1884), 188–205. Parts of this chapter draw on my article "Neera's Refiguring of Hysteria as *Nervosismo* in *Teresa* and *L'Indomani*," in "Rethinking Neera," ed. by Katharine Mitchell and Catherine Ramsey-Portolano, special supplement, *The Italianist* 30 (2010): 101–22.

2 Alberto Banti, "Italy and the Emotions: Perspectives from the Eighteenth Century to the Present" (roundtable discussion, Association for the Study of Modern Italy Annual Conference, IGRS, London, 28 November 2009).

3 Barbara H. Rosenwein, *Emotional Communities in the Early Middle Ages* (Ithaca, NY: Cornell University Press, 2006), 25–6. For recent work in Italian studies on the emotions, see Penelope Morris, Francesco Ricatti, and Mark Seymour, eds., *Politica ed emozioni nella storia d'Italia dal 1848 ad oggi* (Rome: Viella, 2012).

4 Rosenwein, *Emotional Communities*, 3–4.

5 Neera, "Nervosismo," in *Dizionario d'igiene per le famiglie*, 2nd ed. (1881, reprint; Florence: R. Bemporad and Figlio, 1901), 236–8: "Il nervosismo assume tutte le forme, intacca tutti gli organi, esalta e deprime; prende una persona nel pieno rigoglio delle sue forze e la prostra con convulsioni terribili; le toglie la facoltà di camminare, di lavorare, di pensare, la rende impotente, e per colmo di tortura le lascia la sensibilità profonda della sua disgrazia." I use the terms "nervousness" and "anxiety"

interchangeably. Sianne Ngai notes that anxiety "has a history of being gendered in Western culture, particularly in the discursive arenas where it has played the largest role. Psychoanalysis is the strongest example, since its primary model of gender differentiation, the castration complex, relies partly on the affective categories to fully distinguish 'masculine' and 'feminine' attitudes toward a perceived loss." See Sianne Ngai, *Ugly Feelings* (Cambridge, MA: Harvard University Press, 2005), 213.

6 Mantegazza, "Isterismo," in *Dizionario d'igiene per le famiglie*, 2nd ed. (1881; reprint, Florence: R. Bemporad and Figlio, 1901), 196.

7 In *L'Indomani* the *dottorone* – who is a non-practising doctor whose title (ironically suffixed) relates to having a degree – uses the term "isteriche." Sympathizing with women's lot, he comments on their social oppression, describing their "milioni di isteriche." See Neera, *L'Indomani* (1889; reprint, Palermo: Sellerio editore, 1981), 60. Also in Neera's *Teresa*, the narrator describes the eponymous protagonist's 'melancholy hysterics' and how Doctor Tavecchia pronounced Teresa's symptoms of unconsciousness as ashen-looking, her teeth clamped together, as "nervous hysterics." See Neera, *Teresa*, trans. Martha King (Evanston, IL: Northwestern University Press, 1998), 171.

8 See Elaine Showalter, *The Female Malady: Women, Madness, and English Culture, 1830–1980* (London: Virago Press, 1985), 160.

9 La Marchesa Colombi, *Prima morire* (Rome: Lucarini, 1988). Augusto commits suicide at the end of the novel upon receiving a request from Eva, his former lover, to leave the city. As a male protagonist who suffers out of love to the extent that he feels he can no longer live, he represents an exception in women writers' realist fiction.

10 La Marchesa Colombi, *A Small-Town Marriage*, trans. Paula Spurlin Paige (Evanston, IL: Northwestern University Press, 2001), 77: "Ci furono le occupazioni inevitabili della casa che mi aiutarono a combattere, se non il mio dolore, almeno le manifestazioni del dolore!"

11 Il dottor Gigi, "L'arte di vivere," *Vita Intima*, 10 June 1890.

12 Matilde Serao, "Checchina's Virtue," trans. Tom Kelso in *Writing to Delight: Italian Short Stories by Nineteenth-Century Women Writers*, ed. Antonia Arslan and Gabriella Romani (Toronto: University of Toronto Press, 2006), 26: "The Marquis paid her an exquisite compliment. He was truly elegant ... When he spoke he fixed a serious and thoughtful gaze on the eyes of his interlocutor, while a slight smile appeared beneath the blonde arch of his mustache and his soft hands toyed with his knife." (Il marchese le fece un complimento squisito. In verità, egli fu finissimo ... Parlando, fissava negli occhi il suo interlocutore, col suo sguardo serio,

pensoso, mentre un lieve sorriso compariva sotto l'arco biondo dei mustacchi e la mano morbida scherzava col coltello.)

13 La Marchesa Colombi, *Il tramonto di un ideale* (Ferrara: Luciana Tufani Editrice, 1997), 54: "Continuarono a camminare in silenzio, con una grande mestizia sul volto ed un gran peso sul cuore, stringendosi le mani per confortarsi a vicenda, muti e gravi, come chi ha compiuto un atto solenne." (They continued walking in silence, with a great sadness in their faces and a heavy weight in their hearts, holding one another's hands to comfort one another close by, silent and serious, like someone who has committed a solemn act.)

14 Luigi Capuana, *Giacinta* (Milan: Mursia, 1980), 205.

15 Matilde Serao, *Il castigo* (1893; reprint, Rome: Armando Curcio, 1977), 141: "– Ah, la gran cosa, la gran risorsa, essere uomo! Bellissima fortuna: peccato che io non la possa apprezzare! Tu sei donna, è vero, ma è la sorte delle donne, quella di soffrire; e tutte le loro facoltà sono fatte per questa condizione, ma l'uomo è fatto per essere felice, e niente in lui è adatto al dolore; tu sei donna, puoi disperarti, io sono un uomo e non posso e non debbo; tu sei donna, puoi piangere; io non posso e non debbo piangere. Un uomo, già: bel guadagno! Soffro come mille donne prese insieme e non posso né gridare, né torcermi le mani, né strapparmi i capelli."

16 Neera, *L'amor platonico* in *Neera*, ed. by Benedetto Croce, 2nd ed. (Milan: Garzanti, 1943), 765: "È errore di superficiale esperienza il credere l'uomo meno suscettibile che non la donna di affetti sentimentali. Bisogna senza dubbio ricordarsi che tra uomo e donna (non se l'abbiano a male gli egualitari [*sic*]) corrono distanze di abisso, che non tutti gli uomini sono come io dico, ma molti, ripeto, sì, ed assai più che non si supponga. La sola differenza è che negli uomini la vita sentimentale è più nascosta e di breve durata; più nascosta per un particolare *pudore maschile* che li rende renitenti alle confidenze di simile genere, che è loro quasi imposto dalla compagnia rozza e inevitabile degli altri maschi."

17 La Marchesa Colombi, "Teste alate" in *Serate d'inverno* (Ferrara: Luciana Tufani Editrice, 1997), 63: "Se avessi secondato il primo impulso, mi sarei stretto Gustavo al cuore, avrei pianto con lui. Ma per quello sciocco riserbo che ci fa arrossire de' nostri sentimenti migliori, e ne imbriglia le manifestazioni, mi limitai a stringergli le mani ..."

18 Matilde Serao, *Cuore infermo* (Rome: Lucarini, 1988), 12: "Avrebbe voluto scoppiare in grida, in singhiozzi, bestemmiare, urlare, ficcarsi le unghie nel petto e dilaniarlo, rotolarsi per terra come un indemoniato, per cacciar via quel tormento, quell'odio."

19 Serao, *Il castigo*, 67.
20 La Marchesa Colombi, *Prima morire*, 133: "… in una continua alternativa, tra una prostrazione assoluta, ed un delirio violento … prodotta da una grande contrarietà morale."
21 La Marchesa Colombi, *A Small-Town Marriage*, trans. Spurlin Paige, 76: "Mi sentivo divenir tutta fredda, e tremavo, tremavo, e non potevo dir altro. / Mi pareva che tutti i vincoli che avevo colla vita si fossero spezzati ad un tratto, e che, dopo quella grande rovina, dovessi morire; che fosse finito … / I singhiozzi cominciavano a gonfiarmi il petto e stringermi la gola. Resistetti un minuto, poi m'abbandonai nelle sue braccia, piangendo disperatamente, ed esclamando che volevo morire, che volevo farmi monaca, che non volevo più stare a Novara neppure un giorno, e che tutti vedendomi avrebbero riso di me, e che sarei morta di vergogna."
22 Neera, *L'Indomani*, 65: "Alberto entrava e non si scambiavano neppure un bacio; lui serenamente freddo, lei distratta, paralizzata nella realtà dalle false sensazioni subìte prima. Tutto il fisico di Marta si risentiva di questo stato patologico. Era magra, coll'occhio spento; soffriva lunghe malinconie; già più volte, senza una ragione apparente, era corsa a nascondersi nella sua camera per piangere."
23 La Marchesa Colombi, *A Small-Town Marriage*, trans. Spurlin Paige, 23: "Allora lospettacolo cominciò ad interessarmi moltissimo. Come faceva ad innamorarsi? Oh, con che ansietà aspettavo quel momento! Quando Faust si curvava amorosamente verso Margherita, e le gorgheggiava delle belle cose con una voce dolce dolce, mi sentivo struggere di tenerezza, come se le avesse gorgheggiate a me … Di tutto il dramma non capii gran cosa. Ma mi restarono in mente le scene d'amore."
24 Neera, *Teresa*, trans. King, 60: "Teresina era rapita in estasi; il bello dell'arte si rivelava al suo cuore, già aperto all'amore. Ella seguí con ansia angosciosa lo svolgersi dell'azione drammatica; si spaventò al ratto di Gilda, pianse con Rigoletto, ebbe sdegno e disprezzo per i cortigiani, e attese, palpitante, il ritorno di Gilda sulla scena."
25 Ibid.: "Dovette ritirarsi, nell'ombra, a nascondervi le sue lagrime."
26 La Marchesa Colombi, "Una vocazione," in *Cara Speranza*, ed. by Silvia Benatti and Emmanuelle Genevois (Novara: Interlinea, 2003), 104: "Quando [egli] fu scomparso, le ragazze affrettarono i punti al ricamo, vergognose di quell'idea che stava fra loro, sentendosi offese nel loro pudore delicato di giovinette, e non osando parlarne."
27 Ibid.: "Le tremava la mano, ed il respiro le si faceva corto ed affannoso. Sentiva il bisogno di sfogare l'amarezza che le si accumulava in cuore di minuto in minuto."

28 Ibid., 115: "L'idea di trovarsi in casa in quel momento le dava i brividi."
The story has distinct similarities with Anna Banti's later 'Vocazioni indis-
tinte' (1938), which is more overt about the betrayal of women by society,
and in which the heroine suffers nervousness. See Anna Banti, *Il coraggio
delle donne: racconti* (Milan: La Tartaruga, 1983), 61–100.

29 Gustave Flaubert, *Madame Bovary*, trans. unknown (1857; reprint, London:
Penguin, 1995), 239: "The mad scene was little to Emma's taste, and Lucy
seemed to her to be overacting" (La scène de la folie n'intéressait point
Emma, et le jeu de la chanteuse lui parut exagéré).

30 Ibid.: "À partir de ce moment, elle n'écouta plus; et le choeur des conviés,
la scène d'Ashton et de son valet, grand duo en *ré* majeur, tout passa pour
elle dans l'éloignement, comme si les instruments fussent devenus moins
sonores et les personnages plus reculés."

31 Ibid., 234–6:

> Elle se retrouvait dans les lectures de la jeunesse, en plein Walter Scott. ... le sou-
> venir du roman facilitant l'intelligence du libretto, elle suivait l'intrigue phrase à
> phrase, tandis que d'insaisissables pensées qui lui revenaient se dispersaient aus-
> sitôt sous les rafales de la musique ... Lucie entama d'un air brave sa cavatine en
> *sol* majeur; elle se plaignait d'amour, elle demandait des ailes. Emma, de même,
> aurait voulu, fuyant la vie, s'envoler dans une étreinte ... La voix de la chanteuse
> ne lui semblait être que le retentissement de sa conscience, et cette illusion qui la
> charmait quelque chose même de sa vie ... Mais ce bonheur-là, sans doute, était
> un mensonge imaginé pour le désespoir de tout désir. Elle connaissait à présent
> la petitesse des passions que l'art exagérait. S'efforçant donc d'en détourner sa
> pensée, Emma voulait ne plus voir dans cette réproduction de ses douleurs qu'une
> fantaisie plastique bonne à amuser les yeux ...

32 Capuana, *Giacinta*, 58: "Gerace aveva anche una singolar maniera di
lanciar le note verso Giacinta; ed essa, che se n'era accorta, se le sentiva
aggirare attorno alla persona, posar sulla fronte, strisciar lievemente sulle
guance e sul collo, solleticanti."

33 See Elisabeth Bronfen, "Gustave Flaubert's *Madame Bovary* and the Discourse of Hysteria," *Nineteenth-Century Prose* 23, no. 1 (1998):68. Bronfen posits that Emma Bovary's hysteria is "a realistic representation of
psychosomatic distress, where illness stands in for fantasies gone awry,"
though she does not appear to acknowledge the "hysteric" as a male
fantasy, a symptom of men's fears of castration at a time when women
started to move away from their preordained social roles. For an account of hysteria's cultural history, see the introduction in Janet L. Beizer,
Ventriloquized Bodies: Narratives of Hysteria in Nineteenth-Century France

(Ithaca, NY: Cornell University Press, 1994), 4–5. Describing hysteria's eruption in the nineteenth century as the equivalent of a media event, Beizer mentions how hysteria was conceptualized without contestation as a female disease, a uterine disorder from Egyptian antiquity until the seventeenth century. The earliest medical record on hysteria, the Egyptian *Kahun Papyrus* (dating roughly from 1900 BC), attributed various behavioural anomalies to the workings of a mobile uterus, which roamed around the body crowding other organs, or alternatively, to "starvation" of the uterus. Greek and Roman contributions to the theory were predominantly derivative. Plato's *Timaeus*, 91c, represents the wandering womb. Hippocrates (460–377 BC) was the first to use the term *hysteria*, derived from the Greek *hystera*, "uterus." During the Middle Ages, hysteria ceased to be considered a malady related to abstinence and became a sign of sexuality, as it was troubling to think that sexual continence, ostensibly a virtue, could generate disease. Beizer states that the first clear expression of hysteria as a cerebral disease affecting both genders can be traced to Charles Lepois in 1618, although the uterine theory continued to predominate well into the nineteenth century, and the battle between the cerebral or neurological schools of thought was waged for more than three centuries.

34 Flaubert, *Madame Bovary*, 221: "On crut qu'elle avait le délire; elle l'eut à partir de minuit: une fièvre cérébrale s'était déclarée ... elle ne parlait pas, n'entendait rien et même semblait ne point souffrir, – comme si son corps et son âme se fussent ensemble reposés de toutes leurs agitations."

35 Capuana, *Giacinta*, 47–8: "Giacinta impallidiva, sudava freddo. Come sull'orlo di un precipizio, gli occhi le s'intorbidavano; le girava il capo ... Buttata sul letto, mezza spogliata, la faccia affogata fra i guanciali, i capelli disfatti e le mani che brancicavano le coperte, Giacinta singhiozzava, convulsa."

36 Désiré Bourneville and Paul Régnard, *Iconographie photographique de la Salpêtrière*, 3 vols. (Paris: Delahaye and Co., 1876–80).

37 Elisabeth Bronfen, *The Knotted Subject: Hysteria and its Discontents* (Princeton, NJ: Princeton University Press, 1998), 190.

38 Ibid., 193.

39 Ibid., 197–8.

40 See Catherine Clément, *Opera, or the Undoing of Women*, trans. by Betsy Wing (Minneapolis: University of Minnesota Press, 1988), 201. Donizetti's *Lucia di Lammermoor* after Sir Walter Scott's novel *The Bride of Lammermoor* (1819) features its heroine's mad scene. When Emma Bovary from Flaubert's novel watches a performance of the opera, the image of the hysteric

from realist fiction (Emma Bovary) is superimposed onto that of the romantic hysteric (Lucia). See Romana Margherita Pugliese, "The Origins of *Lucia di Lammermoor*'s Cadenza," *Cambridge Opera Journal* 16 (2004): 23–42.

41 Sigmund Freud and Joseph Breuer, *Studies in Hysteria*, trans. Nicola Luckhurst with an introduction by Rachel Bowlby (London: Penguin Books, 2004).

42 Anna O was treated by Breuer between 1880 and 1882 and was the first patient of psychoanalysis. In the early 1890s, Freud persuaded Breuer to write up the story of Anna O's treatment as the first of a series that became the *Studies on Hysteria*. See also Lisa Appignanesi and John Forrester, *Freud's Women* (London: Penguin, 2000), part 2: "Inventing Psychoanalysis," 63–116. As Appignanesi and Forrester note, Freud always insisted that psychoanalysis had been discovered by Josef Breuer in his treatment of Anna O: "Much of the credit for [the invention of the 'talking cure'] must go to Bertha herself; in his later accounts Freud conscientiously paid tribute to both Bertha and Breuer" (73). For a further definition of how Freud perceived hysteria, see Elaine Showalter, *Hystories: Hysterical Epidemics and Modern Culture* (London: Picador, 1997), 84: "Freud believed … hysterics were unable to tell a complete, 'smooth and exact' story about themselves; they left out, distorted, and rearranged information because of sexual repression. And this incapacity to give 'an ordered history of their life' was not simply characteristic of hysterics – it was the *meaning* of hysteria."

43 La Marchesa Colombi, *A Small-Town Marriage*, trans. Spurlin Paige, 38: "Nella nostra solitudine uggiosa, nella monotonia dei giorni piovosi … sballottavo il bimbo, che frignava perché metteva i denti, tutta assorta in quel mio pensiero, figurandomi d'essere non so dove, sola con lui, e già sua moglie …"

44 Neera, *Teresa*, trans. King, 109–10: "Non faceva altro che pensare a Orlandi; ma sempre, giorno e notte, senza posa, con un sacrificio completo di tutti gli altri affetti; e non ne provava alcun rimorso … In realtà la sua vita si era arricchita di una sorgente inesauribile di gioie. Quando sedeva nel vano della finestra, occupata per ore intere a rattoppare, chi poteva impedire alla sua fantasia di rinnovare cento volte, mille volte, fino a sazietà completa il suo colloquio con Orlandi?"

45 Ellie Ragland-Sullivan, "Hysteria," in *Feminism and Psychoanalysis: A Critical Dictionary*, ed. by Elizabeth Wright (Oxford: Blackwell, 1992), 164.

46 Bollas puts forward the view that he may be "an artful histrion," "precocious," "flirtatious," "charming," "is generally lying" but nevertheless is "always loveable and loving," in Christopher Bollas, *Hysteria* (London: Routledge, 2000), 173.

47 Neera, *Teresa*, trans. King, 171: "Ebbe un eccesso di vera disperazione, durante il quale sentì agitarsi nel fondo delle viscere un torrente d'odio, di passioni malvagie, di invidie non mai provate. / Si torceva sul letto, mordendo le coperte con una voglia pazza di fare del male a qualcuno, col desiderio mostruoso di veder scorrere del sangue insieme alle sue lagrime. / La trovarono sfinita, livida in volto, coi denti serrati. / Il dottor Tavecchia, chiamato per tranquillizzare lo spavento della madre, accennò a un isterismo nervoso e prescrisse dei calmanti."

48 See Catherine Ramsey-Portolano, "Neera the Verist Woman Writer," *Italica* 81 (2004): 359: "It is ... Neera, and not Teresa, who identifies the conflict between natural impulses and social constraints as the source of Teresa's hysteria ... Neera denounces the *fin de siècle* familial customs that place the daughter's right to fulfillment second to that of the son and the social structures that place woman's only possibility for fulfillment in marriage."

49 See Bruno Wanrooij, *Storia del pudore: la questione sessuale in Italia 1860–1940* (Venice: Marsilio, 1990), 14.

50 Marina Warner describes the self-sacrificing feminine ideal embodied in the Madonna figure as "an instrument of a dynamic argument from the Catholic Church about the structure of society, presented as a God-given code." See Marina Warner, *Alone of all Her Sex: The Myth and the Cult of the Virgin Mary* (London: Picador, 1985), 62.

51 Jan Goldstein, "The Hysteria Diagnosis and the Politics of Anticlericalism in Late-Nineteenth-Century France," *Journal of Modern History* 54 (1982): 209–10.

52 See Mark S. Micale, *The Mind of Modernism: Medicine, Psychology, and the Cultural Arts in Europe and America, 1880-1940* (Stanford: Stanford University Press, 2004), 24; and Henry Maudsley, *Fisiologia e patologia dello spirito*, trans. Domenico Collina (Naples: Vincenzo Pasquale, 1872).

53 Appignanesi and Forrester, *Freud's Women*, 69. I can think of no examples where male characters belonging to the working class experience hysteria in realist fiction by male writers.

54 Ibid., 63.

55 Showalter, *The Female Malady*, 55.

56 Carroll Smith-Rosenberg, *Disorderly Conduct: Visions of Gender in Victorian America* (New York: Oxford, 1985), 204.

57 Ibid., 206.

58 Capuana, *Giacinta*, 171: "Noi donne siamo pazze. Ci tendiamo da noi stesse una fitta rete di inganni. La colpa non è forse tutta nostra; abbiamo la testa debole."

59 Georges Didi-Huberman, *Invention de l'hystérie. Charcot et l'iconographie de la Salpêtrière* (Paris: Macula, 1982).

60 Bronfen, *The Knotted Subject*, 193.

61 Capuana, *Giacinta*, 157:

> Il Follini ... studiava Giacinta con la fredda curiosità d'uno scienziato di fronte a *un bel caso*. L'eredità naturale, le circostanze sociali glielo spiegavano fino a un certo punto. Ma per lui, già discepolo del De Meis all'università di Bologna, per lui che, se non credeva nell'anima immortale, credeva all'anima e allo spirito, una passione come quella non poteva esser soltanto il prodotto delle cellule, dei nervi e del sangue. E voleva scoprirne tutto il processo, l'essenziale. Gli interessava pel suo libro *Fisiologia e patologia delle passioni* a cui lavorava da due anni. Perciò, quando gli capitava, mettevasi a interrogare destramente Giacinta, a confessarla, come ella diceva, ingegnandosi di sorprendere i sintomi nella loro spontanea attività. / Una sera che la contessa pareva allegrissima e faceva scoppiettare attorno a lei le sue frasi vibranti e frizzanti, il dottore s'era seduto in un angolo, fuori di vista, per osservarla con piú comodo. (The italics are the author's.)

62 Flaubert, *Madame Bovary*, trans. unknown, 221–2: "On crut qu'elle avait le délire; elle l'eut à partir de minuit: une fièvre cérébrale s'était déclarée. / Pendant quarante-trois jours Charles ne la quitta pas. Il abandonna tous ses malades; il ne se couchait plus ... Ce qui l'effrayait le plus, c'était l'abattement d'Emma; car elle ne parlait pas, n'entendait rien et même semblait ne point souffrir, – comme si son corps et son âme se fussent ensemble reposés de toutes leurs agitations. / ... Tantôt elle souffrait au coeur, puis dans la poitrine, dans le cerveau, dans les membres; il lui survint des vomissements où Charles crut apercevoir les premiers symptômes d'un cancer."

63 Neera, *L'Indomani*, 60: "La donna non è sempre vittima ... – ella si vendica, come può, quando può. Ella risponde alla mostruosa ingiustizia dell'amore civile coi suoi milioni di isteriche, coi suoi miliardi di adultere. Colpita, colpisce; ingannata, inganna; niente di più logico."

64 Serao, "Checchina's Virtue," trans. Kelso, 40–1: "Ogni mattina Toto gliene inventava una. – Sarà stata la braciola di maiale che t'ha fatto male, Checca mia. – Se ti senti male, perché non prendi del citrato di magnesia effervescente? È una bibita piacevole e ti spazza lo stomaco come una scopa. – Checca mia, più ti guardo e più mi pare che tu debba avere della coprostasi: perché non ti decidi addirittura per un po' d'olio di mandorle? Fresco, spremuto, da Garneri, è una bellezza." In Charlotte Perkins Gilman's short story "The Yellow Wallpaper" (1892), the assurances of the protagonist's husband, who is also a doctor, and who is certain his wife is better, are also

shown to be untrue. Convinced that she is getting worse, the first-person narrator is reassured by her husband confidently and condescendingly before she commits suicide: "You really are getting better, dear, whether you can see it or not. I am a doctor, dear, and I know." Charlotte Perkins Gilman, *The Yellow Wallpaper*, 15th ed. (1899; reprint, London: Virago, 2005), 23–4.

65 Neera, *Teresa*, trans. King, 188: "– Nulla. Il cuore non ha nulla … esternamente."

66 Il dottor Gigi, "L'arte di vivere," *Vita Intima*, 17 June 1890: "Lunghe passeggiate, buona nutrizione, possibilmente un po' di ginnastica domestica, tutto quello insomma che può favorire lo sviluppo muscolare."

67 Matilde Serao, "L'impero della nevrosi," *Il Mattino*, 12–13 April 1892.

68 Neera, *Teresa*, trans. King, 187: "Teresa sentiva quello sguardo penetrarle nelle viscere e nei pensieri: non lo incontrava, ma anche fuggendolo, ne avvertiva l'intensità, e in questo caso le si palesava anche piú forte, per cui prese il partito di guardarlo essa pure, attratta da un magnetismo che la dominava; finché stette immobile, improvvisamente calmata."

69 Ibid., 188–9: "Tornò qualche giorno dopo, per vedere l'esito della cura, ed essendo comparso all'improvviso davanti a Teresina, ella arrossí, tutta confusa, con un sentimento recondito di vergogna. Quella specie di intimità con un uomo giovane, senza il legame dell'amore, la turbava. Era meravigliata di non trovare maggior avversione al contatto, di sorprendere nei suoi sensi una vita autonoma, indipendente dal cuore e dalla volontà."

70 Ibid., 193–4: "Il dottore parlava, con quella voce maschia, che faceva fremere Teresina. Il suo pensiero era lontano, ma la solita corrente magnetica, di un magnetismo puramente fisico, la faceva stare attenta alle parole del giovane … Senza sapere in qual modo avesse incominciato, si trovò a parlar d'amore. – … L'amore, il vero, nasce da un complesso di circostanze, di affinità intime e continue. È un certo modo di guardare, di sentire, di esporre le idee; è una piega del labbro, la voce, il gesto, la forma della mano, l'odore della pelle. È l'attrazione prolungata dei corpi, per cui piú si sta vicini e piú si starebbe; è lo scambio rapido e completo dei pensieri; è l'afferrare insieme la stessa sensazione, il fondersi, il completarsi l'un l'altro in un assorbimento progressivo dell'anima e dei sensi."

71 Ibid., 195: "Ella si sentiva morire in un rapimento di voluttà, nella delicata eccitazione di quella voce d'uomo che parlava d'amore."

72 Ibid., 43: "Il destarsi, all'indomani, in una camera nuova, fu per Teresa sorgente d'altri piaceri."

73 Ibid.: "Stava voltata di fianco, colle mani raccolte sul petto, i ginocchi un po' rialzati, la testa abbandonata sul guanciale basso."

74 Ibid.: "Teresina non pensò se quell'acconciatura andasse o no d'accordo
colle tradizioni classiche; vedeva quella bella signora vestita di rosa in
mezzo a tante altre vestite di bianco, e il giovane Telemaco fra esse."

75 Ibid., 44: "Incominciò a vestirsi lentamente, gustando il piacere di correre a piedi nudi sul tappetino del corsetto e di girellare in sottana, senza
busto, rialzando ad ogni po' lo spallino della camicia che le scivolava sul
braccio."

76 Ibid., 44–5: "Come erano bianche le sue braccia! Ella non aveva mai avuto
tempo di guardarle, e le apparivano ora come le braccia di un'altra persona, cosí sottili, rotonde e bianche. Proprio non sapeva capacitarsi come
fossero bianche, mentre il colorito del volto tendeva al bruno, ed anche il
collo era bruno; solo scendendo sotto la clavicola, dove principiava il petto,
il bianco riappariva."

77 Ibid., 45: "Si pose ad esaminarsi cosí minutamente, da vicino, che il suo
fiato appannò il cristallo."

78 Ibid. "– Incomincio a *stimarmi* anch'io! – Disse cosí, sorridendo a se stessa
nello specchio, per l'idea buffa ch'ella potesse *stimarsi*, e restò immobile,
colpita dallo scintillo che vide davanti a sé su quelle labbra rosse, tumide,
e su quei denti di una candidezza abbagliante. Tornò a sorridere. Che cosa
bizzarra! Tutto il suo viso cambiava. Faceva dunque quell'effetto lí, lei,
quando rideva?"

79 Ibid., 49: "Moriva; ma non ebbe il coraggio di confessarlo, inebbriata dal
moto, dalla musica saltellante, dal calore di quel corpo stretto al suo,
e dall'odore di gelsomini, acutissimo, che emanavano i capelli del suo
ballerina."

80 Ibid., 50:

> Le venivano in mente i ritornelli dell'organetto, e si stringeva al materasso, col
> braccio sinistro arrotondato in alto, il braccio destro teso, nell'illusione di ballare
> ancora. All'alba si addormentò. / Il primo pensiero, svegliandosi, fu per lui; ma
> invece di essere un pensiero gaio e sorridente, le si affacciò quasi come un dolore,
> come una spina acutissima passata nella pelle. / Inoltrando il giorno, la sua ma-
> linconia cresceva. Non aveva mai provato una simile tristezza. Si sentiva cambiata,
> come se un gran numero d'anni le si fosse aggravato sopra; aveva pensieri mesti di
> morte, di malattie, uno sconforto, un vuoto. Si toccava l'abito qui, lí, dove lo aveva
> toccato lui; e le veniva una gran voglia di piangere. / All'ora del pranzo aveva il
> cuore cosí oppresso, che non poté quasi ingoiare cibo.

81 Neera, *L'Indomani*, 116–17: "Le venivano in mente cose tragiche: la morte
di suo padre, un fanciullo ch'ella aveva visto cadere da una finestra,
le crociere degli ospedali, i manicomi; e poi un dolore al cuore ch'ella

aveva provato, da giovinetta, e che avrebbe potuto essere vizio cardiaco incurabile. Guardava Alberto con una passione, con uno struggimento di tutto il suo essere che le affilava il volto, che le toglieva qualsiasi altra sensazione."

82 Showalter, *The Female Malady*, 134.
83 Neera, *L'Indomani*, 75:

> L'attesa, dapprima calma e rassegnata, volgeva col volgere delle ore, ad una inquietudine generale … Ritta nel mezzo della stanza pareva una statua; le sue sensazioni si concentravano in un immenso, in uno sfrenato desiderio di vedere Alberto. / Il tempo passava, e dall'immobiltà angosciosa Marta entrava in uno stato di allucinazione sensuale. Con mano inconscia slacciava i ganci dell'abito, allentava i nastri, cedendo a una sensazione misteriosa di abbandono, con dei brividi a fior di pelle, la bocca assetata, arida, le braccia aperte disperatamente. / Incapace a reggersi piegava il capo sopra un guanciale, su una spalliera di poltrona, su tutto ciò che poteva darle l'illusione di una carezza. Perduta nelle immagini d'amore scioglieva i capelli, e attorcigliandoseli sul volto ne aspirava l'aroma giovanile, gemendo il proprio nome – Marta, Marta! – che la notte raccoglieva e agli echi deserti della campagna ripeteva – Marta, Marta! / Il tempo passava ancora, finché l'eccitazione illanguidendosi la lasciava sfinita, con le membra rotte, gli occhi pesti e vacillanti.

84 La Marchesa Colombi, *A Small-Town Marriage*, trans. Spurlin Paige, 19:
   "Dopo quel famoso discorso della matrigna sulla bellezza, mi parve impossibile di potermi coricare al buio. Accendevo il lume, e mi scioglievo le trecce dinanzi allo specchietto di due decimetri quadrati, la sola concessione fatta alla vanità nel mobiglio della nostra camera, e che, prima d'allora, ci aveva servito pochissimo."
85 Serao, "Checchina's Virtue," trans. Kelso, 39–40:

> Checchina sentiva crescere in sé, di nuovo, il desiderio, vivo, forte, di andare, quel venerdì, dalle quattro alle sei, in quell'appartamento di via Santi Apostoli. Nella notte, nella solitudine, fissando gli occhi ardenti che l'insonnia spalancava, nelle tenebre, ella si sentiva piena di coraggio. Questo grosso uomo che russava in tutti i toni, e ogni tanto si rivoltava sotto le coperte di un botto solo, come mosso da un saltaleone, non le faceva più paura … Andare, sì, doveva andare, poiché aveva detto sì, quella sera, quando egli l'aveva baciata … E con la lucidità di visione dei cervelli che la veglia notturna esalta, ella si vedeva partire di casa, alle quattro …; si vedeva entrare in casa di lui, che l'aspettava … qui tutti i suoi nervi tremavano in una vibrazione, ed ella nascondeva la faccia nel cuscino … Le pareva di avere una forza nuova che non aveva mai sentito in sé, un coraggio grande, un'audacia che fa superare allegramente qualunque ostacolo, una volontà così ferma che nulla poteva vincerla o spezzarla … Poi, dopo aver rifatto venti volte, ampliando, lo stes-

so progetto ... arrivava sempre all'estremo del suo sogno, a quell'arrivo in quella casa, da lui che l'aspettava ... e tutto s'inabissava in una confusione di fantasie sognanti le sensazioni della mitezza ombrosa, della molezza calda, del silenzio profondo, della carezza voluttuosa delle cose ricche e belle.

86 La Marchesa Colombi, *A Small-Town Marriage*, trans. Spurlin Paige, 52: "Poi mi confidò che lui era un uomo fatale. E lo provò con un fatto ... che lui farebbe la disgrazia della donna di cui s'innamorerebbe e che s'innamorasse di lui."

87 Showalter, *The Female Malady*, 160.

88 Cited in Appignanesi and Forrester, *Freud's Women*, 146.

5. Female Friendships, Sibling Relationships, Mother-Daughter Bonds

1 Sally Mitchell, "Sentiment and Suffering: Women's Recreational Reading in the 1860s," *Victorian Studies* 21(1977): 45.

2 Kate Flint, *The Woman Reader, 1837–1914* (Oxford: Clarendon Press, 1993), 36. Feelings of identification and desire to which Flint refers on behalf of women readers towards the female protagonist in literary fiction have a great deal in common with those experienced by female spectators watching performing female artists (singers, dancers, actresses) at the theatre prior to the rise of Italian silent film.

3 Ibid., 42.

4 Matilde Serao, "Girls' Normal School," in *Unmarried Women: Stories*, trans. Paula Spurlin Paige (Evanston, IL: Northwestern University Press, 2007), 11. Normal schools (*scuole normali*) were teacher-training schools predominantly for girls who were around the ages of fifteen and sixteen.

5 Serao, *Fantasia*, in Matilde Serao, *Opere*, ed. P. Pancrazi, 2 vols. (Milan: Garzanti, 1944–6), 23–4.

6 La Marchesa Colombi, *Prima morire* (Rome: Lucarini Editore, 1988), 5: "Una lettura che esalta, che dà la febbre' ... 'che mi fanno piangere a calde lagrime, che mi tengono afflitta qualche volta una settimana intera per qualche catastrofe improbabile."

7 Flint, *The Woman Reader*, 32.

8 Janet Todd, *Women's Friendship in Literature* (New York: Columbia University Press, 1980), 3–4. See also Karen Hollinger, *In the Company of Women: Contemporary Female Friendship Films* (Minneapolis: University of Minnesota Press, 1998). On relationships between men in literature, see Eve Kosofsky Sedgwick, *Between Men: English Literature and Male Homosocial Desire* (New York; Guildford: Columbia University Press, 1985).

9 Karen Hollinger suggests that social female friendship representations also contain a strong political message, albeit of a conservative nature. See Hollinger, *In the Company of Women*, 9.

10 Nancy Chodorow, *The Reproduction of Mothering: Psychoanalysis and the Sociology of Gender* (Berkeley: University of California Press, 1978), 110.

11 Ursula Fanning, *Gender Meets Genre: Woman as Subject in the Fictional Universe of Matilde Serao* (Dublin: Irish Academic Press, 2002), 153–4. See also Helene Deutsch, *The Psychology of Women: A Psychoanalytic Interpretation* (New York: Grune and Stratton, 1944), v.

12 Fanning, *Gender Meets Genre*, 153.

13 La Marchesa Colombi, *La gente per bene: leggi di convenienza sociale* (Novara: Interlinea, 2000), 66: "Una signorina potrà accettare di pranzare da un'amica, e rimanerci, anche sola, sotto la custodia della signora di casa."

14 De Giorgio, *Le italiane dall'Unità a oggi: modelli culturali e comportamenti sociali* (Rome: Laterza, 1992), 119.

15 Serao, "Girls' Normal School," 5: "Si vedeva bene lo sguardo che Amelia Bozza, una convittrice del primo corso, fissava su Caterina Borelli, l'esterna del terzo corso …, e Caterina Borelli girava fra le dita una rosa appassita che Amelia Bozza le aveva data tre giorni prima." In *Saper vivere*, Serao applauds the creation of female sections for girls at boys' high schools in Germany, and calls for the creation of the same in Italy. See Serao, *Saper vivere: norme di buona creanza* (1900; reprint, Florence: Passigli, 1989), 186.

16 Fanning, *Gender Meets Genre*, 190–2.

17 Serao, "Girls' Normal School," 19–20: "Il gruppo delle sante, il gruppo mistico, le due sorelle Santaniello, Annina Casale, la Pessenda, la Scapolatiello, la Borelli, Maria Valente, si mostravano severe e scandolezzate; … si chiamavano sorelle, fra loro."

18 La Marchesa Colombi, "Racconto alla vecchia maniera," in *Cara Speranza*, ed. by Silvia Benatti and Emmanuelle Genevois (Novara: Interlinea, 2003), 121: "L'Amelia, risentita che la sua amica avesse scelto per l'appunto un altro invece di suo fratello, s'era messa a trattarla con freddezza, a stare a distanza, e poco dopo s'era sposata, ed era partita col marito per Oleggio."

19 De Giorgio, *Le italiane dall'Unità a oggi*, 128.

20 Ibid., 128. See also Sofia Bisi Albini, *Le nostre fanciulle. Norme e consigli* (Milan: Vallardi, 1922), 138–9.

21 Fanning, *Gender Meets Genre*, 154.

22 La Marchesa Colombi, *A Small-Town Marriage*, trans. Paula Spurlin Paige (Evanston, IL: Northwestern University Press, 2001), 74: "[D]opo il suo matrimonio non m'aveva più parlato d'Onorato, e si lasciava vedere di rado a casa nostra."

23 Neera, *Teresa*, trans. Martha King (Evanston, IL: Northwestern University Press, 1998), 29: "Studiava, studiava, stringendosi colle mani la zucca, finché il terribile babbo lo stava guardando – salvo a prendersi poi la rivincita, fuori, nelle vie solitarie coperte d'erba, dove i suoi compagni lo aspettavano, bighellonando, nelle ore tiepide del meriggio; e sull'argine, verso i boschi, dove la riva digrada a filo d'acqua, dove crescono abbondanti i cespugli delle more sotto l'ombra lunga dei pioppi."

24 La Marchesa Colombi, *A Small-Town Marriage*, 51: "Avevano affittata una camera, appunto vicino a casa nostra, già da vari anni. E la sera andavano là, si mettevano un fez, e fumavano nella pipa, e si chiamavano Athos, Portos, Aramis e d'Artagnan."

25 Ibid., 8: "Mettevano un panchettino dinanzi alla finestra, tiravano quattro poltroncine basse basse intorno, poi sedevano loro due e facevano seder noi, mettendo tutte e quattro i piedi sullo stesso panchettino 'per star più vicine' dicevano; come se fossimo in gran confidenza. Ma noi, per vicine che si fosse, non si sapeva mai cosa dire. Però loro erano così belline e gentili, e sapevano tante cose, che eravamo contente soltanto di guardarle, e di star a sentire le loro chiacchierine del collegio dov'erano state, e della campagna dove andavano."

26 See Deborah Cartmell and Imelda Whelehan, Introduction to *Sisterhoods: Across the Literature/Media Divide*, ed. by Deborah Cartmell, I.Q. Hunter, Heidi Kaye, and Imelda Whelehan (London: Pluto, 1998), 2.

27 La Marchesa Colombi, "Una Vocazione," in *Cara Speranza*, ed. by Silvia Benatti and Emmanuelle Genevois (Novara: Interlinea, 2003), 106.

28 La Marchesa Colombi, *A Small-Town Marriage*, trans. Spurlin Paige, 33: "Dopo esserci abbracciate e baciate, rimanemmo un po' confuse, perché quelle dimonstrazioni non erano nelle nostre abitudini … Rimanemmo mortificate di quella scena che avevamo fatta, e non osavamo guardarci." See chapter 3 for a discussion of the notion of "social purity" and its significations in the context of early post–Unification Italy.

29 Ibid., 72: "Come mi parvero noiosi quell'anno gli apparecchi del Natale, che in casa nostra si cominciavano otto giorni prima della festa. Di solito si rideva molto con mia sorella, quando si saliva in piedi sui fornelli, sulle tavole, sulla credenza, e fin sul piano del camino per incoronare di lauro le casseruole appese al muro."

30 Neera, *Teresa*, trans. King, 15: "Ne' suoi doveri di giovane massaia aveva ancora l'incertezza dell'inesperienza; ma si sentiva compresa della sua missione di aiutare la mamma."

31 Ibid., 85: "Le gemelle già grandette – avevano dodici anni – nutrivano un sentimento di gelosia per quella sorella a cui tutti volevano bene

e che, nella sua qualità di sorella maggiore, godeva qualche piccolo privilegio."

32 Ibid., 16.: "A un tratto si accostò a suo fratello, passandogli un braccio intorno al collo, chinandosi lievemente, fino ad accarezzare colla guancia i capelli di lui corti ed ispidi come le setole di una spazzola. Egli non avvertí la carezza."

33 Ibid., 73: "[Teresa] gli rimase accanto, aspirando l'odore dello sigaro che gli usciva dalle labbra, beata, finché presa da una vertigine di tenerezza lo baciò improvvisamente nell'angolo della bocca. Egli la respinse, dolcemente, piú dolcemente d'una volta, dandole una palmatina sulla guancia. E poi le chiese a bruciapelo: – Hai l'amante tu?"

34 De Giorgio, Le italiane dall'Unità a oggi, 50.

35 Juliet Mitchell, Siblings: Sex and Violence (Cambridge: Polity Press, 2003), 71.

36 Lucetta Scaraffia, "Essere Uomo, Essere Donna," in La famiglia italiana dall'Ottocento a oggi, ed. Piero Melograni and Lucetta Scaraffia (Rome: Laterza, 1988), 202.

37 Ibid., 204.

38 See also Scaraffia, "Essere Uomo, Essere Donna," 198.

39 Ibid., 205.

40 Ibid., 206.

41 Neera, Fotografie matrimoniali (Catania: Niccolò Giannotta editore, 1898), 14–15:

> Sofia rammenta certe ore lontane, quando adolescente appena nell'angolo quasi buio del focolare, ascoltava i racconti delle Fate e in quel buio le appariva più splendente che mai il manto d'oro della Fata benefica e l'abito tutto a stelle che la sfortunata Cenerentola aveva trovato dentro ad una castagna. E poi altre ore più recenti, altre fantasie vagheggiate nel buio della cameretta di fanciulla, sognando sveglia i rosei misteri dell'amore. Ma non osò dir nulla a suo marito; egli avrebbe tornato a ridere; egli non capiva. Peccato! Era pur un giovine intelligente, buono, gentile. Sarebbe mai vero (come ella aveva udito dire una volta dalla mamma) che gli uomini hanno una maniera d'amare tutta differente da quella delle donne? Ma pure Romeo era un uomo!

42 Neera, Teresa, trans. King, 123: "Arse dallo struggimento femminile che le spinge tutte, religiose ed amanti, a donarsi sopra un altare; a farsi schiave dell'uomo o schiave di Dio. Questo profondo desiderio delle catene, che tormenta le belle anime di donna, ha in sé una voluttà straordinaria; esse attingono nella debolezza quelle gioie medesime che vengono all'uomo dalla forza, e trovano nel cedere una ebbrezza ancor maggiore che gli altri non trovino nel conquistare."

43 See Jessica Benjamin, *The Bonds of Love: Psychoanalysis, Feminism, and the Problem of Domination* (New York: Random House, 1988).

44 Neera, *Teresa*, trans. King, 12: "– Almeno fosse un maschio! – sospirò ancora la signora. – Non ne ha abbastanza di Carlino? – Oh! non per me; ma le ragazze, poverette, che cos'hanno di buono a questo mondo?"

45 De Giorgio, *Le italiane dall'Unità a oggi*, 292.

46 La Marchesa Colombi, *A Small-Town Marriage*, trans. Spurlin Paige, 84; Neera, *Teresa*, trans. King, 178.

47 Eduardo De Albertis, "Non è la logica che preside il matrimonio," in *Il Giornale delle donne*, 5 December 1902: "Vediamo adesso il perché prenda marito la donna. Lo prende primieramente perché le rincresce rimanere zitella, ché anzi, se stesse in lei, lo prenderebbe a diciotto anni, e meno. Lo prende per farsi una posizione … Lo prende per amore … poche volte."

48 De Giorgio, *Le italiane dall'Unità a oggi*, 346–7.

49 Author unknown, "Piccola Posta," *Cordelia*, 15 January 1919: "Trovo che se hai solamente vent'anni puoi attendere in pace anche un lustro per lo meno. Quante si sono sciupate facendo un matrimonio infelice per il timore di rimanere zitelle!"

50 Neera, *Fotografie matrimoniali*, 5: "Ieri appena, fanciulla; oggi, sposa."

51 La Marchesa Colombi, *A Small-Town Marriage*, trans. Spurlin Paige, 83–4.

52 Neera, *L'Indomani* (Palermo: Sellerio editore, 1981), 10: "Era … strano ch'ella si trovasse chiusa nella stessa camera con un uomo che due mesi prima non conosceva neppure."

53 Maria Minicuci, *Notes sur la condition féminine dans un village du sud de l'Italie*, in *Peuples méditerranéens*, nos. 22–23 (1983), cited in Scaraffia, "Essere Uomo, Essere Donna," 199.

54 Neera, *Fotografie matrimoniali*, 6–9: "Salgono in *coupé*. Sofia è molto nervosa, molto commossa', 'Due momenti di silenzio … Silenzio eterno."

55 Matilde Serao, "Checchina's Virtue," trans. Tom Kelso, in *Writing to Delight: Italian Short Stories by Nineteenth-Century Women Writers*, ed. Antonia Arslan and Gabriella Romani (Toronto: University of Toronto Press, 2006), 85–92.

56 Neera, *L'Indomani*, 36: "Quante domande sulle labbra di Marta! Quella donna maritata da dieci anni avrebbe potuto scioglierle una quantità di problemi, ma non osò."

57 Ibid., 57: "Un abisso la separava dall'uomo a cui s'era data, che le era straniero, che non aveva lo stesso sangue, né gli stessi pensieri, né la stessa anima, che aveva vissuto trent'anni senza di lei, ch'ella non aveva mai visto piangere, che trovava inutile dirle: ti amo … e un bisogno irresistibile l'assalse, il bisogno di gettarsi nelle braccia di sua madre."

58 Fanning, *Gender Meets Genre*, 151–2.
59 Neera, *L'Indomani*, 85: "Casa nostra è molto più comoda, più elegante, non ci manca nulla; io lo adorerei, vorrei spiegare per lui solo la mia bellezza, il mio ingegno; so parlare anch'io, non sono una sciocca, ma, a quanto pare, Toniolo, Merelli e gli altri valgono più di me. Io però ho lasciato per lui mia madre, le mie amiche, tutto; e mi basterebbe lui!"
60 Ibid., 85.
61 Serao, "Checchina's Virtue," 22.
62 La Marchesa Colombi, *A Small-Town Marriage*, trans. Spurlin Paige, 40–1: "... l'abitudine di affidare le ragazze ad una serva, press'a poco della loro età, e meno educata di loro ... Ci mettemmo d'accordo per dire alla serva che non ne parlasse con nessuno e via di corsa, perché era assai lontana quella chiesa."
63 Serao, "The State Telegraph Office (*Women's Section*)," in *Unmarried Women: Stories*, trans. Paula Spurlin Paige (Evanston, IL: Northwestern University Press, 1998), 140.
64 See the appendix in this volume, page 156; Serao, "Checchina's Virtue," 20: "... ladra, insolente ... se ne va per ore intiere dalla casa."
65 Serao, "Checchina's Virtue," 21.
66 Serao, "Terno secco," in *La virtù delle donne* (Rome: Avagliano Editore, 1999), 85: "Poi [la serva] guardò in viso la sua signora e le due madri s'intesero, tacitamente, tanto era il turbamento della giovane, tanto era l'affettuosa compassione della più vecchia."
67 Luigi Capuana, *Giacinta* (Milan: Mursia, 1980), 33: "Alle figliuole dovevan badare le mamme. Se fosse stato un bambino, allora sí, sarebbe toccato a lui [il padre]!"
68 Ibid., 31–2: "Non avea fatto gran piacere alla sua mamma [per la quale] [l]a maternità fu ... un peso insopportabile, un impiccio odioso."
69 Serao, "Silvia," in *Dal vero*, ed. by Patricia Bianchi (Naples: Libreria Dante and Descartes, 2000), 188: "Essa sel [*sic.*] sapeva. I figli non possono restare senza madre sulla terra."
70 Neera, *Le idee di una donna e confessioni letterarie* (Florence: Vallecchi, 1977), 7: "Lei morta, tutto peggiorò: il genere di vita, le relazioni, le abitudini. Avevo avuto appena un barlume della società, quando la casa si chiuse in un silenzio di chiostro."
71 See Naomi Segal, "Motherhood," in *Feminism and Psychoanalysis: A Critical Dictionary*, ed. by Elizabeth Wright (Oxford: Blackwell, 1992), 269: "How is feminism to identify a maternal subject incorporating the two 'unknowns': the mother's knowledge and the mother's desire? French post-Lacanian feminists attempt the latter. In their search for a

representable femininity which displaces phallocentrism, Cixous, Irigaray and Kristeva look to a language (written, spoken, or something else)
of female bodily identity. The connectedness of mother and daughter,
the fluidity of women's *jouissance* and plurality of its organs, the ecstasy
of birth, the idea of a matriolatry free of Christianity's virginity cult,
and utterance tied to the maternal/pre-Oedipal – all these are ways of
putting desire outside the symbolic." See also Adrienne Rich, *Of Woman
Born: Motherhood as Experience and Institution* (1977; reprint, London:
Virago, 1986).

72 De Giorgio, *Le italiane italiane dall'Unità a oggi*, 353.
73 Serao, "Silvia," 181: "Camminando a passi cheti e moderati, dritta nelle
   pieghe rigide, quasi monacali, del suo abito nero ... parlando poco, sorridendo molto meno, pensando pochissimo."
74 Ibid., 182: "La donna di prima, lettera morta, pagina bianca, era scom-
   parsa ... ed era subentrata la donna completa, viva, forte e buona: la madre."
75 Neera, *L'Indomani*, 143: "Sentiva le sue viscere commoversi sotto un
   impulso di persona viva, colla strana rivelazione di un altro essere in se
   stessa. Sembrava una piccola mano che battesse contro il suo seno, una piccola mano che voleva dire: Aprimi, io sono l'amore e la verità."
76 Neera, *Teresa*, trans. King, 14:

> Lo sguardo della signora Soave si arrestò con compiacenza sopra un bambinel-
> lo di cera coperto da una campana di vetro. Quel bambinello giallino, con due
> puntini neri al di sopra di un piccolo rialzo che simulava il naso; quel bambinello
> dall'espressione dolce e rassegnata, coricato da più che vent'anni in mezzo ai fiori
> di carta e alle striscioline d'argento che gli ornavano la culla; quel bambino nudo
> e santo attirava in modo particolare la tenerezza della signora che si sentiva strug-
> gere di amore e di rispetto; con una voglia di piangere, una voglia di baciarlo, e una
> voglia di raccomandarsi alle sue manine benedette. La grandezza di Dio, rappresen-
> tata da quel piccolo bambino, la colpiva di uno stupore pietoso e devoto. Si alzò, e,
> movendosi a stento, andò a deporre un bacio sulla campana di vetro; restando poi
> immobile, colle mani giunte, assorta in una contemplazione dolorosa."

77 Angela Dalle Vacche, *Diva: Defiance and Passion in Early Italian Cinema*
   (Austin: University of Texas Press, 2008), 7.
78 See Ursula Fanning, "Maternal Prescriptions and Descriptions in Post–
   Unification Italy," in *Women and Gender in Post-Unification Italy: Between
   Public and Private Spheres*, ed. Katharine Mitchell and Helena Sanson
   (Oxford: Peter Lang, 2013), 13–38, for recent work on motherhood. For a
   recent study of motherhood in Neera's works, see Catherine Ramsey-
   Portolano, "A Modern Feminist Reading of the Maternal Instinct in

Neera," in "Rethinking Neera," ed. by Katharine Mitchell and Catherine Ramsey-Portolano, special supplement, *The Italianist* 30 (2010): 50–68. In her article "Parturition, Parting, and Paradox," Cristina Mazzoni argues that turn-of-the-century Italian literary texts repeatedly try to break the silence that enshrouds the subjects of childbirth. See Cristina Mazzoni, "Parturition, Parting, and Paradox in Turn-of-the-Century Italian Literature (D'Annunzio, Aleramo, Neera)," *Forum Italicum*, 31 (1997): 343–66. Her analysis examines how Neera's novels identify childbirth with woman's pain, undoing and death. Discussing Neera's *Teresa*, Mazzoni draws attention to the portrayal of Teresa's mother, who, having recently given birth, "would look down at her thin breast where yet another daughter was attached, and feel even sadder" (30), and Teresa's aunt, who "had had sixteen or seventeen children, but had never known love, never been loved. Continually nursing or pregnant, she was absorbed in these cares and, beguiled or satisfied by the appearance of love, she didn't feel the lack of it" (36).

79 Paolo Mantegazza and Neera, *Dizionario d'igiene per le famiglie* (1881; reprint, Florence: R. Bemporad and Figlio, 1901), 9–12. In 1870, Eugenio Fazio in his *La Donna. Pensieri* (Women. Thoughts) cited Letourneau's reference to puberty in his *Fisiologia delle passioni* (Physiology of passions, 1870), pathologizing women's bodies by referring to menstruation as "*a continuous illness.* [Women] receive a love-wound every month," 47. Fazio's italics. Antonio Marro's *La pubertà studiata nell'uomo e nella donna* (Puberty studied in man and woman) (Turin: Fratelli Bocca Editore, 1897) was the first major scientific study on adolescence in the new Italy.

80 Neera, "Paolina," trans. Elena Past, in *Writing to Delight: Italian Short Stories by Nineteenth-Century Women Writers,* ed. Antonia Arslan and Gabriella Romani (Toronto: University of Toronto Press, 2006), 61. See "Paolina" [1881] in *Neera,* ed. by Benedetto Croce (Milan: Garzanti, 1943), 661: "Tu sei oramai una donnetta e certe cose le puoi comprendere ... Sai che devono accadere grandi cose? ... Diedi un balzo, come i puledri quando accennano ad imbizzarrire. Ero retrograda fino al midollo delle ossa; tutti i cambiamenti mi sgomentavano."

81 Neera, *Teresa*, trans. King, 14: "Questa notte avrai un altro fratellino ... sono cose che capirai piú tardi ... ma già sei la maggiore tu, devi pur saperlo."

82 Ibid., 15: "Teresina rimase immobile, appoggiata allo stipite dell'uscio, con una oppressione in gola e un turbamento improvviso ... Le poche parole

della madre, pronunciate lí sull'uscio, nel turbamento della notte, l'avevano profondamente impressionata. Si sentiva a un tratto fatta donna – con un presentimento improvviso di dolori lontani, con una responsabilità nuova, con un pudore bizzarro, misto di una straordinaria dolcezza."

83 See *The Irigaray Reader*, ed. by Margaret Whitford (Oxford: Blackwell, 1991), 2.

84 The italics are mine. See Margaret Whitford, "Mother–Daughter Relationship," in *Feminism and Psychoanalysis: A Critical Dictionary*, ed. Elizabeth Wright (Oxford: Blackwell, 1992), 263: "Horizontal relations between women – sisterhood – will only be possible if the vertical relationship – the maternal genealogy – has been given cultural recognition, if, that is, women's desire for, and love of, the mother is given a voice."

85 See Graziella Parati and Rebecca West, eds., *Italian Feminist Theory and Practice. Equality and Sexual Difference* (London: Associated University Press, 2002), 21.

86 Libreria delle Donne di Milano, *Non credere di avere dei diritti* (Turin: Rosenberg and Sellier, 1987), 18.

87 Serao, "Terno secco," 84.

88 Neera, *Teresa*, trans. King, 179: "Teresina viveva quasi esclusivamente in compagnia della madre inferma – riparate tutte e due dall'aria, coi piedi sullo stesso sgabello, sorridendosi tristamente."

89 Ibid., 53–4: "Teresina aveva un desiderio pazzo di raccontarle [alla signora Soave] il suo segreto, ma in quel momento non osò ... L'occasione era favorevole, sulle labbra della fanciulla bruciava il nome di Cecchino: ella non aveva parlato del ballo che per giungere a parlare di lui; voleva dir tutto, tutto alla mamma. Ma quel nome non uscí. Due o tre sforzi ancora rimasero infruttuosi; un nodo inesplicabile le stringeva la gola, il cuore le batteva disordinatamente."

90 Ibid., 83: "Per sua madre, Teresina aveva una tenerezza, un culto; e la madre la ricambiava con un affetto triste, pieno di sottintesi dolorosi. Non si erano mai fatte confidenze, non ne avevano il temperamento, fors'anche era mancata l'occasione di incominciare: ma quando nelle ore di riposo, durante i sonni o le assenze dell'Ida, le due donne sedevano accanto alla eterna finestra, il loro silenzio aveva una voce."

91 Ibid., 134: "Ella non sapeva dell'amore di sua figlia per fatti o confidenze avute; ma lo vedeva aleggiare nell'aria, lo intuiva dagli sguardi vaganti della fanciulla – forse si illudeva, nel suo cieco affetto di madre, nella sua tenerezza di donna, che l'amore ha resa infelice e che sorride ancora all'amore. Certo non ebbe bisogno di chiedere il nome dell'amante di Teresina."

92 Ibid., 137: "Madre e figlia piansero nel leggerla."
93 Sandra Gilbert and Susan Gubar, *The Madwoman in the Attic*, 2nd ed. (New Haven: Yale University Press, 2000), 504.
94 Marianne Hirsch, *The Mother/Daughter Plot: Narrative, Psychoanalysis, Feminism* (Bloomington: Indiana University Press, 1989), 33.
95 Neera, *L'Indomani*, 71: "… perché non le avevano detto: Tu entrerai, ignota, nel letto di un ignoto; il vostro contatto sarà senza delirio e i vostri cuori si avvicineranno senza fondersi?"
96 Ibid., 136: "… un pudore ed un orgoglio di donna."
97 Ibid.: "Tacquero, trascinate entrambe dai loro pensieri, divise per modo che dopo un po' di tempo si guardarono in faccia disorientate. Molto c'era da dire da una parte e dall'altra; immenso il desiderio di chiedere, di confidare … Per farla parlare, la signora Oldofredi si interessò alle nuove relazioni di sua figlia."
98 Ibid., 143: "… vivere nella continua illusione dell'amore; per questo abbiamo la religione e la maternità."
99 Ibid.: "Marta non udiva, delle parole di sua madre, che il bisbiglio."

Conclusion

1 Salvatore Battaglia, *Grande dizionario della lingua italiana*, 1st ed. (Turin: UTET, 1998), 487: "… vincolo naturale e affettivo che unisce le sorelle; complicità femminile, solidarietà fra donne."
2 Niccolò Tommaseo and Bernardo Bellini, *Dizionario della lingua italiana* (Turin: UTET, 1861–79), 1015.
3 Michela De Giorgio, *Le italiane dall'Unità a oggi: modelli culturali e comportamenti sociali* (Rome: Laterza, 1992), 126.
4 See Alba della Fazia Amoia, *Twentieth-Century Italian Women Writers: The Feminine Experience* (Carbondale: Southern Illinois University Press, 1996), 93; Antonia Arslan, *Dame, galline e regine: la scrittura femminile italiana fra '800 e '900*, ed. by Marina Pasqui, with a preface by Siobhan Nash-Marshall (Milan: Guerini Studio, 1998), 165.
5 "Buoni libri," *Museo di famiglia*, 15 January 1877 (author unknown): "Foggiato alla moderna, scritto con garbo, e che si legge con gran piacere."
6 Emilia Mariani, "Lettera Aperta a Matilde Serao," *La Donna*, 10 October 1883; Adele Maiani Nulli, "Lettera Aperta a Neera," *L'Italia femminile*, 16 April 1899.
7 Lucienne Kroha, *The Woman Writer in Late-Nineteenth-Century Italy: Gender and the Formation of Literary Identity* (Lewiston, NY: E. Mellen Press, 1992), 16–17.

8 Elaine Showalter, *A Literature of Their Own: From Charlotte Brontë to Doris Lessing* (London: Virago, 1999), 15–16.

9 Mary Poovey, *The Proper Lady and the Woman Writer* (Chicago: University of Chicago Press, 1984), x.

Appendix

1 Torriani's mother, Carolina Imperatori, was required to work after her husband's death. She was employed at a "Canobiane" primary school for girls; the name derives from Amico Canobio who founded the first state schools in Novara. She taught a class of forty-eight pupils and earned 350 lire per annum. She worked there for six years while raising her two children and doing extra work to pay off debts. See Giovanni Silengo and Silvia Benatti, "Immagini e documenti di una vita," in *La Marchesa Colombi: una scrittrice e il suo tempo*, ed. Silvia Benatti and Roberto Cicala (Novara: Interlinea Edizioni, 2001), 222.

2 See La Marchesa Colombi, *La creola e il violino di Cremona: i libretti d'opera della Marchesa Colombi*, ed. by Maria Grazia Cossu (Padova: Il poligrafo, 2011).

3 La Marchesa Colombi, *La gente per bene: leggi di convenienza sociale* (Novara: Interlinea, 2000), 83: "La lettera comincia con quello che s'ha a dire, e finisce quando non s'ha più nulla a dire. Ecco la sola regola ch'io ammetto. Non si firmino mai *serva*, perchè le signore non sono mai serve di nessuno."

4 Neera, *Una giovinezza del secolo XIX* (Milan: Feltrinelli, 1975), 119: "Scrivevo non pensando a scrivere. Se i libri e la penna mi confortavano nel tedio monotono della mia esistenza, non è tuttavia su di essi che fissavo lo sguardo per l'avvenire." For a recent collective study on Neera, see Katharine Mitchell and Catherine Ramsey-Portolano, eds., "Rethinking Neera," special supplement, *The Italianist* 30, Supplement-1 (2010).

5 Neera, *Il libro di mio figlio*, in *Neera*, ed. by Benedetto Croce, 2nd ed. (1891; reprint, Milan: Garzanti, 1943), 701–49; Neera, *Battaglie per un'idea* (Milan: Galli di Baldini, Castoldi e c., 1898), now available in full-text on the Italian Women Writers' database at http://www.lib.uchicago.edu/efts/IWW (accessed 17 July 2013); Neera, *L'amor platonico*, in *Neera*, 751–75.

6 Neera, "Preface," *Le idee di una donna*, 37: "La donna non si riconosce più nella integrità del proprio valore, ed è questo valore suo che difendo con schietto ardore, dedicando i miei sforzi alle donne che accettano con semplicità e nobilmente la loro grande missione, facendo cioè del femminismo vero."

7 Antonia Arslan, *Dame, droga e galline: romanzo popolare e romanzo di consumo fra '800 e '900* (Padova: CLEUP, 1977), 95.

8 See Matilde Serao, *Unmarried Women: Stories*, trans. Paula Spurlin Paige (Evanston, IL: Northwestern University Press, 2007).

9 Cited in *Donne del giornalismo: da Eleonora Fonseca a Ilaria Alpi: dizionario storico bio-bibliografico, secoli XVIII-XX*, ed. by Laura Pisano (Milan: Franco Angeli, 2004), 342.

10 Serao transferred the column to future newspapers that she worked on and/or founded: *Corriere di Roma; Corriere di Napoli; Il Mattino; La Settimana. Rassegna di Lettere, arti e scienze; Il Giorno.*

Bibliography

Aleramo, Sibilla. *A Woman*. Translated by Rosalind Delmar. Berkeley: University of California Press, 1980.

–. *Una donna*. 1906. Reprint, Milan: Feltrinelli, 1998.

Allum, Percy. "Catholicism." In *The Cambridge Companion to Modern Italian Culture*, edited by Zygmunt G. Barański and Rebecca West. 2nd ed. Cambridge: Cambridge University Press, 2004.

Althusser, Louis. *Lenin and Philosophy, and Other Essays*. Translated by B. Brewster. London: New Left Books, and New York: Monthly Review Press, 1971.

Amoia, Alba della Fazia. *Twentieth-Century Italian Women Writers: The Feminine Experience*. Carbondale: Southern Illinois University Press, 1996.

Appignanesi, Lisa, and John Forrester. *Freud's Women*. London: Penguin, 2000.

Armstrong, Nancy. *Desire and Domestic Fiction: A Political History of the Novel*. Oxford: Oxford University Press, 1987.

Arslan, Antonia. *Dame, droga e galline: romanzo popolare e romanzo di consumo fra '800 e '900*. Padova: CLEUP, 1977.

–. "Un'amicizia tra letterate: Vittoria Aganoor e Neera. (Con appendice di lettere)." *Quaderni veneti* 4, no. 8 (1988): 35–74.

–. "Un progetto culturale temerario e il suo fallimento: 'Vita Intima' (1890–91)." In *Donne e giornalismo: percorsi e presenze di una storia di genere*, edited by Silvia Franchini and Simonetta Soldani, Studi e Ricerche di Storia dell'Editoria, 23. Milan: Franco Angeli, 2004.

Arslan, Antonia, and Gabriella Romani, eds. *Writing to Delight: Italian Short Stories by Nineteenth-Century Women Writers*. Toronto: University of Toronto Press, 2006.

Attfield, Judy. *Wild Things: The Material Culture of Everyday Life*. Oxford: Berg, 2000.

Baccini, Ida. *La mia vita*. Rome: Società Editrice Dante Alighieri, 1904.

Balbo, Cesare. *Delle speranze d'Italia*. Florence: Le Monnier, 1844.

–. *Pensieri ed esempi*. Turin: UTET, 1857.

Baldacci, Luigi. "Nota introduttiva." In Neera, *Teresa*, Centopagine 42. Turin: Einaudi, 1976.

Banti, Alberto. *Il Risorgimento italiano*. Rome: Laterza, 2004.

Banti, Anna. *Il coraggio delle donne: racconti*. Milan: La Tartaruga, 1983.

–. *Serao*. Turin: UTET, 1965.

Battaglia, Salvatore. *Grande dizionario della lingua italiana*. Vol. 5, *L'età contemporanea e l'italiano odierno*. Turin: Unione Tipografico-Editrice, 1998.

Baym, Nina. *Woman's Fiction: A Guide to Novels by and about Women in America, 1820–1870*. Ithaca, NY: Cornell University Press, 1978.

Beizer, Janet L. *Ventriloquized Bodies: Narratives of Hysteria in Nineteenth-Century France*. Ithaca, NY: Cornell University Press, 1994.

Belsey, Catherine. *Critical Practice*. London: Routledge, 1980.

Benjamin, Jessica. *The Bonds of Love: Psychoanalysis, Feminism, and the Problem of Domination*. New York: Random House, 1988.

Bertoni Jovine, Dina. "Funzione emancipatrice della scuola e contributo della donna all'attività educativa." In *L'emancipazione femminile in Italia: un secolo di discussioni*. Florence: La Nuova Italia, 1963.

Bisi Albini, Sofia. *Le nostre fanciulle. Norme e consigli*. Milan: Vallardi, 1922.

Boggio, Maricia. *Anna Kuliscioff*. Venice: Marsilio, 1977.

Bollas, Christopher. *Hysteria*. London: Routledge, 2000.

Bourneville, Désiré, and Paul Régnard. *Iconographie photographique de la Salpêtrière*. 3 vols. Paris: Delahaye and Co., 1876–80.

Briganti, Alessandra. "Matilde Serao: un profilo." In *Svelamento, Sibilla Aleramo: una biografia intellettuale*, edited by Annarita Buttafuoco and Maria Zancan. Milan: Feltrinelli, 1988.

Bronfen, Elisabeth. "Gustave Flaubert's *Madame Bovary* and the Discourse of Hysteria." *Nineteenth-Century Prose* 23, no. 1 (1998): 65–99.

–. *The Knotted Subject: Hysteria and Its Discontents*. Princeton, NJ: Princeton University Press, 1998.

Brooks, Peter. *Realist Vision*. New Haven: Yale University Press, 2005.

Butler, Judith. *Gender Trouble: Feminism and the Subversion of Identity*. 1990. Reprint, New York: Routledge, 1999.

Buttafuoco, Annarita. *Questioni di cittadinanza: donne e diritti sociali nell'Italia liberale*. Siena: Protagon Editori Toscani, 1997.

Caldwell, Lesley. *Italian Family Matters: Women, Politics and Legal Reform*. London: Macmillan, 1991.

Capuana, Luigi. *Giacinta*. 1879. Reprint, Rome: Riuniti, 1980.

Cartmell Deborah, and Imelda Whelehan. Introduction to *Sisterhoods: Across the Literature/Media Divide*, edited by Deborah Cartmell, I.Q. Hunter, Heidi Kaye, and Imelda Whelehan. London: Pluto Press, 1998.

Cattaneo, Carlo. "Sul romanzo delle donne contemporanee in Italia." In *Opere edite e inedite*, edited by Agostino Bertani. Florence: Le Monnier, 1863.

Cento Bull, Anna. "Social and Political Cultures in Italy from 1860 to the Present Day." In *The Cambridge Companion to Modern Italian Culture*, edited by Zygmunt G. Barański, and Rebecca J. West. Cambridge: Cambridge University Press, 2001.

Chodorow, Nancy. *The Reproduction of Mothering: Psychoanalysis and the Sociology of Gender*. Berkeley: University of California Press, 1978.

Cixous, Hélène. "The Laugh of the Medusa." In *The Signs Reader: Women, Gender, and Scholarship*, edited by Elizabeth Abel and Emily K. Abel. Chicago: University of Chicago Press, 1983.

Clark, Martin. *Modern Italy*. 10th ed. London: Longman, 1995.

Clément, Catherine. *Opera, or the Undoing of Women*. Translated by Betsy Wing. Minneapolis: University of Minnesota Press, 1988.

Colley, Linda. *Britons: Forging the Nation, 1707–1837*. London: Vintage, 1996.

Cometto, Maria Teresa. *La Marchesa Colombi: la prima giornalista del Corriere della sera*. Turin: Blu, 1996.

–. "Marchesa Colombi e Neera." In *Ritratto di signora: Neera (Anna Radius Zuccari) e il suo tempo*, edited by Antonia Arslan and Marina Pasqui. Milan: Comune di Milano, 1999.

Covato, Carmela. "Educate ad educare: ruolo materno ed itinerari formativi." In *L'educazione delle donne: scuole e modelli di vita femminile nell'Italia dell'Ottocento*. 2nd ed. Milan: Franco Angeli, 1991.

Croce, Benedetto. *Neera*. 2nd ed. Milan: Garzanti, 1943.

Crowley, John E. "Inventing Comfort: The Piazza." In *American Material Culture: The Shape of the Field*, edited by Ann Smart Martin and J. Ritchie Garrison. Winterthur, DE: Henry Francis du Pont Winterthur Museum, 1997.

Dalle Vacche, Angela. *Diva: Defiance and Passion in Early Italian Cinema*. Austin: University of Texas Press, 2008.

Darwin, Charles. *L'origine dell'uomo e la scelta in rapporto col sesso*. Translated by A. Di Michele Lessona. Turin: Unione tipografico-editrice, 1871.

–. *Sull'origine delle specie per elezione naturale, ovvero Conservazione delle razze perfezionate nella lotta per l'esistenza*. Translated by Giovanni Canestrini e Leonardo Salimbeni. Modena: N. Zanichelli e Soci, 1864.

Dau Novelli, Cecilia. "Modelli di comportamento e ruoli familiari." In *Borghesi e imprenditori a Milano: Dall'Unità alla prima guerra mondiale*, edited by Giorgio Fiocco. Bari: Laterza, 1984.

Davidoff, Leonore. "Regarding some "Old Husbands' Tales": Public and Private in Feminist History." In *Worlds Between: Historical Perspectives on Gender and Class*. Cambridge: Polity Press, 1995.

De Certeau, Michel. *The Practice of Everyday Life*. Translated by Steven Rendall. Berkeley: University of California Press, 1984.

De Fort, Ester. *Storia della scuola elementare in Italia*. Vol. 1, *Dall'Unità all'età giolittiana*. Milan: Feltrinelli, 1979.

De Giorgio, Michela. *Le italiane dall'Unità a oggi: modelli culturali e comportamenti sociali*. Rome: Laterza, 1992.

–. "The Catholic Model." In *A History of Women in the West*. Vol. 4, *Emerging Feminism from Revolution to World War*, edited by Geneviève Fraisse and Michelle Perrot. Cambridge, MA: Belknap Press, 1993.

De Nicola, Francesco, and Pier Antonio Zannoni. *Scrittrici, giornaliste: da Matilde Serao a Susanna Tamaro*. Venice: Marsilio, 2001.

De Nunzio Schilardi, Wanda. *L'invenzione del reale: studi su Matilde Serao*. Bari: Palomar, 2004.

Deutsch, Helene. *The Psychology of Women: A Psychoanalytic Interpretation*. New York: Grune and Stratton, 1944.

Didi-Huberman, Georges. *Invention de l'hystérie. Charcot et l'iconographie de la Salpêtrière*. Paris: Macula, 1982.

Eger, Elizabeth, Charlotte Grant, Cliona Ó Gallchoir, and Penny Warburton, eds. *Women, Writing and the Public Sphere 1700–1830*. Cambridge: Cambridge University Press, 2001.

Fanning, Ursula. "Enclosure, Escape and the Erotic: Shadows of the Self in the Writings of Grazia Deledda." In *Grazia Deledda: The Challenge of Modernity*, edited by Sharon Wood. Leicester: Troubador, 2007.

–. *Gender Meets Genre: Woman as Subject in the Fictional Universe of Matilde Serao*. Dublin: Irish Academic Press, 2002.

–. "Maternal Prescriptions and Descriptions in Post–Unification Italy." In *Women and Gender in Post–Unification Italy: Between Public and Private Spheres*, edited by Katharine Mitchell and Helena Sanson. Oxford: Peter Lang, 2013.

Farinelli, Giuseppe. *Storia del giornalismo italiano: dalle origini ai nostri giorni*. Turin: UTET, 1997.

Flaubert, Gustave. *Madame Bovary*. Translator unknown. 1857. Reprint, London: Penguin, 1995.

Flint, Kate. *The Woman Reader, 1837–1914*. Oxford: Clarendon Press, 1993.

Franceschi-Ferrucci, Caterina. *Della educazione morale della donna: libri tre*. 3rd ed. Florence: Le Monnier, 1875.

Franchini, Silvia. "Cultura nazionale e prodotti d'importazione: alle origini di un archetipo italiano di 'stampa femminile.'" In *Donne e giornalismo*, edited by Silvia Franchini and Simonetta Soldani, Studi e Ricerche di Storia dell'Editoria, 23. Milan: Franco Angeli, 2004.

–. "Donne e Stampa Periodica: Un Nuovo Repertorio Regionale." In *Giornali di donne in Toscana: Un catalogo, molte storie (1770–1945)*. Florence: Leo S. Olschki, 2007.

Freud, Sigmund, and Joseph Breuer. *Studies in Hysteria*. Translated by Nicola Luckhurst, with an introduction by Rachel Bowlby. London: Penguin Books, 2004.

Gabrielli, Patrizia. "Protagonists and Politics in the Italian Women's Movement: A Reflection on the Work of Annarita Buttafuoco." *Journal of Modern Italian Studies* 7, no. 1 (2002): 74–87.

Genevois, Emmanuelle. "Da Maria Antonietta Torriani a 'La Marchesa Colombi': gli esordi di una scrittrice tra giornalismo e letteratura." In *La Marchesa Colombi: una scrittrice e il suo tempo: Atti del Convegno Internazionale, Novara 26 maggio 2000*, edited by Silvia Benatti and Roberto Cicala, with an introductory essay by Antonia Arslan. Novara: Interlinea Edizioni, 2001.

Gibson, Mary. *Prostitution and the State in Italy, 1860–1915*. New Brunswick, NJ: Rutgers University Press, 1986.

Giglio, Raffaele. *Per la storia di un'amicizia: D'Annunzio, Hérelle, Scarfoglio, Serao: documenti inediti*. Naples: Loffredo, 1977.

Gilbert, Sandra M., and Susan Gubar. *The Madwoman in the Attic*. 2nd ed. New Haven: Yale University Press, 2000.

Gilman, Charlotte Perkins. *The Yellow Wallpaper*, 15th ed. 1899. Reprint, London: Virago, 2005.

Ginzburg, Natalia. "La condizione femminile." In *Vita immaginaria*. Milan: Mondadori, 1974.

–. "Le donne negli scritti di Matilde Serao." *La Stampa*, 6 January 1977.

–. *Lessico famigliare*. Turin: Einaudi, 1966.

–. "Nota introduttiva." In La Marchesa Colombi, *Un matrimonio in provincia*. Centopagine, 23. Turin: Einaudi, 1973.

Goldstein, Jan. "The Hysteria Diagnosis and the Politics of Anticlericalism in Late-Nineteenth-Century France." *Journal of Modern History* 54 (1982): 209–39.

Gori, Claudia. "Oltre domani: futuro, progresso e divino nell'emancipazione italiano tra Otto e Novecento." *Storia delle donne* 1 (2005): 239–55.

Gramone, Antonella. "La Marchesa Colombi tra mode e modelli." In *La Marchesa Colombi: una scrittrice e il suo tempo*. Novara: Interlinea Edizioni, 2001.

Habermas, Jürgen. *The Structural Transformation of the Public Sphere: An Enquiry into a Category of Bourgeois Society*. Translated by Thomas Burger, with the assistance of Frederick Lawrence. 9th ed. Cambridge: Polity Press, 2006.

Hallamore Caesar, Ann. "Crossing the Public/Private Divide: The *Salotto* and the Theatre in Late-Nineteenth-Century Italy." In *Theatre, Opera, and Performance in Italy from the Fifteenth Century to the Present: Essays in Honour of Richard Andrews*, edited by Brian Richardson, Simon Gilson and Catherine Keen. Leeds: Maney, 2004.

–. "Women Readers and the Novel in Nineteenth-Century Italy." *Italian Studies*, 56 (2001): 80–97.

–. "Writing by Women in Post-Unification Literary Culture: The Case for De-segregation." In *Women and Gender in Post-Unification Italy: Between Public and Private Spheres*, edited by Katharine Mitchell and Helena Sanson. Oxford: Peter Lang, 2013.

Hallamore Caesar, Ann, and Michael Caesar. *Modern Italian Literature*. Cambridge: Polity Press, 2007.

Hallamore Caesar, Ann, Gabriella Romani, and Jennifer Burns, eds. *The Printed Media in Fin-de-Siècle Italy: Publishers, Writers, and Readers*. London: MHRA and Maney, 2011.

Hamon, Philippe. *Expositions: Literature and Architecture in Nineteenth-Century France*. Translated by Katia Sainson-Frank and Lisa Maguire. Berkeley: University of California Press, 1992.

Harrowitz, Nancy. *Antisemitism, Misogyny, and the Logic of Cultural Difference: Cesare Lombroso and Matilde Serao*. Lincoln: University of Nebraska Press, 1994.

Hirsch, Marianne. *The Mother/Daughter Plot: Narrative, Psychoanalysis, Feminism*. Bloomington: Indiana University Press, 1989.

Hollinger, Karen. *In the Company of Women: Contemporary Female Friendship Films*. Minneapolis: University of Minnesota Press, 1998.

Hosker, Lucy. "The Spinster in the Works of Neera and Matilde Serao: Other or Mother?" In *Women and Gender in Post–Unification Italy: Between Public and Private Spheres*, edited by Katharine Mitchell and Helena Sanson. Oxford: Peter Lang, 2013.

Infusino, Gianni. "Aristocrazia e popolo (Le donne negli scritti di Matilde Serao)." In *Matilde Serao tra giornalismo e letteratura*, edited by Gianni Infusino. Naples: Guida Editori, 1981.

Irigaray, Luce. *This Sex Which Is Not One*. Translated by Catherine Porter, with Carolyn Burke. Ithaca, NY: Cornell University Press, 1985.

James, William. "What Is an Emotion?" *Mind* 9 (1884): 188–205.

Jones, Verina. "Journalism, 1750–1850." In *A History of Women's Writing in Italy*, edited by Letizia Panizza and Sharon Wood. Cambridge: Cambridge University Press, 2000.

Kristeva, Julia. *Desire in Language*. Translated by Leon S. Roudiez. Oxford: Basil Blackwell, 1980.

Kroha, Lucienne. *The Woman Writer in Late-Nineteenth-Century Italy: Gender and the Formation of Literary Identity*. Lewiston, NY: E. Mellen Press, 1992.

La Marchesa Colombi. *A Small-Town Marriage*. Translated by Paula Spurlin Paige. Evanston, IL: Northwestern University Press, 2001.

–. "Dear Hope." Translated by Lina Insana. In *Writing to Delight: Italian Short Stories by Nineteenth-Century Women Writers*, edited by Antonia Arslan and Gabriella Romani. Toronto: University of Toronto Press, 2006.

–. "In provincia." In *Serate d'inverno*. Ferrara: Luciana Tufani Editrice, 1997.

–. *Il tramonto di un ideale*. 1882. Reprint, Ferrara: Luciana Tufani Editrice, 1997.

–. *La creola e il violino di Cremona: i libretti d'opera della Marchesa Colombi*, edited by Maria Grazia Cossu. Padova: Il poligrafo, 2011.

–. *La gente per bene: leggi di convenienza sociale*. 1877. Reprint, Novara: Interlinea Edizioni, 2000.

–. "Learn a Trade for a Rainy Day." Translated by by Lina Insana. In *Writing to Delight: Italian Short Stories by Nineteenth-Century Women Writers*, edited by Antonia Arslan and Gabriella Romani. Toronto: University of Toronto Press, 2006.

–. "Paolina." Translated by Elena Past. In *Writing to Delight: Italian Short Stories by Nineteenth-Century Women Writers*, edited by Antonia Arslan and Gabriella Romani. Toronto: University of Toronto Press, 2006.

–. *Prima morire*. 1881. Reprint, Rome: Lucarini Editore, 1988.

–. "Racconto alla vecchia maniera." In *Cara Speranza*, edited by Silvia Benatti and Emmanuelle Genevois. Novara: Interlinea, 2003.

–. *Serate d'inverno*. 1879. Reprint, Ferrara: Luciana Tufani Editrice, 1997.

–. *Un matrimonio in provincia*. 1885. Reprint, Novara: Interlinea, 1999.

–. "Una Vocazione." In *Cara Speranza*, edited by Silvia Benatti and Emmanuelle Genevois. Novara: Interlinea, 2003.

–. "Winter Evenings." Translated by Lina Insana. In *Writing to Delight: Italian Short Stories by Nineteenth-Century Women Writers*, edited by Antonia Arslan and Gabriella Romani. Toronto: University of Toronto Press, 2006.

Lefebvre, Henri. *Everyday Life in the Modern World*. London: Penguin, 1971.

–. "The Everyday and Everydayness." *Yale French Studies* 73 (1987): 7–11.

–. *The Production of Space*. Translated by Donald Nicholson-Smith. Oxford: Blackwell, 1996.

Libreria delle Donne di Milano, *Non credere di avere dei diritti* . Turin: Rosenberg and Sellier, 1987.

Lombroso, Cesare, and Guglielmo Ferrero. *Criminal Woman, the Prostitute, and the Normal Woman*. Translated by Nicole Hahn Rafter and Mary Gibson. Durham, NC: Duke University Press, 2004.

Mack Smith, Denis. *Italy: A Modern History*. Ann Arbor: University of Michigan Press, 1969.

–. *Modern Italy. A Political History*. New Haven: Yale University Press, 1997.

Manacorda, Giuliano. "L'opera di Matilde Serao entro l'ipotesi gramsciana di una lettura nazional-popolare." In *Matilde Serao tra giornalismo e letteratura*, edited by Gianni Infusino. Naples: Guida Editori, 1981.

Mantegazza, Paolo, and Neera. *Dizionario d'igiene per le famiglie*. 1881. Reprint, Florence: R. Bemporad and Figlio, 1901.

Marchesini, Daniele. "L'analfabetismo femminile nell'Italia dell'Ottocento: caratteristiche e dinamiche." In *L'educazione delle donne: scuole e modelli di vita femminile nell'Italia dell'Ottocento*, edited by Simonetta Soldani. 2nd ed. Milan: Franco Angeli, 1991.

Maudsley, Henry. *Fisiologia e patologia dello spirito*. Translated by Domenico Collina. Naples: Vincenzo Pasquale, 1872.

Mazzoni, Cristina. "Parturition, Parting, and Paradox in Turn-of-the-Century Italian Literature (D'Annunzio, Aleramo, Neera)." *Forum Italicum*, 31 (1997): 343–66.

Meehan, J. ed., *Feminists Read Habermas: Gendering the Subject of Discourse*. New York: Routledge, 1995.

Merrick, Elizabeth. *This Is Not Chick Lit: Original Stories by America's Best Women Writers*. New York: Random House, 2006.

Micale, Mark S. *The Mind of Modernism: Medicine, Psychology, and the Cultural Arts in Europe and America, 1880–1940*. Stanford: Stanford University Press, 2004.

Mill, John Stuart. *La servitù delle donne*. Translated by Anna Maria Mozzoni. Milan: F. Legros, 1870.

Mitchell, Juliet. *Siblings: Sex and Violence*. Cambridge: Polity Press, 2003.

Mitchell, Katharine. "La Marchesa Colombi, Neera, Matilde Serao: Forging a Female Solidarity in Late Nineteenth-Century Journals for Women." *Italian Studies* 63, no. 1 (2008): 63–84.

–. "Narrativizing Female Experience in Late Nineteenth-Century Italy through Domestic Fiction." *Rethinking History: the Journal of Theory and Practice* 15, no. 3 (2010): 483–501.

–. "Neera's Refiguring of Hysteria as *Nervosismo* in *Teresa* and *L'Indomani*." In "Rethinking Neera," edited by Katharine Mitchell and Catherine Ramsey-Portolano, special supplement, *The Italianist* 30, Supplement 1 (2010): 101–22.

–. "Sorelle in arte (e politica)': The 'Woman Question' and Female Solidarity at the *Fin de Siècle.*" In *Women and Gender in Post–Unification Italy: Between Public and Private Spheres*, edited by Katharine Mitchell and Helena Sanson. Oxford: Peter Lang, 2013.

Mitchell, Sally. "Sentiment and Suffering: Women's Recreational Reading in the 1860s." *Victorian Studies* 21(1977): 29–46.

Modleski, Tania. *Loving with a Vengeance: Mass Produced Fantasies for Women.* 2nd ed. New York: Routledge, 2008.

Moers, Ellen. *Literary Women.* London: W.H. Allen, 1977.

Moi, Toril. *Sexual/Textual Politics: Feminist Literary Theory.* 2nd ed. London: Routledge, 2002.

Morandini, Giuliana. *La voce che è in lei: antologia della narrativa femminile italiana tra '800 e '900.* Milan: Bompiani, 1980.

Morelli, Salvatore. *La donna e la scienza, o la soluzione dell'umano problema.* Naples: Stab. tip. dell'Ancora, 1861.

Morris, Penelope, Francesco Ricatti, and Mark Seymour, eds., *Politica ed emozioni nella storia d'Italia dal 1848 ad oggi.* Rome: Viella, 2012.

Mullan, John. *Sentiment and Sociability: The Language of Feeling in the Eighteenth Century.* Oxford: Clarendon, 1988.

Neera. *Dizionario d'igiene per le famiglie,* 2nd ed. 1881. Reprint, Florence: R. Bemporad and Figlio, 1901.

–. "Falena". Translated by Martha King. In "Rethinking Neera," edited by Katharine Mitchell and Catherine Ramsey-Portolano, supplement to *The Italianist* 30, Supplement-1 (2010): 154–6.

–. *Fotografie matrimoniali.* Catania: Niccolò Giannotta Editore, 1898.

–. *Il libro di mio figlio.* In *Neera,* edited by Benedetto Croce. 2nd ed. Milan: Garzanti, 1943.

–. *L'amor platonico.* In *Neera,* edited by Benedetto Croce. 2nd ed. Milan: Garzanti, 1943.

–. *Le idee di una donna e confessioni letterarie.* 1903. Reprint, Florence: Vallecchi, 1977.

–. *L'Indomani.* 1890. Reprint, Palermo: Sellerio, 1981.

–. *Lydia.* 1887. Reprint, Lecco: Periplo, 1995.

–. *Teresa.* 1886. Reprint, Lecco: Periplo, 1995.

–. *Teresa.* Translated by Martha King. Evanston, IL: Northwestern University Press, 1998.

–. *Una giovinezza del secolo XIX.* 1919. Reprint, Milan: Feltrinelli, 1975.

Nevers, Emilia. *Il galateo della borghesia: norme per trattar bene.* Turin: Biblioteca per le signore, 1877.

Ngai, Sianne. *Ugly Feelings.* Cambridge, MA: Harvard University Press, 2005.

Nichols, Bill. *Representing Reality: Issues and Concepts in Documentary.* Bloomington: Indiana University Press, 1991.

Nietzsche, Friedrich. *The Will to Power.* Translated by Walter Kaufmann and R.J. Hollingdale. New York: Vintage, 1968.

Ojetti, Ugo. *Alla scoperta dei letterati.* Milan: Dumolard, 1895.

Ortaggi Cammarosano, Simonetta. "Labouring Women in Northern and Central Italy in the Nineteenth Century." In *Society and Politics in the Age of the Risorgimento,* edited by John A. Davis and Paul Ginsborg. Cambridge: Cambridge University Press, 1991.

Pacifici, Sergio. *The Modern Italian Novel from Capuana to Tozzi.* London: Feffer and Simons, 1973.

–. *The Modern Italian Novel from Manzoni to Svevo.* London: Feffer and Simons, 1967.

Panizza, Letizia, and Sharon Wood, eds. *A History of Women's Writing in Italy.* Cambridge: Cambridge University Press, 2000.

Parati, Graziella, and Rebecca West, eds. *Italian Feminist Theory and Practice: Equality and Sexual Difference.* London: Associated University Press, 2002.

Percoto, Caterina. *Racconti.* Florence: Le Monnier, 1858.

Peroni Bortolotti, Franca. *Sul movimento politico della donna. Scritti inediti,* edited by Annarita Buttafuoco. Rome: Utopia, 1987.

Pisa, Beatrice. *Venticinque anni di emancipazionismo femminile in Italia: Gualberta Alaide Beccari e la rivista "La Donna" (1868–1890).* Rome: Elengraf, 1982.

Poovey, Mary. *The Proper Lady and the Woman Writer: Ideology as Style in the Works of Mary Wollstonecraft, Mary Shelley, and Jane Austen.* Chicago: University of Chicago Press, 1984.

Puccini, Sandra. "Condizione della donna e questione femminile (1892–1922)." In *La questione femminile in Italia dal '900 ad oggi,* edited by G. Ascoli, N. Fusini, M. Gramaglia, L. Menapace, S. Puccini, and E. Santarelli. Milan: Franco Angeli, 1979.

Pugliese, Romana Margherita. "The Origins of *Lucia di Lammermoor'*s Cadenza." *Cambridge Opera Journal* 16 (2004): 23–42.

Radway, Janice A. "Women Read the Romance: The Interaction of Text and Context." *Feminist Studies* 9, no. 1 (1983): 53–78.

Ragland-Sullivan, Ellie. "Hysteria." In *Feminism and Psychoanalysis: A Critical Dictionary,* edited by Elizabeth Wright. Oxford: Blackwell, 1992.

Ragone, Giovanni. "La letteratura e il consumo: un profilo dei generi e dei modelli nell'editoria italiana (1845–1925)." In *Letteratura italiana* II: *Produzione e consumo.* Turin: Einaudi, 1983.

Raicich, Marino. "Liceo, università, professioni: un percorso difficile." In *L'educazione delle donne: scuole e modelli di vita femminile nell'Italia dell'Ottocento.* 2nd ed. Milan: Franco Angeli, 1991.

Ramsey-Portolano, Catherine. "Neera the *Verist* Woman Writer." *Italica* 81, no. 3 (2004): 351–66.

Re, Lucia. "Passion and Sexual Difference: The Risorgimento and the Gendering of Writing in Nineteenth-Century Italian Culture." In *Making and Remaking Italy: The Cultivation of National Identity around the Risorgimento*, edited by Albert Russell Ascoli and Krystyna von Henneberg. Oxford: Berg, 2001.

Rendall, Jane. "Women and the Public Sphere." *Gender & History* 11, no. 3 (1999): 475–88.

Rich, Adrienne. *Of Woman Born: Motherhood as Experience and Institution*. 1977. Reprint, London: Virago, 1986.

Rizzo, Domenico. "Marriage on Trial: Adultery in Nineteenth-Century Rome." In *Gender, Family and Sexuality: The Private Sphere in Italy, 1860–1945*, edited by Perry Wilson. Basingstoke: Palgrave Macmillan, 2004.

Rosenwein, Barbara H. *Emotional Communities in the Early Middle Ages*. Ithaca, NY: Cornell University Press, 2006.

Rosmini, Antonio. *Filosofia del diritto*. Naples: Batelli, 1845.

Rowbotham, Sheila. *Hidden from History: 300 Years of Women's Oppression and the Fight against It*. London: Pluto, 1973.

Rubin, Gayle. "The Traffic in Women: Notes on the 'Political Economy' of Sex." In *Feminism and History*, edited by Joan Wallach Scott. Oxford: Oxford University Press, 1996.

Salvati, Mariuccia. "A proposito di salotti." In *Donne e spazio*, edited by Dianella Gagliani and Mariuccia Salvati. Bologna: CLUEB, 1995.

Sanson, Helena. "Women Writers and the Questione della Lingua in Ottocento Italy: The Cases of Caterina Percoto, La Marchesa Colombi, and Matilde Serao." *Modern Language Review* 105, no. 4 (2010): 1028–52.

Santoro, Anna. *Narratrici italiane dell'Ottocento*. Naples: Federico and Ardia, 1987.

Santovetti, Olivia. "The Cliché of the Romantic Female Reader and the Paradox of Novelistic Illusion: Federico De Roberto's *L'Illusione*, 1891." In *The Printed Media in Fin-de-siècle Italy: Publishers, Writers, and Readers*, edited by Ann Hallamore Caesar, Gabriella Romani, and Jennifer Burns. London: MHRA and Maney, 2011.

Saredo, Luisa. *Le farfalle di provincia: scene della vita reale*. Milan: G. Daelli, 1857.

–. "Pia de' Monteroni". In *Racconti*. Florence: Le Monnier, 1878.

Scaraffia, Lucetta. "Essere Uomo, Essere Donna." In *La famiglia italiana dall'Ottocento a oggi*, edited by Piero Melograni and Lucetta Scaraffia. Rome: Laterza, 1988.

–. "'Christianity Has Liberated Her and Placed Her alongside Men in the Family': From 1850 to 1988 (Mulieris Dignitatem)." In *Women and Faith: Catholic Religious Life in Italy from Late Antiquity to the Present*, edited by

Lucetta Scaraffia and Gabriella Zarri. Cambridge, MA: Harvard University Press, 1999.

Sedgwick, Eve Kosofsky. *Between Men: English Literature and Male Homosocial Desire*. New York: Columbia University Press, 1985.

Segal, Naomi. "Motherhood." In *Feminism and Psychoanalysis: A Critical Dictionary*, edited by Elizabeth Wright. Oxford: Blackwell, 1992.

Serao, Matilde. "Checchina's Virtue." Translated by Tom Kelso. In *Writing to Delight: Italian Short Stories by Nineteenth-Century Women Writers*, edited by Antonia Arslan and Gabriella Romani. Toronto: University of Toronto Press, 2006.

–. "Girls' Normal School." In *Unmarried Women: Stories*. Translated by Paula Spurlin Paige. Evanston, IL: Northwestern University Press, 2007.

–. *Fantasia*. In Matilde Serao, *Opere*, edited by P. Pancrazi. 2 vols. Milan: Garzanti, 1944–6.

–. *Il castigo*. 1893. Reprint, Rome: Armando Curcio, 1977.

–. *Il romanzo della fanciulla*. 1886. Reprint, Naples: Liguori, 1985.

–. "O Giovannino o la morte." In *La virtù delle donne*. Rome: Avagliano Editore, 1999.

–. *Ricordando Neera*. Milan: Fratelli Treves Editori, 1920.

–. *Saper vivere: norme di buona creanza*. 1900. Reprint, Florence: Passigli Editori, 1989.

–. "Silvia." In *Dal vero*, edited by Patricia Bianchi. Naples: Libreria Dante and Descartes, 2000.

–. "The State Telegraph Office (*Women's Section*)." In *Unmarried Women: Stories*. Translated by Paula Spurlin Paige. Evanston, IL: Northwestern University Press, 2007.

Seymour, Mark. *Debating Divorce in Italy: Marriage and the Making of Modern Italians, 1860–1974*. New York: Palgrave Macmillan, 2006.

–. "'Till Death Do Them Part? The Church-State Struggle over Marriage and Divorce, 1860–1914." In *Gender, Family and Sexuality: The Private Sphere in Italy, 1860–1945*, edited by Perry Wilson. Basingstoke: Palgrave Macmillan, 2004.

Showalter, Elaine. *A Literature of Their Own: From Charlotte Brontë to Doris Lessing*. Princeton: Princeton University Press in 1977; London: Virago, 1999.

–. *Hystories: Hysterical Epidemics and Modern Culture*. London: Picador, 1997.

–. *The Female Malady: Women, Madness, and English Culture, 1830–1980*. London: Virago Press, 1985.

Silengo, Giovanni and Silvia Benatti, "Immagini e documenti di una vita." In *La Marchesa Colombi: una scrittrice e il suo tempo*, edited by Silvia Benatti and Roberto Cicala. Novara: Interlinea Edizioni, 2001.

Smith-Rosenberg, Carroll. *Disorderly Conduct: Visions of Gender in Victorian America*. New York: Oxford, 1985.

Soldani, Simonetta. "Premessa." In *L'educazione delle donne: scuole e modelli di vita femminile nell'Italia dell'Ottocento*, edited by Simonetta Soldani. 2nd ed. Milan: Franco Angeli, 1991.

Tellini, Gino. *Il romanzo italiano dell'Ottocento e Novecento*. Milan: Bruno Mondadori, 1998.

Todd, Janet. *Women's Friendship in Literature*. New York: Columbia University Press, 1980.

Tommaseo, Niccolò. *Degli studi che più si convengono alle donne*. Milan: Agnelli, 1868.

–. *La donna. Scritti varii ed inediti*. Milan: Agnelli, 1868.

Tommaseo, Niccolò, and Bernardo Bellini. *Dizionario della lingua italiana*. Turin: UTET, 1861–79.

Valisa, Silvia. "Gendered Quests: Analysis, Revelation, and the Epistemology of Gender in Neera's *Teresa, Lydia* and *L'Indomani*." *The Italianist* 28 (2008): 92–112.

–. "Still Figures: Photography, Modernity and Gender in Neera's *Fotografie matrimoniali*." In "Rethinking Neera," edited by Katharine Mitchell and Catherine Ramsey-Portolano, special supplement, *The Italianist* 30, Supplement 1 (2010): 26–49.

Vickery, Amanda. "Golden Age to Separate Spheres: A Review of the Categories and Chronology of Women's History." *Historical Journal* 36, no. 2 (1993): 383–414.

Wanrooij, Bruno. *Storia del pudore: la questione sessuale in Italia 1860–1940*. Venice: Marsilio, 1990.

Warner, Marina. *Alone of all Her Sex: The Myth and the Cult of the Virgin Mary*. London: Picador, 1985.

Watt, Ian. *The Rise of the Novel: Studies in Defoe, Richardson and Fielding*. London: Hogarth Press, 1987.

Whitford, Margaret, ed. *The Irigaray Reader*. Oxford: Blackwell, 1991.

Wilson, Perry, ed. *Gender, Family and Sexuality: The Private Sphere in Italy, 1860–1945*. Basingstoke: Palgrave Macmillan, 2004.

Wood, Sharon. *Italian Women's Writing, 1860–1994*. London: Athlone Press, 1995.

Wood, Sharon, and Joseph Farrell. "Other Voices: Contesting the Status Quo." In *The Cambridge Companion to Modern Italian Culture*, edited by Zygmunt G. Barański and Rebecca J. West. Cambridge: Cambridge University Press, 2001.

Woolf, Virginia. *A Room of One's Own*. 1919. Reprint, London: Penguin Books, 1945.

Wright, Elizabeth, ed. *Feminism and Psychoanalysis: A Critical Dictionary.*
Oxford: Blackwell, 1992.
Zambon, Patrizia. "Riviste fiorentine e milanesi dell'ultimo Ottocento nel
carteggio Angiolo Orvieto-Neera." In *Il sogno aristocratico. Angiolo Orvieto
e Neera: corrispondenza 1889–1917,* edited by Antonia Arslan and Patrizia
Zambon. Milan: Guerini Studio, 1990.

Index

active life, endorsement of 40–1
actresses 43, 54, 61
adultery 11, 41–2, 47
Aleramo, Sibilla 19–20, 21, 46, 57
Althusser, Louis 23
American domestic fiction 15
Amoia, Fazia 151
Amoretti, Maria Pellegrina 165n28
Anna O 106, 205–6n42
"Api, Mosconi e Vespe" column
    (Serao) 58, 159
appearance, description of 25–6
architecture, depiction of 60
Armstrong, Nancy 62, 91–2
arranged marriages 11, 30, 134
Arslan, Antonia 18, 151, 158,
    177n51
art, and women 51
Austen, Ann 18
Austen, Jane 18, 27, 152–3
author, role of 36
authority 36, 133, 141; author's 32,
    36; criticism of 61; father's 34, 38,
    142; husband's 56; of male heads
    of households 11; mother's 143
autobiographical narrative
    169n32
auto-eroticism 96, 115–21

Balbo, Cesare 60
balconies 77–8, 79
Baldacci, Luigi 4, 56–7, 158
Banti, Alberto 94
Banti, Anna 57
Barthes, Roland 36
Battaglia, Salvatore 150–1
Battaglie per un'idea (Neera) 48, 51,
    52–3, 58, 157
Bauer, Ida 121
Beccari, Gualberta Alaide 37, 45, 151;
    La Donna 11, 17–18
bedrooms 69–73
behaviour: guidance 48–51; proper
    91; in threshold spaces 78–9, 80;
    value of proper 48
Belsey, Catherine, *Critical Practice* 23
Benjamin, Jessica 136
Bernhardt, Sarah 54
Bianchi, Celestino 16
Bisi, Sofia 129
body, the 96, 103, 115–21
Bollas, Christopher 108
Bonghi, Ruggiero 16
Bortolotti, Franca Pieroni 10
Bourneville, Désiré, and
    Paul Régnard, *Iconographie
    photographique de la Salpêtrière* 105

spaces 75, 79; use of language
27–8; women's relationship with
the home 66
Una donna (Aleramo) 20
Una giovinezza del secolo XIX (Neera)
19, 21; and female solidarity 54;
use of language 28
"Una Vocazione" (La Marchesa
Colombi) 80, 86, 102, 132
Unification ix, x, 4, 9, 34, 48, 108, 151;
post-Unification 7, 13, 31, 33, 59,
95, 123, 127–8,
United States of America: La
Marchesa Colombi on 37;
women's rights in 46
universities 12, 39, 165n28

Valisa, Silvia 77
values 38
Vassallo, Luigi 159
Verga, Giovanni 6, 24–5, 25, 42, 139
verismo 6–7, 24–8
Vespucci, Americo 38
vicarious participation 123–4
Virgin Mary 70, 109, 143–4
virtue 49, 51
Vita Intima 32, 42–5, 97, 113, 157
Vivanti, Annie 21, 44
voting rights 9, 13, 58

Wanrooij, Bruno 48
Watt, Ian 16–17
Whelehan, Imelda 132
windows 72, 77, 78–9, 83
Wollstonecraft, Mary 152–3
woman question, the 5–6, 11, 55, 59,
151, 153
women: acceptable professions
12–13; agency 52, 102, 120;
American 37; autonomy 145;

and cafés 91; in doorways 76,
76–7; easily substituted 134–5;
emotional suffering 99–103;
exhibiting themselves 78–9;
gender socialization 87; hysterical
protest 121; ideal 43; intellectual
inferiority 52; intelligence
51–3; isolation 140–1; legal
subordination to men 11–12, 30;
life cycle 40–1, 43; medicalization
of 6; natural reactions 125; need
to be accompanied 80; Neera on
44–5; numbers 18; objectification
51; ostracized 66; and pain 53;
the *passeggiata* 81–2; politicized
10; portrayal of 6–7; power 135;
proper place 59–60, 157–8; in the
public sphere 61–2, 63, 80–1, 81–3;
relationship with the home 64–7;
role of 5, 10, 18, 19–20, 29, 39, 45,
51, 61, 121, 136; sense of failure
110; submission 77; sympathy for
91–3; and windows 79–80
women lawyers 34, 47
women writers: absence of
genealogy 21, 152–3; anxiety of
authorship 19–20; collaboration
42, 47; conservatism 47, 51, 150;
contribution 58; emergence of 15–22;
female solidarity 151; female-
authored reviews 151–2; influences
18, 27; newspapers columns 32–5;
and realism 24–8; relationship with
readers 123–6; rise in popularity
18–19; self-perception 21–2;
solidarity with readers 20–1
women's emancipation movement 3,
10–12, 13
women's organizations 53–4
women's rights 3, 11, 15, 46

Lightning Source UK Ltd.
Milton Keynes UK
UKOW02n0719170915

258743UK00002B/13/P

9 781442 646414